Pat Lowther's Continent

Pat Lowther's Continent
HER LIFE AND WORK

TOBY BROOKS

Toby Brooks

gynergy
books

Technical editing: Jane Billinghurst
Cover art: © Anne Meredith Barry
Cover photo: Mike Kelly, used with permission of Pat Lowther's Estate
Photo on p. 106: Peter Hulbert, used with permission of *The Vancouver Sun*
All other photos: Courtesy of Pat Lowther's children
Printed and bound in Canada

Gynergy books acknowledges financial support for our publishing activities from the Government of Canada through the Book Publishing Industry Development Program (BPIDP), and the Canada Council for the Arts.

Published by:
gynergy books
P.O. Box 2023
Charlottetown, PEI
Canada   C1A 7N7

Canadian Cataloguing in Publication Data

Brooks, Toby, 1936-

    Pat Lowther's continent

    Includes bibliographical references.
    ISBN 0-921881-54-1

1. Lowther, Pat, 1935-1975. 2. Poets, Canadian (English) — 20th century — Biography.* I. Title.

PS8573.09Z57 2000   C811'.54   C00-950037-5
PR9199.3.L66Z54 2000

As I tell Pat Lowther's story, I think of two women I cared for at Interval House of Ottawa-Carleton, a shelter for battered women. Like Pat's, their lives were taken by the men who said they loved them. Both women had left their men before the murders. I grieve also for the loss of a fourth life: young Sharon Nasin Mohamed was felled by a man her mother had rejected. Sometimes I imagine that Sharon's spirit occupies the same corner of the cosmos as Pat's. Pat the mother, Sharon the open-hearted child, you are with me.

Contents

Preface

In 1975, just as people with influence in Canadian literature were starting to take notice of the work of Patricia Louise Lowther, the body of this forty-year-old Vancouver poet was found in Furry Creek, a mountain stream that runs into Howe Sound, British Columbia. She had been bludgeoned to death with a hammer. Her husband, Roy Lowther, was later convicted of the murder. He died in jail, never having admitted to the crime.

During her life, Pat's poetry attracted a small but ardent readership. Immediately after her death, a number of short articles were published about Pat, but interest seemed to dwindle: one thesis, a couple of articles, a workshopped play. Perhaps the lack of original documents contributed to the inattention. During her lifetime, Pat lost a number of manuscripts. The losses continued after Pat's death. Roy admitted to having destroyed many of her papers, including unfinished and unpublished poems. At the time of his arrest, he and the children were living in a rented house. In the harried move during the murder trial, more paper was undoubtedly lost.

After Pat's death, her family succeeded in collecting some of her unpublished poems and papers, and they were consigned to a trunk in her son's attic. Twenty years passed. Some of the horror of Pat's death lessened and her daughter Beth Lowther opened the trunk. It held letters, an old notebook, journals with her published work, and some books of poetry that were gifts from other writers. In addition, there was a brown briefcase containing early versions of published poems, as well as unfinished poems. In the trunk was also a collection of poems that Pat had been preparing for publication. Beth Lowther put the poems together in manuscript form and

Time Capsule: New and Selected Poems was published by Polestar in Victoria in the spring of 1997.

At the time of Pat's death, I was gripped by her-poetry. Pat Lowther's work has a lot to say to anyone, but it touches a particular chord inside women who were adults before the 1960s. My explanation is that the feminist thinking of the 1960s was led mostly by young women in their twenties who were figuring out how, if at all, to relate to men. Those of us who were older and already had established relationships may have been sympathetic to the young women's search but it was different from ours. Pat gave us a compass that could guide us in thinking about the relationships we were in and how they fit into life on planet Earth.

As an admirer of her poetry, I was saddened by her death, but at the time it did not affect me personally. Then, in 1976, I got a job as a counsellor in a shelter for battered women. As did most workers who had no personal experience of violent homes, I had my eyes opened by the women and children who came to the house. I worked at the shelter for thirteen years, and that experience forever changed my understanding of human relationships. Day after day I met remarkable women, women who somehow kept their humanity while living with terror. Pat stayed in my mind.

In the early 1980s, I decided I wanted to do something in Pat's memory. Maybe I could write a tribute to this woman whose poetry sang in my head. I wrote letters, asking for information about her. A librarian of a close friend of Pat's gave me the name Allan Safarik, and he referred me to Dona Sturmanis, who had written several articles about Pat and who was considering writing a biography. I offered to help Dona with her research, and she responded by generously offering me co-authorship. We worked together for a time, and then Dona left the project because of other commitments.

In the 1970s, I needed Pat Lowther to put my vague feelings into words. Pat did that for me. Now I'm doing what I can to tell her story. I extend my sincere thanks to those who retold this painful story; perhaps together we can broaden the understanding of why Pat's life was cut short and celebrate the continent she has left behind.

Toby Brooks
March 2000

Acknowledgements

Virginia Tinmuth, Pat's remarkable mother, who passed away in 1998, gave me the basic information about Pat's life as well as countless cups of tea. Brenda, Pat's sister, gave me glimpses of Pat that only a sister could provide. I also thank her for helping me find my way around North Vancouver. John Tinmouth, Pat's brother, gave me information and resuscitated my tape recorder. Barry Wilks, Pat's cousin, talked about Mayne Island. The work would not have been possible without the information, cooperation and support of Pat's children: Alan Domphousse, Kathy Lyons, Beth Lowther and Christine Lowther, each one of whom is remarkable in his or her own way. Ruth Lowther Lalonde kindly allowed me to use her father's papers.

These friends and colleagues of Pat's granted me interviews: bill bissett; Stephen Michael Bersensky; Brian Brett; Brian Campbell; Ward Carson; Professor Fred Candelaria; Professor Fred Cogswell; Judith Copithorne; Maxine Gadd; the late Professor Réshard Gool; Elizabeth Gourlay; Police Inspector Ken Hale; Professor Robert Harlow; Michael Koziniak; Rita Lalik; Arlene Lampert; Elizabeth Lane; Ed Livingston; Professor George McWhirter; Joe Rosenblatt; Allan Safarik; Bethoe Shirkoff; Professor Hilda Thomas; Lorraine Vernon; and Hilda Woolnough. The help of the late Professor Réshard Gool was unique. He arranged for Pat Lowther's reading trip to Prince Edward Island in 1975, and he and his wife, Hilda Woolnough, were kind to Pat when she arrived. Later, Gool was kind to Pat's literary memory by writing a radio script about her; he also preserved documents and a tape of the reading. That tape saved Pat's physical voice for posterity. Thirteen years later, Gool and Woolnough repeated their kindness to Pat by hosting me and committing hours of their time to my interview questions about their experiences with Pat. Réshard Gool died on May 1, 1989. We shall not easily find another man so uncompromising about fairness and generosity.

Although the following people did not know Pat Lowther, they granted me interviews that helped put together the pieces of her life, her work and her death: Howard Engel; Attorney John Hall; Mr. Justice A.G. Henderson; Professor D.G. Jones; Dr. David Wylie Norman; Aviva Ravel; and Leandro Urbina.

Dona Sturmanis' ideas, together with our conversations over the past eight years, have contributed a great deal to my work. The most important thing that she did was reassure me, when I doubted myself, that I could write this book. In addition, some of the research and interviews from Dona's unpublished manuscript are incorporated into this book. Her manuscript builds on the original research on Pat's murder that Vancouver journalist Sean Rossiter prepared and generously gave to her.

I thank my many friends who were touched by Pat's story and gave me help to make sure that it was told. Enid Valerie gave me untold hours of stylistic and editorial help and was always available when I had questions about Spanish punctuation.

Professor Seymour Mayne has been encouraging since I did a student paper in 1985. He was Pat's first editor and spoke to me in detail about that experience. Following that he gave me a great deal of practical help and generally stuck by me. Professor L.T.R. McDonald pointed out the importance of Pat's poetry to his students and encouraged my work. Helen Kauleity kept me spiritually well during a dark period in writing this painful story. Della Golland, with whom I organized a tribute to Pat Lowther in 1995, permitted me to use her thesis on Pat Lowther and was available for advice. Laurie Joe answered legal questions and was always encouraging. Sharon Abron Drache and Candis Graham gave me advice about publishing. Linda MacLeod discussed with me the meaning behind the statistics on murdered women. As I write this, I am thankful for the steadfastness of my former co-workers at an Ottawa shelter for battered women, who have spent their careers trying to prevent similar tragedies.

I thank Phyllis Wilson and William Toye of Oxford University Press for the use of their files. Betty Gustafson kindly allowed me to consult the Ralph Gustafson Collection at the McLennan Library of McGill University, where I found the staff of Rare Books and Special Collections to be most helpful. Antje Helmuth, librarian at the British Columbia Ministry of Human Resources, dug out social service regulations dating back over twenty years. Similarly, Maureen Wight of the Cultural Services Branch of the British Columbia Ministry of Small Business, Tourism and Culture retrieved twenty-year-old records of the British Columbia Arts Board. I thank as well my kindly critics: Claire Devlin, Maureen Cullingham, Professor Seymour Mayne and Andrea Kunard — for reading and criticism — and Wendy McPeake — for criticism and publishing advice. While researching the book I made several trips from my home in Ottawa to British Columbia, where many kind people housed, fed, transported and generally cared for me. Thank you to Marilyn Fuchs, Cathy Ford, Dorothy Elias, Sheila Gilhooly, Glenda MacPherson, Dona Sturmanis, Fran and the late Leon Kraintz and Ellen Frank. Chris Jang made me tea and transported me. Warren Rudd transported me and coped valiantly with my hearing problem. Greg and Priah Morley hosted and transported me in Victoria. Kate Nonesuch and Evelyn Battell gave me unwavering encouragement. Christine Lowther hosted me at her island home and showed me the beauties of the British Columbia rainforest. Beth Lowther, as the caretaker of her mother's papers, ceded her dining-room table to me for many hours.

I was schooled in an era before computers and they remain mysterious even after I have used one to write a book. My dear friend and neighbour Paul Gross tamed my computer and sent countless electronic messages for me. Members of my family all played essential roles. My daughter, Naomi Brooks, kept insisting that I am smarter than my computer; my daughter-in-law, Nella Cotrupi, gave me literary and legal advice; my son, Jake Brooks, gave me creative marketing ideas and helped organize the twentieth Pat Lowther Memorial Tribute in 1995. My life partner, David Brooks, gets credit for my first involvement with Pat Lowther because he gave me one of her books as a gift. Later, when I worked on this book, he gave me help with grammar that was always welcome. He also gave me computer help that was not always welcome, occasionally speaking in the computer's defense. In spite of those lapses, I am sincerely grateful for David's help.

I would also like to thank The League of Canadian Poets for allowing me the use of their files in the Public Archives of Canada.

A sincere thanks to Louise Fleming and Sibyl Frei of gynergy books and to my editor Jane Billinghurst for guiding this book into print at last.

I would like to extend a particular thank you to Pat Lowther's children, who have been so generous in granting permission to use her published and unpublished work.

CHAPTER 1

First Things

The plainness of first things
trees
gravel
rocks
naive root atom
of philosophy's first molecule

— Pat Lowther[1]

PAT LOWTHER STOOD BEFORE HER CLASS in creative writing at the University of British Columbia. A lecturer standing in front of a class might not sound remarkable, but, to Pat, getting this job was remarkable beyond words. Not only did it give her a chance to share her gift with others; it might also be her ticket to financial independence. The slim woman at the front of the classroom had an "interesting face ... high cheekbones, alert eyes under a clear brow."[2] What she did not have was a degree from any university, or even a diploma from any high school. Nor did she have much money. Pat had left school at sixteen to work as a keypunch operator. Then she married and had children. Four years later, she divorced, went back to work, got married again and had more children. Amidst diapers and spilled porridge, she honed her craft. Her students caught her enthusiasm for poetry and her commitment to the power of words. After class, one of them proclaimed, "It's going to be a great course!"[3] Two weeks later, the woman who had recently been hailed as a poet of "impeccable verbal appropriateness"[4] was dead. Her second husband, Roy Lowther, was convicted of her murder; his weapon was a hammer.

In the forty years given to her, Pat published two books of poetry and a broadsheet. In subject, her poetry ranges from examining tiny craneflies to grappling with the cosmos. Between these two poles, she feels the landscape in her body, ponders evolution, and explores human beings on both a personal and a political level. Readers are easily caught up in the singing quality of Pat's writing, but it is her subjects that really take hold. Throughout her work, one can sense the struggle of a woman and mother trying to live with integrity in a landscape that often seems indifferent to life. That landscape is physical and metaphysical, political and personal. Women readers, especially, have identified strongly with Pat's work. Those who grew into adulthood before the 1960s can read it with thundering recognition. Pat's poetry looks at birth and mothering, and tries to understand problems in relationships. In spite of its focus on family, her poetry also exhibits a pull from the outside. The new feminist movement was beginning to question sex roles and women's relationships with men; many women in the 1960s and 1970s felt that this examination was long past due. Pat Lowther's poetry does strenuous work on both sides of the issue.

Patricia Louise Tinmouth was born on July 29, 1935. Her parents, Virginia and Arthur Tinmouth, were down-to-earth people who lived in North Vancouver, British Columbia. What made them out of the ordinary was their love of words and music.

Scientists may not be able to show that the love of poetry is carried in the genes, but, if Pat's family members could, they would surely trace Pat Lowther's poetic gift back to her maternal grandfather, James Wilks, who was born in 1867. "My father was great with words," says Pat's mother. "He loved poetry and would quote Shakespeare at the drop of a hat."[5] Although James Wilks was a well-read man, he did not have much formal schooling. Virginia thinks of him as educated because "he was so broadminded." The little schooling James did receive was at a Catholic mission school run for Native Canadians, although it is not clear how a child who was neither Native Canadian nor Roman Catholic had qualified to attend such a school. Perhaps there was a vacancy at the right time.

According to her birth certificate, issued in Chesterfield, England, Virginia's mother was born Annie McCane, although the family name was also spelled McCain. In her poem "History Lessons," Pat preserves this lively story of her grandmother's sister, Eliza.

> Eliza McCain,
> height five foot one,
> when the governor ordered striking coal miners
> (and everyone else)
> off the streets of Nanaimo,
> threatened to thrash a six-foot militiaman
> with her umbrella …
> until the poor fellow,
> fumbling his hat and rehearsing
> alternative explanations for his superior,
> let her pass
> with shopping list triumphant.
>
> Unfortunately, the stores were closed. [6]

The Wilks family came to British Columbia from a coal-mining area in Northumberland, England. James' father hoped that his sons would be spared the hard and dangerous life that he had had, working in the mines. As luck would have it, the man with the dream died young, and James' brothers moved to the United States. James was left to support his mother and, in spite of his father's hopes, he became a miner. It was while living in Vancouver that he met and married Annie McCane.

James Wilks believed that life could be better for coal miners and he helped organize the Vancouver Island Mine Workers' Association, which operated in the western part of the United States and Canada a little after the turn of the twentieth century. For his growing family, this meant moving around from place to place. It was while the Wilks family was living in Montana that Virginia Louise Wilks was born. She was named after another daughter who had died several years earlier. In all, the Wilks family had seven children, six of whom survived. Eventually the family moved back to British Columbia, and James became the operator of the first liquor store in North Vancouver. He also kept his hand in public affairs and did some ghost-writing for politicians. He died when Pat was about eighteen months old, so she never did get to know the grandfather from whom she may have inherited her love of words.

Virginia Tinmuth, who would live to become a great-grand-mother, is a person who speaks her mind. "My daughters are soft-spoken. They're not like me," she affirms. She also says that, as a child, she was "puny." Her parents thought physical activity would be the thing to build her up, so, for her health, they sent her to the Grace Goddard Dance School. This was in 1915, when the school had a central location in downtown Vancouver at Granville and Davie Streets. More than Virginia's health responded to dance. She discovered that dancing was to be her great passion, and it was not long before she became a teacher and a performer with the Atree DanceTroupe. When this dance company "barnstormed around B.C. in a big Hudson sedan," Virginia Wilks was with them.

Virginia's travels took her to New York City. One day she wandered into a rehearsal at the Rockefeller Theater. As she watched the young women going through their routine, she was

Pat's mother, Virginia Louise Wilks,
was a dancer in her youth. (circa 1921)

approached by the dance teacher and choreographer for the company.

"Have you come for rehearsal?" he asked.

"No," she answered.

"Are you looking for a job? Do you have any experience?"

"I can do what those girls are doing."

That is how Virginia Wilks was hired as a dancer with the famous Rockettes. She soon left to join another touring group, the Russell Markerd Dancers. This company toured the eastern United States in a show called "The New Americana." Virginia recalls that the dancers made $55 a week, which was very good money for the late 1920s. Then the stock market crashed, and desperate people in New York began jumping out of windows. Virginia realized that the boom-and-bust life was not to her liking and she returned to British Columbia, where she was lucky enough to find a job demonstrating wax products for $18.50 a week.

Not long after her return to Canada, Virginia met Arthur Tinmouth. One of the things Arthur and Virginia had in common was their enjoyment of music. "Arthur was very musical. He could play anything. He could sit at a piano and pick up a tune. He could also play the harmonica, guitar, accordion, trumpet and the swinette." (A swinette was whatever dishpan or washboard was handy when Arthur was seized with a need to make music.) It was 1933, and, in the custom of the times, Virginia gave up her job when she and Arthur married. Arthur was earning $150 a month. In those years, thrifty people could set up a household with that amount of money. Virginia explains: "We had a house fully furnished when we got married."

The name "Tinmuth" or "Tinmouth" comes from the name of a town, Tynemouth, on the mouth of the River Tyne in Northumberland, England. When Virginia married Arthur, they spelled their name "Tinmouth," closer to the name of the town. Later, at Arthur's mother's suggestion, they dropped the "o." Both spellings continue to be used.[7]

Pat's father, Arthur Tinmouth, was the son of Harriet and Arthur Tinmouth, Sr. He was born in Sunderland, England, in 1908 and was the last of eight children. Arthur Sr. had been a journeyman strip caulker in a shipyard. The eldest son, John, found work in the coal mines, the same English coal mines that so many people were fleeing. Hoping to improve their fortune, the Tinmouths immigrated to Canada, first settling in Redcliffe, Alberta, and then moving to Halifax, Nova Scotia. In Nova Scotia, they heard that experienced shipyard workers were needed in Vancouver. On the journey west, Arthur's four-year-old sister was struck with diphtheria and died. That was just the beginning of their troubles in the new country. After they settled in Vancouver, Arthur Sr. lost his life when he fell into a hold at the shipyard. No one saw him fall in, and he was trapped when they closed the hatch as usual. Harriet Tinmouth was left with six children to raise on her own. The pension she received as a result of the accident would have been small comfort.

After Arthur Jr. and Virginia married, they lived in a small house at the Lynn Creek Waterworks Intake Station, where Arthur worked as a caretaker. At the intake station, water ran from the creek into big tanks that supplied the water for North Vancouver. It was Arthur's job to make sure that everything worked. The station was built in the woods above North Vancouver, a beautiful but lonely setting.

The Tinmouths started their family life during the Great Depression and, even though Arthur had a job, like a lot of people they worried about the way things were going. As Virginia puts it, "Everybody was a socialist and everybody was a communist." The Tinmouths became active in the Liberal party, and Virginia was even president of the Liberal riding association for a while. "Later," she says with a chuckle, "Arthur and I saw the light and joined the CCF." The CCF, the Co-operative Commonwealth Federation, would later become the New Democratic Party.

Virginia wonders if her children absorbed their political ideas from the songs she sang to them when they were babies. "If one of my children needed extra cuddling or nursing, I'd sing 'The Red Flag.' It's a great tune to walk back and forth with." "The Red Flag" was a rallying song for Communists in the 1930s and is sung to the tune of "O Tannenbaum." The chorus of this rousing ditty goes, "Then raise the scarlet banner high / Beneath its folds we'll live and die." During those economically depressed years, people did not have to be Communists to be influenced by the hopefulness of a group that had a vision of how to deal with the problems of their day.

Pat was Arthur and Virginia's first child. Carrying on a tradition from the Wilks side of the family, they gave their baby the middle name Louise. According to her mother, Patricia Louise Tinmouth was "a pretty little girl with golden brown curls." Pat had the advantage of parents who sang and danced with her, but she had the disadvantage of having no playmates. She grew to be a quiet child who responded to the solitude of Lynn Creek by looking within her imagination. She created Bonnie, a grown-up friend who

Pat about age 4. (circa 1939)

wore a long skirt that swept the floor and walked without feet. More wonderful still, Bonnie came from a place where it never got dark. Pat explained to her mother that, if she went away with Bonnie, she would never have to go to bed.

Pat's early surroundings wove themselves into her character. Having had to accept physical and spiritual solitude in her early years, she later celebrated in her poetry not only people, animals and plants but the minerals that feed growth. The world of her mind was the place where she lived. She set herself the task of piercing the barrier around solid things so that she could unite the world of matter with her mind. In one poem she invites an unnamed someone to her secret island, where "We'll lie on the sand / and feel the galaxy / on our cheeks and foreheads."[8]

Hardly had Pat learned to talk than she wanted to read. Her parents responded by getting her a little blackboard. They taught her to read "Pat" and went on to teach her words like "sat," "hat" and "cat." It wasn't long before they found she could read the words on the label of a Campbell's soup can. Soon, Pat was reading all on her own. By the time she was two, she had learned to recognize every word in her book *Polly and Her Friends*. At age three, not satisfied with the children's books that her parents read to her, she would pick up their books and ask, "What's in there?"

At three and a half, Pat wrote what may have been her first poem: "I love to sit on the cool green grass, / Sit there on my little ass."[9] Whatever else may be said of this rhyme, it shows that Pat was already writing about her feelings and touching nature with her body. Becoming one with nature would become a hallmark of her work.

When Pat was about four years old, a friend of Virginia's ran for the British Columbia legislature, and, when Virginia went to vote, she brought Pat along. At the polling station, someone said, "Here's the little girl who knows how to read." Another person doubted it. So Virginia picked up the closest piece of paper, which happened to be "Instructions for Poll Clerks," and Pat read it out loud with no trouble. "Of course, she didn't understand what it meant, but she could read all the words."

When Pat was four, her sister, Brenda, was born, and, like every other first child who is no longer an only child, she saw herself nudged from the centre of the family nest. Although there is no information showing that Pat was badly upset by the arrival of her sister, her poem "Watershed" could be about the changes that the new baby brought into Pat's life. Whether describing her own life or observing another child's experience, Pat recorded the life-shaping nudge from the centre.

> Here the road ends
> the mountains ring
> with woodpeckers
> my parents made a nest
> …
> my father took my
> mother's nipple,
> squirted milk at me:
> "See, it doesn't
> like you any more.
> It belongs to the new baby." [10]

As a tot, Brenda adored her elder sister and tried to do everything that "sisah" did, but the girls had very different personalities. "Brenda was a doer. She was always making things," Virginia remembers, whereas Pat always had a book in her hand and was a little removed from the people around her. Brenda is more explicit: "You never felt you had her full attention. She would talk to people while holding a book at arm's length, continuing to read."

Being a little removed was something that Pat carried into everyday activities. There were many little practical things she never learned to do. "She wasn't incompetent, but she could make others think she was" is Brenda's assessment. Brenda remembers wanting Pat to go skating with her, whereas Pat would have preferred to stay at home and read. At times like that, Pat took advantage of Brenda's adulation. She would agree to go skating, but only if Brenda put on Pat's skates and laced them up for her.

As Pat grew, her memory was remarkable. Virginia says that Pat could read a book, put it down and quote it so closely you would think she was reading it. Once, at a children's party, they played a memory game. The hostess put twenty-two assorted objects on a tray, the children looked at it for a few minutes and then the tray was taken away. Most of the children remembered four or five of the objects. Pat remembered all twenty-two.

By the time that Pat was six years old, she had read all the *Oz* books. "We would go to the library and get armfuls of children's books. She had read way beyond the reading material a six-year-old would have," Virginia recalls. Before Pat started school, she was also writing plays. This was, of course, before the days of home television and videos, and, during the late 1930s and early 1940s, it would have been a rare treat for a small child to see a play. Her mother remembers that Pat included stage directions such as "very coyly."

To make it easier for Pat to get to school, the family moved from the intake station to a large rented house on Third Street East in North Vancouver, which they shared with Virginia's mother and brother, Annie and Bob Wilks. After a few years, they bought a house of their own at 233-12th Street East, which Virginia remembers as a lovely house, "the best place we ever lived."

The school that Pat entered was Ridgeway Elementary School, built in 1913 and, as of 1997, was still in use. It features a bell tower with blue trim that is visible many blocks away. In the custom of 1913, the words "GIRLS" and "BOYS" are carved in stone over the two front doors, a holdover from an era when boys and girls were usually not allowed to play together. The explanation often given was that boys were "rough."

Patt wrote her first play before
starting school. (circa 1942)

Pat was enrolled at Ridgeway in September 1941. No one has recorded whether Pat's early mastery of reading was a problem for her first-grade teacher. Perhaps Pat was quiet enough in school not to be troublesome, but she must have been painfully bored with her Grade One reading lessons. She may have learned that school had little to teach her.

When Virginia discovered that she was pregnant with her third child, Arthur pointed out that nine months is a long time for children to wait for an event, so they decided not to tell Pat and Brenda until closer to the birth. Unfortunately, the woman next door told her little girl that the Tinmouths were going to have a new baby. Then, the little girl told Pat and Brenda. The Tinmouth girls were indignant at having learned family news from a neighbour, especially news as important as this. Pat's attraction to babies was at her core right from her childhood, and her poetry celebrates the power of new life. In "May Chant,"[11] which critics consider one of her best works, she uses the power of birth as a potion against evil. When she was asked for a brief biography for a reading in Prince Edward Island, she opened it by saying: "Born in North Vancouver. Worked in offices and grew children."

The Tinmouth's third child was born in 1946. When the family was trying to think what to call the new baby, Pat suggested the name Arden. Brenda remembers that there was a boy named Arden in their school on whom both she and her sister had a crush. Unhappily, the baby given this romantic name was born with cerebral palsy. At the time of his birth, doctors thought he might live ten to thirteen years. He is now a man in his fifties.

Pat was always very fond of Arden. As the oldest girl, Pat was expected to help with her brother and he was dependent upon Pat for companionship. Although there are few comments to be found about Pat's attitude on helping with her brother, it is likely that her relationship with her disabled brother served to increase her sensitivity about the good and bad luck that visits people. Her poetry never looks away from bad events, but tries to make them fit into the whole universe. For example, at the conclusion of "In the Continent Behind My Eyes," Pat imagines what it might have been like living at the dawn of the Ice Age. Her character's response to that catastrophe is to carve the story of her people on the wall of a cave.[12]

After Arden, there was one more child born to the Tinmouths. John was born in 1949, and he grew up to be a warm-hearted man with a well-developed sense of humour. John is another musical Tinmouth. He went on to sing, and play guitar and keyboard in a band.

Pat quietly stood out in school. By the time she was ten, officials wanted to find out just what her abilities were, so she was singled out to take a series of intelligence tests. Virginia brought Pat to the school-board office, and Pat took two days of intensive tests. Pat had always been a frail child, and these tests were physically hard on her. After the second day, Virginia told the authorities that Pat had endured as much as she could. The woman giving the tests told Virginia that Pat had scored 137, well above average, and that, given more time, she could have scored even higher.

Virginia always regretted that she could not provide a more intellectual environment for her gifted daughter. She had three other children to care for, and Arden's health problems would rule the family's life and finances until he was grown. "I used to say she learned by osmosis. She was way ahead of me, anyhow. That's why I wasn't much help," Virginia muses. "If Pat had been born into a different family, she'd have had a much better chance. I really didn't have time." Be that as it may, the family never stood in Pat's way when she wrote. At age ten, Pat won her first recognition for poetry. She sent a poem to "Uncle Ben's Sunray Club," a children's column in *The Vancouver Sun*. The prize she received for her verse was a book of poetry.

What was going on within this quiet, studious girl? In "Woman," a poem Pat would write many years later, she says, "As a child I climbed trees / ... in its closed veins, a closed system."[13] Everything she touched seemed to increase her wonder at the universe and how the parts connected to the whole. Unhappily, that wonder inevitably was mixed with the pain in relationships. If the unpublished poem "Advice to Young Women" is based upon her personal life, Pat had a friend who broke a confidence when she was a little girl. She warns us: "Beware indecent exposure / of wounds (here's where my best friend betrayed me / at seven years old ...)."[14] Betrayal, for a sensitive child, would have been crushing. If this did happen, it was probably one of those things that taught Pat to keep a step back from the laughing crowd.

Pat was deeply influenced by her early experiences along Lynn Creek, when her father took her on outdoor adventures. Her poem "In the Continent Behind My Eyes" speaks about going with him on his rounds at the intake station.

> When I was a child
> my father worked with water,
> adjusting flow and level,
> going out from his bed
> into 3 in the morning storms
> to keep the screens clear
> And once he took me to Rice Lake
> where no one is allowed —
> the water was flat as pavement
> papered with fallen leaves
> and flat wooden walkways
> and there I walked on water [15]

When Pat was a child, the family often visited Arthur's mother, Harriet Tinmouth, on Sunday afternoons for English-style tea. Brenda recalls these trips to Gramma Tinmouth's house. To get there, they had to drive across the Second Narrows Bridge. If Vancouver is a city generally famous for its fog, its Second Narrows Bridge is exceptionally so. Brenda remembers a particular stretch where they sometimes had to have someone walk in front of the car so the driver knew where the road was. At other times, Arthur would negotiate his way by standing on the running board of the car with one hand inside on the steering wheel.

Harriet Tinmouth would live to the age of ninety, as worthy as any Eliza McCain. As her years advanced, Brenda remembers her grandmother saying, "When I go, they'll have to take me out and shoot me."

Mayne Island. (circa 1960)

The family's favourite times together were on Mayne Island in the southern Gulf Islands in the Strait of Georgia. Virginia's brother, Bill Wilks, and his wife, Elsie, owned land on the island. Mayne is unique: although nature placed it off the coast of Canada, it has a Mediterranean climate and the most moderate temperatures in the country. Mayne shares the vegetation of the other southern Gulf Islands with their growths of Garry oak, prickly pear cactus and Pat's beloved arbutus. As well, it has animals like the Bendires shrew and the California bat. And, of course, there are chipmunks, squirrels, western spotted skunk, and even black-tailed deer.

This mixture of woods and sandy beaches provided the setting where the Tinmouths and the Wilkses spent their happiest times. Pat's daughter Beth says, "Mayne Island has a distinctive smell," a particular fragrance undoubtedly rising from its special ecology.

There is a small handwritten note among Pat's papers that says simply, "Some things can't be changed like the view from the cabin." Pat loved the island for its natural beauty and also because, while there, she could be with her dearly loved aunt Elsie and uncle Bill.

Virginia's brother, Bill Wilks, was a singular man. He owned a small trucking business that operated mostly in North Vancouver. Although he did not drink, one of his business activities was delivering beer. He was not a big man, but the work of loading and unloading beer barrels gave him muscular forearms that would have been the envy of body builders.

Like his father, James, Bill was concerned about the problems of working people. His father's solution had been trade-union work; Bill's was the Communist Party. He was a humane, hard-working fellow who saw greed as the source of unnecessary misery. He believed that people would treat the earth and one another with care if they would only think about things. Bill did what he could in his own neighbourhood in North Vancouver. He was bothered that the teenagers did not have wholesome activities, so he organized dances at the high school and hired popular bands of the day. Then, he would supervise the evening. Bill had the knack of spotting possible troublemakers and getting them to leave before they became rough. His manner was gentle, but it was backed up by that well-muscled body.

Bill and Elsie were in their forties when they moved their family permanently to Mayne Island; as their son, Barry, explained, "they got tired of the rat race in the city." On Mayne Island, Bill undertook several activities to support his family. He ran the general store, grew both field and hot-house tomatoes, and raised sheep. From time to time, he was a logger and a builder as well. Although two generations of Wilkses were supported by the resources that the land provided, they used the land gently. Years after Bill's death, Parks Canada acquired the land for a heritage park, describing it as still having strong ecological integrity. Bill Wilks had carried on his work carefully, long before "environment" became a household word.

It is clear that Bill and Elsie passed on their love of Mayne Island to Pat. It resonates in her poetry as she writes about and tries to understand the earth, the water and all the two-, four-, six- and eight-legged animals that slithered, crawled, walked, swam or flew past her. The island gave her the material to write poems called "Anemones," "Craneflies in Their Season," "Octopus" and "Hermit Crabs."[16] She even wrote a poem about those creatures much dreaded by gardeners, slugs, whose slime, she tells us, makes a crystal rope. Then she really shakes our way of seeing by imagining herself behaving as slugs do.

> they are twined
>   together
> in a perfect spiral
>   flowing
>   around
>   each other
>   spinning
>   gently
>   with their motions
> *Imagine*
>   making love like that[17]

The poem "Song" was probably inspired by Mayne Island as well. It is a conditional invitation to the reader to join her on what she calls "my island," giving directions on how to get there and how to behave after arriving. The poem also works as a metaphor for testing whether or not the reader can be trusted.[18]

As Pat's brother Arden grew, his special health needs continued. Since this was before the days of public health insurance, his medical expenses were a constant worry for the family. Thinking that their living expenses would be lower on Mayne, in 1947 they sold their beloved house on 12th Street, their furniture and their washing machine, and moved to the island, hoping to run a store there. But a life on Mayne Island was not meant to be. The same month that they moved there, the only doctor on the island left. To care for Arden, they had to make frequent trips to Vancouver for medical appointments. This proved too difficult and too expensive, and so, after only four months, they moved back to Vancouver.

The Tinmouths returned to North Vancouver with no extra money, so the solution was to move in with family. They found space in the basement of Annie Wilks' house on Capilano Road. Arthur took a job as a sheet-metal worker at the Burrard Shipyards and, by 1950, the family had saved up enough money to buy a lot on 10th Street in North Vancouver. There they built a prefabricated house that Arthur put together with the help of two other men. The house remains the Tinmouth family home to this day. Life mostly went well after that, but they had to get through a strike at the shipyard, with loss of pay, at about the same time that they moved to 10th Street.

As Pat and Brenda grew, they continued to be very different. When Brenda walked home from school with a gang of friends, Virginia could hear them laughing half a block away. By contrast, Pat would come home quietly and go down to her bedroom in the basement. Her mother knew that she was home only when she saw Pat's shoes neatly parked by the door. Then, Virginia would call a greeting downstairs to her and Pat would answer, "Hello, Mother," then go back to her reading. "She was a no-fuss person. Everything she did was with no fuss," Virginia concludes.

Living safely on the Canadian side of the ocean did not insulate the Tinmouth family from being personally affected by World War II. From 1939 to 1945, headlines blared the latest details of campaigns, and newsreels echoed the shrieks of bombs. Everyone was conscripted for "the war effort." Children at Ridgeway Elementary School, for instance, finished their studies early on Friday

afternoons to sort rivets, roll bandages and learn First Aid. This was
a benign effect of the country's total absorption with war. A more
malevolent result was night terrors. Pat was eleven years old when
the war ended. She would later write a poem that describes such a
nightmare. In "Rumours of War" she says, "I must have heard /
ominous news broadcasts / on the radio; / they must have mentioned / the Black Forest … but the Black Forest / came right up our
ravine / … and Raggedy Ann / and I woke screaming."[19]

Pat's mother told of another memorable event that happened
during Pat's eleventh year. One day Pat came home from school in
uncharacteristic turmoil. When her mother got her to explain, Pat
complained, "It's not fair." What was not fair was that one of her
friends had started to menstruate, and Pat felt that she had an equal
right to the same status. This was typical of Pat. She accepted her
body and did not buy into the old adage that women's cycles are a
curse. Her poem "The Last Room" may be about menstruation,
among other things. It describes a smooth gourd, a dark place and
"former skins."[20]

Throughout much of her childhood and early adolescence, Pat
was burdened with a health problem that might have affected her
personality. The problem started with what looked like a cold sore
on her lip. One of the children in the neighbourhood had had
impetigo, so Virginia brought her daughter to the public health
nurse, who suggested a medication for this condition. The following
day was the school Halloween party, and Pat did not want to miss it.
Virginia put lots of medication on the sore and sent Pat off to school.
Pat came home very sick, with sores inside and outside her mouth.
In the next stage of the disease, these sores broke into blisters.

The problem came and went for years, and the doctors had
trouble diagnosing it. First, they thought it was a tropical disease,
but finally they determined that it was a form of herpes. During the
worst of the outbreaks, Pat was hospitalized for five days. She was
so ill that she had to have the care of a special nurse twenty-four

hours a day. For a long time the treatment consisted of taking sulphur drugs and bathing with antibiotic soap. Then the doctors gave her vaccinations and, instead of blisters, dark spots appeared on her skin. In the end, Pat had to undergo surgery to have a piece of her lip removed. After that, the problem largely subsided, but it left visible and invisible scars. Shaking her head, Virginia comments, "Pat had a real cross to bear on that. She was really sensitive." Living with constant open blisters must have affected her character development and probably contributed to her self-effacing manner.

Young girls worry about their appearance and Pat was no different. From her poetry, we know that she was keenly aware of her body. Pat preserves and communicates the memory of her strong adolescent feelings in "On Reading a Poem Written in Adolescence." "Couldn't write then maybe / but how I could love / … I can almost remember / how many hands I had / hooked in the sky."[21]

Pat's mother had the impression that Pat never had boyfriends in high school. She was friendly with boys on the school paper, but, so far as anyone knows, she never had a high-school sweetheart. Her mother sometimes overheard Pat's telephone conversations with boys who would call and invite her out. Virginia repeatedly heard Pat politely but firmly say, "No, thanks, I don't want to go out with you." Always a private person, Pat may have dated boys and not told her family about it. In her notebook, Pat writes of a place called "The Hive."[22] "I was taken there by T., a boy I was going with." The emphasis in her notebook is not on the young man, however, but on "The Hive," which she describes as a big old house, honeycombed with little cells of rooms. Her fascination was with the large structure made up of intriguing little parts.

When she was sixteen, Pat told her parents that she was quitting school to get a job. Virginia says, "We thought that was terrible. She was such a natural scholar." Years later, Pat's daughter Beth talked the matter over with her grandmother, who explained to her that quitting school, usually to earn money, "in those days and in that neighbourhood, wasn't considered out of the ordinary." Beth's own answer is, "I think she wanted to grow up in a hurry. She wanted to move on. She wanted to make money." In Pat's usual private way, she never did tell her family why she left school. Her mother and her daughter could only speculate.

Pat's family says that they were not aware of any hopes that Pat might have had to continue her education, and Pat never wrote about any such dreams. Yet she saved a certificate issued by the British Columbia department of education, division of examinations, which certifies that Patricia Louise Tinmouth, Candidate Number 12074, had forty-five of the ninety-two credits needed for university standing. At the bottom of the page is the admonition "THIS CERTIFICATE SHOULD BE PRESERVED," which is exactly what Pat did.

In her early school years, officials had Pat tested because they considered her to be gifted, but by the end of high school she was not doing outstanding work. Schooling seems to have played little part in the growth of this child who loved books and writing poetry. Her exceptional memory and imagination were not enough to help her flourish in school. Given her family's finances, Pat would have had to win scholarships to go to university, but no one guided her toward that goal.

Maybe university would have given Pat's mind the exercise it craved. Maybe not. Gifted people are often bored by the routine of school, and Pat's boredom may have started when she entered Grade One already able to read. Going to university demands the investment of a large amount of time and money. Pat's family had always put their money and emotions into caring for one another. Pat might have felt selfish devoting that amount of money to herself. In her poem "The Comet," Pat shows her awareness of her family's financial status when she describes advice offered by one of her aunts: "'Don't ever get your ears pierced. / Robbers could tear your jewels / Right out of your flesh!' As though I, / or any of us, / would ever own jewels."[23]

Pat may have felt that staying in high school, even though there were no tuition fees, was a financial burden on the family. Many young adults see themselves as losing money simply by not having a job. There are also people who leave high school because they cannot afford what they believe are the obligatory brand names. Virginia wonders if Pat wanted to earn money to "afford more stylish clothes." It is unlikely that Pat could be completely influenced by something as frivolous as fashion, but it is easy to believe that she wanted to be like the other girls. Her mother noticed that Pat "went with the more popular, more affluent crowd." Even in their working-class neighbourhood, some people were better off than others.

Given the neighbourhood in which she lived, Pat might never have considered university as a real possibility. By and large, teenagers whose friends are university bound are likely to see themselves doing the same thing. In Pat's North Vancouver neighbourhood, the girls were preparing for clerical jobs until marriage, and many of the boys were eyeing jobs in the shipyards. Neither of these male or female choices would have encouraged her fellow students to think about university. Had Pat talked about higher education in that crowd, she would probably have felt more isolated than she already was. Those compartments she was to write about so eloquently as an adult probably meant that her well-developed mind, with its love of poetry, had to be kept out of exchanges with her classmates.

A couple of days after quitting high school, Pat found a job as a keypunch operator with Evans, Coleman and Evans, a building materials firm. Later, she moved to a similar position at the Burrard Shipyards. There, by age eighteen, she was supervising five people.

It is impossible to guess how Pat Lowther would have fared with more formal education. Living with skin eruptions must have trained her not to push herself forward. When one is a teenager, one's feelings are as soft as baby's hair, and one can spend the rest of one's life with the remains of those early feelings. Maybe life told Pat that she was just not good enough to try certain things.

CHAPTER 2

A Husband and Two Babies

Words were sacred objects to her.

— Stephen Michael Bersensky[1]

As PAT GREW INTO A YOUNG ADULT, her high intelligence was evidently not enough to give her a good opinion of herself. These are the years of trying to figure out who one is and of receiving messages from outside as to how society thinks one should be. The disfiguration caused by the herpes outbreaks of earlier years undoubtedly left Pat convinced that she was unattractive, a flawed person. Her friends say that she often made jokes against herself that made them uncomfortable. Self put-down is a defense tactic that many people use: it is less painful to joke about one's shortcomings and thereby prevent others from dong so.

Fellow poet and friend Professor Fred Cogswell describes Pat's internal and external dilemma: "She could be as fearless as a tigress where injustice to others was concerned, but she had no armour with which to defend herself when these things impinged upon her personally. This seeming contradiction stemmed, as far as I could tell, from an ingrained conviction — which no one who knew her could share — of her own lack of inner grace and beauty. All too often she made unfair comparisons to her own disadvantage between the appearances of others and her own inner knowledge of herself. Could she have been persuaded to see herself as I and her friends saw her, she would have seen as straight, stout-hearted, and loyal a person as it is any one's human privilege to meet."[2]

The devotion of friends like Fred Cogswell seems not to have been convincing to Pat. If she was not worthy in her own eyes, then maybe she could show the world that someone else cared about her. For many young women, claiming the love of a man was the route to self-approval. Perhaps she thought that the acquisition of a husband would be just the medicine she needed to gain respect.

During her childhood, Pat had been friends with a group of girls consisting of the Domphousse sisters and their girl cousins. For years she had been invited to Domphousse family picnics and birthday parties. When Pat started working at the Burrard Shipyards, she took a second look at their brother, Bill, who was then a labourer there. It must have been a look that was well received, because they were married that same year, 1953. Pat was just eighteen. Bill was several years older, and this likely made Pat feel more grown up than her years. The couple moved to Deep Cove, a scenic community up the coast from North Vancouver. Pat gave up her job and devoted herself to being a housewife and then a mother, the grand postwar ideal.

"It would be hard for a man of Bill's nature to put up with a girl like Pat. He was strong, efficient, fast" is Virginia's estimation. Bill was an active man who lived in the world he could see. The world of poetry and allusion did not speak to him. Virginia points out that "Pat was a daydreamer. She was always into books. She had never done any housework or cooking." To someone unaware of the work that Pat was doing in her mind, it could look as if she were spending her day in complete inactivity. She might gaze at the dust on the furniture, look at earthworms in the garden or sit pensively stroking the cat. Then, leaving the furniture undusted and the garden unweeded, she would pick up her pen. When Virginia warned Bill about these differences before the marriage, his response was "Oh, I'll help her," and when he married Pat he did help out, but willing hands were not enough to bridge the gap between them.

Why did two such different people think they should get married? The answer is most likely simple sexual attraction. This, after all, was the 1950s, and once people were sexually involved they often felt that they "had to get married." Common-law relationships were rare. Although a great deal of sexual activity happened before and outside marriage, most — except a few trailblazers — gave in to the social pressure to conceal it.

The most common way of maintaining the fiction that only married women became pregnant was a quick marriage. People would then try to blur the actual date the marriage vows were taken, and chubby, well-developed babies were dubbed premature. In Pat's case, Virginia, who had been raised with the old social codes, said that she had forgotten the date of Pat's marriage to Bill Domphousse. When Pat's second daughter, Beth, pressed her grandmother for details of her mother's first marriage. Virginia, using the language of the 1950s, said, "If you must know, your mother had to get married." Beth honours her mother's later frankness about sexuality and speaks of her frustration with the fiction of "making things look a certain way." Sex was a part of Pat's humanity and gave a texture to her poetry. To a certain extent, she was among the pioneers who made possible the more honest sexuality that was born in the 1960s.

Pat and Bill had two children. Their first child, Alan, was born on the first day of April in 1954. Their second child, Katherine, was born on September 30, 1956, and from the start she was "Kathy." In 1957 Pat managed to vary her domestic life by taking a creative writing course at a community college in North Vancouver. It was there that she became friends with fellow student Ward Carson. Since they both lived in Deep Cove, Carson started driving Pat home after class. He would drop her off and then retire to his "huge old log house" on a remote private beach in Deep Cove. The house was set in a cluster of trees, and not too many people found their way out there. One day Carson answered a knock to find Pat on the doorstep with fresh home baking. After that, their friendship broadened beyond a mutual interest in writing. They shared their political ideas and ideals and, during the next few years, they attended peace marches together.

As Virginia had feared, Pat's marriage to Bill foundered. After about five years of marriage, the couple divorced. It was the judge's idea to award custody of Alan to his father and Kathy to her mother. At twenty-three, Pat returned to work as a keypunch operator and, with her two-and-a-half-year-old daughter, moved into the basement of her parents' home.

Pat's oldest daughter, Kathy.
(circa 1960)

Virginia's recollection of those years is that they were "very calm." When Kathy was old enough, she went to Ridgeway Elementary School — just as her mom had done — and spent her time after school with Gram until Pat got home from work. Pat and Kathy usually had dinner with the family and then retired to their small basement apartment, a big room that Pat had partitioned into two. Kathy's bedroom was on one side of the partition; Pat had a sitting room and sleeping area on the other. Some evenings Pat indulged her love of music, playing her parents' piano or listening to record albums. Carson remembers that she was especially fond of opera, which she often sang on the spur of the moment. She had a collection of more than forty opera albums, impressive on her modest income. Other evenings Pat had groups of friends in to read poetry and discuss politics. Kathy's memories of those years in the Tinmouth home are good ones: "It was a family atmosphere, for sure."

Four-year-old Alan lived with his father, who remarried shortly after the divorce. His new wife had a large number of children from her two previous marriages and, as Virginia describes it, "Alan was lost, but he never complained." He spent a lot of time with the Tinmouth grandparents and he would ask his grandmother, "When am I going to live with my mother again?" Not knowing what to say, she would reply, "Oh, it won't be long." Virginia shakes her head sadly. "I didn't know what the dickens to tell him!"

On Saturdays, Alan would visit his mother and sister, and, on Sundays, Kathy visited her father and Alan. Alan would arrive at his mother's place at 10:00 A.M. and usually find her sound asleep, recuperating from her week-long grind at work. He remembers, "She was the hardest person to wake up I've ever come across." As adults, both Alan and Kathy remember each of them living with one parent and a set of grandparents. They also remember weekends as being the best time.

Pat's feelings about her son come through in several poems that she dedicated to him. In one poem, the boy shows his mother his lucky stone. She responds by advising him, "Carefully fold your fingers, son / With the smooth stone safely locked within. / Tightly grasp and guard its glisten." She ends by telling him why he should so carefully guard his treasure: "Luck's a favour few have owned."[3]

With the dual responsibilities of working and raising her daughter, Pat had little time left over for herself. "She never had enough time to write," Virginia recollects. "She always said, 'I wish I had more time. I wish I had time to do justice to this.' Pat was always reading and she was always writing. Even when she was having a cup of tea, she'd have a piece of paper alongside her tea cup and she'd put a little bit down. She was working on poetry all the time."

Despite the many claims on her time, Pat did manage to squirrel away moments to work on her poetry. In 1959, Mrs. P. Domphousse of Deep Cove, B.C., sent a poem to the *Alberta Poetry Year Book* and won an award in the Short Poetry Class. "Requiem for a Phoenix" points to the dangers of believing wholly in legends. She imagines the bird courting death, believing in its own rebirth and learning too late that death is permanent. Despite the bird's fate, the poem does not dismiss the magic of legends. On the contrary, "Requiem for a Phoenix" couples a profound respect for myth with the logic of a rational modern mind.[4]

After Pat and Bill separated, Pat's friendship with Ward Carson continued. At that time, Pat had an evening job downtown and often telephoned Carson for a drive home. She was twenty-five by now and he was over forty. It is likely they were lovers. Like Pat, Carson was a creative person with little formal education. During World War II he had trained as an airplane mechanic with the Royal Canadian Air Force and had also served for a year in Special Intelligence. Most of his later working life was spent as an electrician at Simon Fraser University.

Carson shared with Pat a fascination for cosmic ideas. He spent much time researching what he calls the "Basic Coordinate System of the Universe." This research included working on the key to a universal equation in astrophysics and a new decimal system, which he called "the universe in proportion." In later years Carson's inventions emphasized his environmental concerns.[5] Carson credits Pat with teaching him a great deal about the craft of writing, and Pat trusted Carson enough to leave original copies of some of her work in his care. Their friendship is the only reason some of her early poems found their way into print after her death.

Carson reports that Pat was sometimes haunted by dark premonitions. If one needs to look for a rational explanation for these feelings, the fact that Pat was often sick as a child could be the reason. Her friend Lorraine Vernon believes that this may have "added to her feeling that life was tenuous." Once, when Carson and Pat were alone together, Pat was silent, with her eyes closed, for a long time; then her arms and legs twitched. After several minutes, Pat opened her eyes, and Carson asked her what she was doing. Pat answered, "I'm travelling." He asked her where she had gone and she answered, "I can't tell you." He never asked her again. Although Ward Carson is a thoroughly practical man, he knew that what Pat was experiencing was just as real as the circuits he wired.

Pat ended her relationship with Carson in about 1961, and he still carries her parting words to him: "I'm tired of *macho* men. I'm going to look for the most effeminate man I can find and be a mother to him." Carson believes Pat said this simply to hurt him. Interestingly, Pat's poetry does not cast people into types, does not seek to hurt, instead it shows how human beings are made up of complicated and changing qualities. Pat's second daughter, Beth, has a partial answer to explain her mother's words. She believes that her mom had a strong "saving mentality." Like many nurturing people, Pat often made the mistake of thinking that she could save people from their problems. Beth also points out that, in her mother's era, feminist thinking was just beginning to work itself out and there were still some rough spots in the logic. When asked to explain this nurturing side of Pat, Carson's response is a comparison gleaned from his electrician's background: "Sides develop between two persons. They form a field between them." People often behave differently, depending upon who their companions are, and they also bring out particular facets of the one they are with.

CHAPTER 3

Poetry in Vancouver

I want to be with the thing.

— Pat Lowther[1]

IN THE EARLY 1960S, THE PAT EVERYONE COULD SEE on the outside was a considerate daughter, breadwinner and loving mother, but the inner Pat was having problems. "Desperation" is the word she used. Sometime after 1959, while still using the name Domphousse, she wrote a covering letter to an unknown person who seems to have asked to see a sample of her work. The name on the letter is illegible, although it could be "Mr. Study."[2] This person may have been in a position to publish or promote Pat's poetry in some way. Pat confides, "Living in a state of desperation for so many years has naturally been reflected in everything I've written." Then she adds with more confidence, "If you're looking for Edna Jackson or Audrey Alexandra Brown, it's not in here." In closing, she tweaks him with: "Can you stand it?"

The note also says that she has enclosed a book with her poem on pages thirty-nine and forty. This had to be "Requiem for a Phoenix," which appeared on those pages of the *Alberta Poetry Year*

Book of 1959. What to make of this? Pat admits to living in a painful state. Yet her ideas about poetry are firm. There are no apologies for being herself or for not following the styles of earlier women poets. It is striking that Pat confides her desperation to someone she addresses as "Mr." and who evidently does not share her views on poetry. Some people use their problems like a letter of reference. Perhaps this is what Pat was doing. Friends such as Allan Safarik, bill bissett and Stephen Michael Bersensky tell of long, soul-searching telephone conversations with Pat, but these people were close friends who shared her poetic and political values. She may have written the letter for herself and never sent it to any Mr. Study. In any case, "Can you stand it?" is an unusual piece of written evidence that Pat sometimes made an effort to tease to get a point across.

At this time of turmoil, Pat was also beginning to find out who she was, and the name that she used when submitting poetry changed. She no longer signed her work as the matron Mrs. P. Domphousse. She dropped the "Mrs.," and a fully first-named Patricia Domphousse of Vancouver had three poems published in the the 1961 *Alberta Poetry Year Book*.[3]

The 1960s were good times for literature in Vancouver, even for that usually poor cousin of the family, poetry. In 1963, the city was the site of a successful gathering, the Vancouver Poetry Conference, which attracted a diverse group of Canadian and American poets. Coffee houses with names like "The Advance Mattress Factory," "The Black Spot" and "The Attic" came into being, largely in the warehouse district along Burrard Inlet. The coffee houses provided congenial places for Pat and other unknown poets to read their work in public.

At that time, Gastown, as it is now known, was a low-cost area, making it possible for small literary presses such as Talon Books, Pulp Press and bill bissett's blewointmentpress to locate in the area. A women's art gallery was another fixture of the neighbourhood during the 1960s. The gallery put on street-theatre productions on matters important to women, such as abortion. The artists fashioned portable cardboard scenery and staged surprise demonstrations for the benefit of astonished shoppers. Once artists had shown the vitality of the area, developers started to emphasize its 19th-century history and put in trendy pubs and restaurants. Real estate prices rose, and today decorative lights and tourist shops line the streets.

These coffee houses of the 1960s were centres of political as well as cultural activity. The politics reflected the concerns of the decade: human rights, justice and peace. Poetry readings were usually run as fundraising events for small presses such as blewointmentpress and Very Stone House, but they sometimes had political goals as well, such as ending the war in Vietnam or helping the League for Socialist Action.

Stephen Michael Bersensky is one of the many Americans who fled the United States to avoid being drafted to fight in Vietnam. He settled in Vancouver and says he became "a poet by the atmosphere." He believes that Pat was also nourished by that atmosphere. Although the drug culture of the 1960s was a factor in the Vancouver poetry world, there is no evidence that Pat either favoured or used drugs. She was, however, sympathetic to some of the concerns of the hippies. This sympathy allowed Pat to have respectful relationships with a variety of poets. Some had university positions and comfortable incomes; others were from the drug culture and had even less financial security than Pat.

Maxine Gadd was among the poets who often shared the program with Pat in those coffee houses with the quirky names. Pat was only seven years older than Gadd, "but she seemed more mature. I was part of the hippy drug culture and Pat lived in her own world with her family. I don't remember toking with Pat." Thinking back to the Pat she knew in the 1960s, Gadd calls her a pre-feminist. She is quick to point out, "By that I don't mean she was an anti-feminist.

She was writing just prior to the new feminist movement of the late 1960s." When the young women of the 1960s were exploring their relationships with men, Pat already had family responsibilities. Gadd does not separate Pat the person from Pat the poet. "Pat's poetic images are womanly ones. They're about birth and sex. The woman is the one who bears." That can involve more than bearing children. It can mean holding up people and ideas or art, and it takes a particular kind of courage — an enduring courage, very different from the swashbuckling kind. Gadd concludes, "Trees that are given too much to bear can break at the stem."

Roy Lowther, whom Pat would meet very shortly, also noted the literary atmosphere. Always short of cash, he walked around Gastown with a shopping bag full of verses for sale. Like an old-fashioned minstrel, he occasionally earned some money for his efforts.

The poetry yeast continued to bubble and, in 1961, Pat received two honourable mentions in the *Alberta Poetry Year Book*. They were for "Pastorale" and "Spring Sunday." In addition, "Alpha Beta" received an award in the short poem class.[4]

"Alpha Beta" examines the frightening majesty of the jaguar, a god figure in the ancient Inca religion. The poem pictures the animal's surroundings: "There in the jungle, dried blood / smelling of lizards and minerals", the big cat makes a home. "Alpha Beta" is clearly influenced by the work of Chilean poet Pablo Neruda, who wrote of the ancient spirits that are connected to places. Many of Neruda's poems are about Latin American jungles and their smells, and he probably wrote about minerals more passionately than any other poet.

"Pastorale," contrary to what the reader might expect, is no dewy-eyed description of nature. Rather, the title seems to be poking fun at traditional pastoral poetry. The poet looks at an old well whose "water would make frogs of princes," and the poem itself is an exchange between the poet's real body and nature.

There I played at modesty
Not with fig leaves
But with leaves of the grape,
The assertive, acid, green grape.
Velvet dust settled upon my hair.

As in traditional pastoral poetry, hints of human sexuality mingle with growing things, but Pat departs from the sentiment of traditional innocence: "All the years I have been angry / Remembering so much wasted on innocence."[5]

In the 1960s women were just beginning to question the sexual codes that had been handed down to them. To talk about sex publicly was to risk being considered a bad girl. Pat took that risk, and in doing so made a contribution to honesty about women's sexuality. She looks at the sensuousness of sex as well as at what sex does to a woman's life. In "The Dig," she describes "the bones of a woman" at an archaeological site.

and sex, that soft explosion
. . .
their bodies thickened like tubers
broke and were remade
again and again crying out
in the heave of breaking
the terrible pleasure
again and again till
. . .
they became bone.
. . .
Will our bones tell
sisters, what we died of? [6]

"Wanting" is probably her best-known poem about women's sexuality. It opens with an apparently masochistic desire "to be broken / utterly." But this is a fully human woman and she cannot separate sexual desire from the core of herself. She fears that the breaking will not let her male lover see "the flower shape of me."[7]

Later poems, such as "The Insider" and "Angel," continue her exploration of what sexuality does to women. In "The Insider," she says,

> I am a woman; all that I might be
> is like a cloud or mist in which I live.
> Dragging my sex like a great dark sack with me,
> I learned this was all I had to give. [8]

In "Angel" she confesses,

> And I have accepted all that love is, the ruthless hand
> in my guts, the rearranging,
> breaking and remaking,
> the flowing of myself
>
> …
>
> And have not kept an essence of myself — [9]

The 1960s may have ushered in an era of sexual frankness, in Pat's poetry and in society at large, but frankness does not — and did not — lead directly to equality. The standards of sexual behaviour were still set by tradition, religion, laws and unspoken custom. Those standards expected a woman to be sexually asleep until she was married. After that, she was to be totally available to her lord and master. Not until 1982 was the Criminal Code of Canada amended to make it an offence for a man to force sex upon his wife. Pat would not live to see the 1980s.

In or outside marriage, the newer, freer sexuality turned out to be a many-sided gem. Sometimes it scratched great gouges out of the wearer. Once a woman entered into a sexual relationship with a man, her standing as a person changed, both in her eyes and in the eyes of others. If her sexual relationship was within a marriage, she was still viewed as her husband's property. If it was outside marriage, she was viewed as somewhat tainted. In neither case was the woman seen as autonomous and entitled to make personal choices. Yet Pat took the risk, saying that her sexual feelings were important and going on to express her anger at being silenced. In "Pastorale," she turns the idea of sexual innocence on its head and condemns it.[10] Being against the code put Pat in danger. As her daughter Beth points out, "The man who would take her life was deeply threatened by her frank openness to sexuality."[11]

Pat's work continued to score points. The Vancouver Poetry Society published "After Rain" and "Diamonds" in a 1962 issue of *Full Tide*, adding this editorial note: "Mrs. Patricia Domphousse is a new member. We note the strength and delicacy of her work and hope to see more of it."[12]

While living as a single mother and trying to be a poet, Pat confessed, in prose, her feelings about writing: "I want to be with the thing. It was with me as I suffered my morning bus ride, straphanging with office workers similar to those among whom I spend the least productive, but most remunerative and respectable, part of my day."[13] "The thing" is the freedom to live inside her mind and write poetry. In her work called "Poetry," she confesses that the poet's job is to sharpen the reader's perception.[14] Pat believed that poetry has the power to change people.

In April 1963, *Full Tide* once again printed Pat's work, this time, "Recollections of Three Dumb Angels" and "On the Bridges."[15] In this period Pat was working on a series she named "Poems for Life." They were signed Pat Domphousse and were found, after her death, among papers stored in a trunk in her son's attic. Although the work is from an early stage in her poetic career, it shows appreciation for irony writ large. The first work in the series, "A Moral Tale," is the story of a lark that refused freedom.[16] The second, "On the Day After Armistice Day," tells the story of a bystander at a parade who was hit by a Civil Defense car.[17] While in hospital, the accident victim is given a blood transfusion that causes his death. The storyteller thinks he died of "someone else's anaemia."

Pat's poems from the early 1960s show that she was already working with the ideas and poetic forms that she would use in her mature work. "The Comet," which is about the death of her mother's sister, was written in that period. A poem of mixed quality — its main weakness being a lack of focus — it is nonetheless valuable for tracing Pat's ideas and poetic progress. In Aunt Belle's younger years, she had told her nieces and nephews of the time she had watched a dazzling comet. As Belle passes from life to death, Pat hopes that she had "a dazzle of comet / after the pain."[18] Pat used the idea later in writing a poem about Pablo Neruda's death, in which she pictures his body as a jewel returning to the elements. In "15 April 1962," which anticipates her better-known "Notes from Furry Creek," she writes:

> Here on my hands grow leaves.
> …
> That floating seaweed is my hair
> And here, to the left of my breastbone,
> That mountain range.
> Beats the shining earth. [19]

"The Motionlessness of Music"[20] opens with a line used in "In the Silence Between," a poem that would become part of her most acclaimed book, A Stone Diary. At this point in Pat's poetic development she was experimenting with different poetic forms to convey the subjects that concerned her. The acceptance of those poems in literary journals must have given her increased confidence in her craft.

CHAPTER 4

Enter, Roy Lowther

a man I love
in every man

— Pat Lowther[1]

PAT'S LIFE IN THE EARLY 1960s was filled with being a poet, caring for Kathy and working as a keypunch operator. Perhaps that would have been a full enough life for some people, but Pat must have felt a certain unfulfilled yearning. In "The Last Room," she writes, "All through the folded hours / I am burning / quietly."[2] It seems that Pat was yearning for a relationship. Then, in 1961, on one of her visits to the Vanguard Book Store, a downtown Vancouver shop that specialized in left-wing books, Pat entered into a conversation with another patron, Roy Armstrong Lowther. Roy was married to Hannah Govorchin at the time, but their marriage was in tatters. They had three children and the family lived on social assistance.[3]

Roy must have seemed different from the other people Pat knew: He wrote poetry and music; he was older and had travelled. In conversation at the bookstore, they certainly would have had a lot to say to each other about politics, and they might have discovered that they both loved hiking in the Furry Creek area overlooking Howe Sound. Pat may have thought that Providence had arranged a match for her. Perhaps she saw a vulnerability in Roy that she thought she could fix.

Furry Creek is just down the road from Roy's boyhood home, the town of Britannia Beach, which grew up because of its copper deposits. The family settled there when Roy's father found work as a watchman-repairman with the Howe Sound Mining Company. His mother taught piano from the family home. The historic marker on the Squamish Highway reads, "The ores of the Britania [sic] Range were first staked by a trapper named Oliver Furry in 1897." The sign proclaims that the mine operated from 1899 to 1974, making it the "oldest continuously worked copper mine in the British colonies." Local people, however, have other memories.

According to local historian Bruce Ramsey, the mine was run by the Britannia Mining and Smelting Company until 1958, when the company got into financial trouble and closed the mine, causing an economic slump in the town. Although the mine was reopened the following year by another company, the town remained depressed. Then in 1963, the Anaconda Copper Company bought the mine.[4] For people moved by poetry, the purchase would not have looked auspicious. Anaconda was one of the companies that worked the mines of Chile. One of Pablo Neruda's major works, Canto General, is made up of 340 poems that tell the natural and political history of South America. One these poems, "Anaconda Mining Company," calls the company a monster with an "insatiable gullet" and sees the result of its activities as "cross after twisted cross, / the only kindling scattered / by the tree of mining."[5]

Pat was profoundly affected by Pablo Neruda's poetry. To her, Anaconda would have signalled trouble. Sure enough, in August 1964, labour disputes caused a seven-month strike. After the strike, the mine operated for another ten years before Anaconda pulled out, leaving the empty smelter to tower above the town. Although Pat would have sympathized with the people left behind after the closing of the mine, the earth and its elements would have had a stronger call on her. There is an unpublished poem in her old notebook called "Rocks in Copper Bearing Water" in which she describes the rocks as "washed with amber and rose."[6] It is likely that she is writing about the rocks near Britannia Beach, possibly those under the waters of Furry Creek. In this poem, after the pollution and harsh economics of mining, nature has its quiet victory.

As a person who saw life in terms of political systems, Roy Lowther was critical of much of the world he saw around him. And he was happy to criticize people as well as systems. Pat wrote an untitled poem about him early in their relationship. This unpublished poem was left in a brown briefcase and stored in a trunk in her son's attic after Pat's death:

> There stands my love all curst and lone
>
> His townfolk feed him with hate and shame,
> With none but me to defend his name;
>
> Come, love away from slander's dirt.
> Come bent and slow and quiet.
> Love cannot heal all hate has hurt,
> But still I'll live to try it! [7]

The "saving mentality" was at work. Pat seldom used this kind of rhyme and rhythm in her poetry, whereas Roy was a strong advocate of formal structure. When she lost her heart to him, it seems that, for a time, he influenced her poetic style.

Pat's friend Bethoe Shirkoff believes that Pat was first drawn to Roy because she "liked his politics and he touched her heart with his sob story." Pat probably thought she had found the man she could "mother," as she had vowed when breaking off with Ward

Carson. Whatever it was that drew Pat to Roy, they were an unlikely looking couple. Pat dressed in jeans and wore her dark hair long. She looked light and youthful; Roy, according to Bethoe, was "grey, heavy and shambling."

Pat's parents had seen Roy a few times as one of Pat's literary visitors. When she told her parents she was going to lend him money so that he could go back to school, they were unprepared. Her dad gave the opinion that a woman should not lend a man money unless they were married. That's when Pat quietly told her parents that she was going to marry Roy. Virginia remembers that Pat's second wedding was done the way Pat did everything. There was no fuss, no noise. It just happened. Pat's brother Arden was the only member of the family who attended the wedding. Pat's parents felt uneasy about the marriage.

Pat and Roy married on July 20, 1963. Years later their daughter Chris would write a poem called "Mother"[8] and observe that her parents' wedding day was just eight days before Pat's twenty-eighth birthday. The couple honeymooned at their beloved spot, Furry Creek.

Notes from Furry Creek

1
The water reflecting cedars
all the way up
deep sonorous green —
nothing prepares you
for the ruler-straight
log fallen across
and the perfect
water fall it makes
and the pool behind it
novocaine-cold
and the huckleberries
hanging
like fat red lanterns

2
The dam, built
by coolies, has outlived
its time; its wall
stained sallow
as ancient skin
dries in the sun

The spillway still
splashes bright spray
on the lion
shapes of rock
far down below

The dam foot
is a pit
for the royal animals
quiet and dangerous
in the stare
of sun and water

3
When the stones swallowed me
I could not surface
but squatted
in foaming water
all one curve
motionless,
glowing like agate.

I understood the secret
of a monkey-puzzle tree
by knowing its opposite:

the smooth and the smooth
and the smooth takes,
seduces your eyes

to smaller and smaller
ellipses;
reaching the centre
you become
stone, the perpetual
lavèd god. [9]

Furry Creek has changed greatly since Pat wrote of its deep, sonorous, green reflections. First, the logging industry transformed the forest into a bald spot; then a developer built luxury condominiums on it. But some things remain the same. A hiker walking along the logging road that alternately parallels and crosses the creek can still look up from the trail and see Mount Capilano. Just as in Pat's poem, there would be fallen logs "making waterfalls." The water, even in June, is still "novocaine-cold."

It's unfortunate that second wives don't ask first wives for letters of reference. If Pat had known the reason Roy's first wife had

Pat often spent time at Furry Creek. (circa 1960)

divorced him, it would have given her a warning. Roy had tried to strangle his first wife and she had been lucky enough to escape with her life. Over thirty years later, Ruth Lowther Lalonde, Roy's daughter from his first marriage, remembers with horror, "It happened in my bedroom. I remember his hands as they were around her neck. I was four years old. I was screaming. A neighbour heard and called the police." Ruth explains her father's behaviour as the result of a mental illness diagnosed as anxiety hysteria. The problems were severe enough for his first wife to place him in a mental hospital for a while in 1960. It is unlikely that Pat knew any of this.

Even though Roy's daughter remembers the attack on her mother with clarity, Roy probably did not admit to it. In a poem called "Trial Separation," which was published in *Alberta Poetry Year Book* in 1966, Roy contends that his wife lied in court and he goes on to blame her for his raised fist by saying, "None watch her

Pat, in front of her parent's home. (1964)

Pat's only son, Alan, age 9. (1965)

years of yell push his fist high."[10] A poem is not hard fact, yet it does
reveal the poet's feelings. The relevant facts are that Roy's first wife
divorced him and, because of his violence, his access to his children
was restricted. This distressed him and he was determined to
replace them.

When Pat and Roy married, their first home was at 5823 Saint
George Street. Pat's six-year-old daughter, Kathy, continued to live
with her mother, and Alan continued to visit on Saturdays. The
Lowther home was a huge old house with a large front porch and
balconies on the top floor. Although there was plenty of play space
for Kathy in both the front- and backyards, that was not the main
attraction for her. The most exciting play area was out back. Kathy
remembers, "You could hop the chain-link fence in the backyard
into the graveyard." Once in this gruesome playground, Kathy and
her friends hid behind the gravestones and jumped out to scare one
another. The children's games prompted Pat to write a meditation

on graveyards, which was never published. To Pat, the graveyard was neither dramatic nor bitter, it was simply there.

A Graveyard, as Landscape

> Though my backyard
>   borders on a cemetery
>   and though all winter
>   the wind blows
>   over the dead
> into my thin-walled bedroom
>   I am unimpressed
>   by the drama
>   of graveyards.
> Even the muchalive children
>   playing
>   among the stones
> go down the mind smoothly
>   like an accustomed meal
>   with no sharp bud
>   of bitterness
>
>   or clot-crystal [11]

In those early days of the Lowther marriage, life was more good than bad. This is probably when Pat wrote an unpublished poem describing her feelings about her new home:

House

> We could be kicked out tomorrow
> And they'd never miss us,
> the little furry creatures
> living among the gas jets,
> the doves growling in the rafters,
> not miss the smell of my cooking,
> nor Mozart arranging tensions

in the living room,
not miss our noisy loving
in the freezing bedroom,
wind blowing through the closed windows
as though they weren't there.
Somebody else would pay
the eighty-five a month
and perpetual arrears
on the gas bill;
keep it a damnsight cleaner.

God I love it. [12]

Pat had played piano since she was a child. The first shadow to fall over her second marriage was Roy's attitude toward her piano playing. Alan remembers that she played only when Roy wasn't home, "because he'd criticize her playing." No one remembers Pat talking about this change in her life. She just quietly lit up another Matinée cigarette. Pat's poetic self was not nipped, however. In December 1963, *Full Tide* published "Stone" and "With Ferns in a Bucket."[13] A revised version of the latter is in her book *This Difficult Flowring*.

In 1964, *Alberta Poetry Year Book* finally awarded Pat a first prize. She submitted a poem called "The Sewing Machine and the Umbrella" for the Humorous Class. This time, her work was signed Patricia Lowther. There was no Mrs. in her name. "The Sewing Machine and the Umbrella" pokes fun at surrealistic painters. She insists that her real life has more incongruities than they could ever imagine. For her house is littered with:

last week's newspapers;
phone bill, poem, child's sandal,
. . .

the dog is sleeping
on top of Pablo Neruda
and a roller skate. [14]

More important to Pat's career, in the summer of 1965, the literary journal *Northwest Review* published "A Water Clock."[15] Recognition for the poem did not stop there. Pacific Books of Palo Alto, California, issued a yearly collection of what it considered the best "original poetry published in magazines for the English-speaking world." "A Water Clock" was among the poems selected for inclusion in *Best Poems of 1965: Borestone Mountain Poetry Awards*.[16] Now Pat had a modest international standing, but she may not have thought it a great achievement. Her unpublished poem, probably from that period, expressing her disappointment in the poetry that gets acclaim:

On Reading an Anthology of "Best Poems"

But the masters of splendour are not
here, for here no quick hard hand
leaps from the language,
knuckled with verbs,
to grapple my soul's nape [17]

Poetry criticism had to share space in Pat's mind with public issues. In the 1950s and 1960s, during the height of the Cold War between the West and the Soviet Union, there was a great deal of testing of nuclear weapons. Were radiation and other types of chemical fall-out dangerous to people's health? The generals were not asking that question; people like Pat were. In an effort to learn the effects of strontium 90, one type of the radioactive fall-out, Pat took part in a study on baby teeth. In 1965, she filled out a form detailing Kathy's date of birth, how long she was breast-fed and the kind of milk she drank in her first year.[18] Pat saved a newspaper clipping telling of the concern some scientists had that nuclear-bomb tests had released strontium 90 into the atmosphere. This was of particular concern to mothers of young children, because strontium 90 is chemically similar to calcium and can be taken into the bones through food, especially milk. Scientists didn't know what effect radioactivity in children's bones might have, but it needed to be questioned. Many mothers switched their children from fresh to powdered milk — the fresher the milk, the higher the concentration of strontium 90. No doubt Pat knew that these actions by themselves would not stop the testing, but she was politically astute enough to know that the strontium 90 research added to public criticism of the arms race.

Protecting the well-being of children was a major part of Pat's life. She had marvelled at new life since she was a little girl. Her ardour for life made her vulnerable to Roy's need to replace the family he had lost. Birth control was not high on Pat's list. She has one short notebook entry comparing the use of a condom to sitting in the dentist's chair. She did not want to tamper with the magic of love and birth.

> Once we've had babies
> we can't stop
> ...
> apple trees can't
> forget the seasons [19]

While the problems with Roy were incubating, so was Pat. Their first child, Heidi Elizabeth, was born on August 9, 1966, and was soon nicknamed Beth. Pat wrote to fellow poet Dorothy Livesay about the event. During her pregnancy, Pat related, she had wondered if she was carrying "two or more whopping boys"; instead she bore "one rather smallish girl."[20]

The birth itself was sudden and violent and gave rise to the poem "Touch Home," published in *Milk Stone* in 1974. An earlier draft of the poem, entitled "Beginning," was among the papers found after her death in the trunk in her son's attic.

Touch Home

My daughter, a statistic
in a population explosion
exploded
      popped
out of my body like a cork.

The doctors called for oxygen,
the birth too sudden, violent,
the child seemed pale

But my daughter lay
in perfect tranquillity
touching   the new air
     with her
elegant   hands. [21]

"Touch Home" cannot help but bring a throb of recognition to any woman who has feared for her child's survival at birth. Pat was among the lucky ones who are first alarmed at the danger to their newborn infant and then relieved by the baby's graceful presence.

Professor Réshard Gool, who knew Pat in later years and wrote about her after her death, was taken with the poem for other reasons. In a radio script, he called the image "touching the new air with her elegant hands" "one of the most perfect and exquisite conclusions to any English-language poem."[22] Editors Gary Geddes and Phyllis Bruce used the poem in their collection *15 Canadian Poets Plus 5*, an anthology used in courses in Canadian literature.[23]

It was probably during that pregnancy that Pat also wrote "Poem for Schizophrenics," which was published in the literary magazine *The Fiddlehead* in the winter of 1966. "Poem for Schizophrenics" is a prayerful hope that the "sullen dwarves and japing clowns" who give torment will relent so that the suffering person can "step into the light."[24] That summer, *The Fiddlehead* published two more of her poems. "A Water Clock," the poem that had earned a Borestone Award the previous year, along with another piece, "with ferns in a bucket,"[25] appeared prominently on page two. Pat was becoming more visible as a poet.

From the start, Roy took an active part in caring for his new baby. His way of caring, however, was to do things for the baby as he saw fit. Even though babies have a noisy way of making their needs known, he refused to pick up clues from the little one he was "helping." Kathy tells of an incident when Beth was a baby. "Roy was feeding her in her crib and she was crying and he kept feeding her and she started to choke. My mother rushed over and tried to take the food from his hand, and he jumped up and hit her with his

Pat's second daughter, Beth,
as an infant. (circa 1967)

arm, sending her from the kitchen into the dining room backwards over a chair."[26]

When Beth was a baby, Pat wrote a poem simply called "Beth." It tells how helpless this mother felt when her child cried and nothing could comfort her. Beth was Pat's third baby, and one can guess that ordinary baby tears would have been taken in stride. These were not ordinary baby tears. Something was seriously distressing Beth, and Pat was at a loss to understand what it was. Scenes such as the one Kathy described must have had a good deal to do with the baby's distress as well as with the poet-mother's concern.

Beth

A human child
So lovely and so right
put smiles in all my corners:
the bends of my elbows,
interstices of all my bones
are lotioned with pleasure

Until the child turns
On an inner spine of pain,
Some nerve whip coil
I cannot know.
All is disharmony.
Her happy reaching symmetry
Is all askew
and I can only cry,
What do you want?
What can I do? [27]

Despite Roy's treatment of Beth, he loved her. He never claimed any affection, however, for Pat's daughter Kathy. He repeatedly tried to get Kathy out of the house. The first time Roy put her out, Kathy was about nine years old. It happened when Pat had gone on a poetry-reading tour. Kathy remembers the family driving her mother to the train. "When we got back, he promptly threw me out of the house for the entire time she was gone, about nine or ten days." Kathy went to stay with a friend. "I don't think I told my mum about that till years later … If I ever did. I knew that she'd flip out." Over time, the resentment between Kathy and Roy grew.

While Kathy struggled in her relationship with Roy, Alan managed to avoid direct conflict with him. When he was a teenager, he played guitar in a rock-and-roll band, an activity he continued into his adult years. When he visited his mother, Alan would bring his guitar. What little communication Alan and Roy had was about music. Asked what kind of a musician Roy was, Alan answers, "He could get by on the piano. He could get by a little bit on the guitar. As far as being a musician, no. But he had an incredible knowledge of the theory of music. I had nothing to tune the guitar with, except the piano. I would keep hitting a note until he would say, 'That's an E'." Here Alan reports the only talent any of Pat's children seem to have seen in Roy Lowther. "He had perfect pitch. You could hit any note on the piano and, from the other room, he could tell you what note it was."

CHAPTER 5

Another Baby
and Some Poets

*Nor can we ever
be done with newness*

— Pat Lowther[1]

PAT HAD NO TROUBLE GIVING LIFE and, the February after Beth was born, she became pregnant again. Pat and Roy Lowther's second child was born on the evening of November 19, 1967. They named her Christine Louise. Now Christine Louise joined grandmother Virginia Louise and mother Patricia Louise in continuing the Wilks family tradition. Christine was named after a little girl called Christie who had been one of Roy's students. That Christie is mentioned in Roy's papers as a child with outstanding singing and writing talent. Throughout her childhood, the newest Lowther was nicknamed "Christie." When she was twelve years old, she chose to call herself "Chris."

Even with a new baby, Pat managed to get out and meet other poets. Pat, El Jean Wilson and Elizabeth Gourlay met several times at Helene Rosenthal's West Vancouver home to help one another with their writing. Elizabeth Gourlay says, "We always meant to get together again, but people got busy and the meetings stopped." Gourlay was about twenty years Pat's senior and believes Pat had understanding beyond her years. Gourlay compares her relatively sheltered life with the stressful marriage and scarce money that were constants in Pat's world. She recalls a poem that Pat read at a workshop, one which Gourlay says she did not understand until she grew older. Although she and Pat did not meet again after the group ended — "It was not likely that we would become friends. We lived in different worlds" — she thinks Pat was "a talented person and a tremendous poet."

"Poem: For All the Mad Poets" came out of this period in Pat's life. Her desire to write poetry is a physical need, as physical as a stone, as sensuous as stroking the palms of hands or touching "lip to lover's tongue."

Poem: For All the Mad Poets

When we remember how it rises,
glimmering in that charged darkness
whiter than any moon,
and how the touch of it upon the mind
is like the shape of water-washed stone
to the palms of the hands,
or the shape of lip to lover's tongue,
the shape and shine so fiercely to be loved,
as though the mind's eye
could become a carnal lover,
and how the thing more demanding than music,
still hovers beyond all senses
where the sensitive surfaces of thought
can only, aching, stretch
and shape its form
where it is not,
and sweat this film of words,
do we wonder that, sometimes, one
falls down that branching dark?[2]

Elizabeth Gourlay says, "[Pat felt] exactly as I do about the making of a poem." She explains that it is more than just observation and a feeling for the sound of words. It's about the senses. It's carnal. "Writing a poem is like making love," says Gourlay. There is also an ingredient that Gourlay calls "magic." Perhaps it's that magic that made Pat fear she might be drawn into the rich contours of her own mind and not return.

"Poem: For All the Mad Poets" was not published until after Pat's death, when Vancouver writer Paul Grescoe included it in a *Canadian Magazine* story about her. There is also an earlier version in a file labelled "Contents of Brown Brief Case." It was written in pencil on the back of a statement by Ward Carson about intolerance and greed. Poetry, social issues, friends: they were all of a piece.

In 1965 a social gathering gave Pat a real break. Dorothy Livesay, who was then a professor at the University of British Columbia, often gave parties to help her students and other hopeful writers get acquainted. In December 1965, Livesay invited people to enjoy her famous dish, Rhodesian chicken. Poet Seymour Mayne, who is now a professor of English literature at the University of Ottawa, describes it as a chicken stew in a piquant sauce, full of fruit and vegetables. The good food and lively conversation drew young writers, such as Stephen Michael Bersensky, Pat Lane, bill bissett, Martina Clinton and Pierre Coupe — most with their partners of the time. Among these budding writers, Mayne met Pat and Roy Lowther. Poet bill bissett also met Pat at that party. His memory of her at that time was of a woman "who was trying to be more of an early Communist-Puritan ideal ... more strict looking, less flowing in case one's gender or sexuality might emerge and that would be against the party line ... She used to wear her hair folded back."

It was at this gathering that Seymour Mayne first interested other people in the idea of starting the small press that was to become Very Stone House. By May 1966, the press was in operation, and Mayne had been joined by Patrick Lane, bill bissett and

Jim Brown. By then, Livesay was away as writer-in-residence at the university in Fredericton, New Brunswick, and for the next two years she sublet her house at 3347 8th Avenue in Kitsilano to Mayne. He rented out some rooms to students and used the rest of the building as the headquarters of Very Stone House. The press was a typical shoestring venture of the 1960s. Mayne was a graduate student at the time and he used his student bursary as collateral for a loan to finance the company. The other partners had even less financial standing than a debt-ridden student. In the years that Very Stone House operated, the four cash-strapped writers managed to pay the printing and stationery bills, although sometimes the bank balance was in the order of $50.[3]

The editors started the press partly to get themselves published, but they also wanted to give other new writers a chance. Pat Lowther and Red Lane, Patrick Lane's younger brother, were at the top of that second list. An advertising sheet dated January 16, 1967, lists forthcoming books. The sheet capitalizes bill bissett's name and playfully spells Seymore's name as "Seemore." It lists *Letters from the Savage Mind* by Pat Lane at the price of $2.00, *Fires in the Temple* by Bill Bissett at $3.00, *The Circus in the Boy's Eye* by Jim Brown at $1.50 and *From the Portals of Mouseholes* by Seemore Mayne at $1.50.[4] The carefully irregular layout used in the original sheet is one that bill bissett would later make his own.

It wasn't long before bill bissett left the group to set up his one-of-a-kind publishing house, blewointmentpress. When Jim Brown left the group to form Talon Books, Patrick Lane and Seymour Mayne were left to run Very Stone House. Mayne was the managing editor from 1966 to 1969.

As the editor of Very Stone House, Seymour Mayne visited Pat at home to work out the details of the manuscript that was to become her first book, *This Difficult Flowring*. He remembers visiting the Lowthers' house on grey Vancouver days, a house with a "lack of colour, and a sense almost of dejection itself." Pat would meet him with "the very haggard and harrowed look on her face," exuding a "very tentative, almost self-abnegating sense." Asked if Pat seemed like a frantic mother of two toddlers, Mayne answers, "[There] was a quiet frantic quality in her life. It was a subterranean stream, you know, inside her. She didn't exude a frantic quality, but inside her, there must have been tremendous anxiety."

Mayne feels Pat's was an unfortunate marriage since "she, no doubt, outgrew him, spiritually and artistically." When her work started to receive more attention than his, it was clear that Roy felt neglected by the literary world. "We wanted to publish her book, not his book. I'm sure it was apparent to him that she was the one who was getting the attention that perhaps he felt he deserved." He goes on to say of Roy: "He was a peculiar person. You sensed bottled up within him a tremendous degree of aggression, I wouldn't say violence, but aggression ... As fate would have it, they grew apart."

It seemed that even life-loving Pat got more than she bargained for with two rapid pregnancies. Stress over housekeeping had been one of the problems in her first marriage, and it remained one in her second. Her struggle shows in the poem "Two Babies in Two Years":

> Now am I one with those wide-wombed
> mediterranean women
> who pour forth litters of children,
> mouthfuls of kisses and shrieks
>
> their hands always wet and full
> in motion [5]

Babies were not the only thing draining Pat. Lack of money was also a strain. When Pat and Roy first married, Roy had a teaching job at the Maple Ridge School Board which he later lost. According to the five-page biography Roy wrote at the back of his journal, he was at Maple Ridge from 1963 to 1968.[6] He lost that job because the principal said he had poor discipline, although Roy did not agree with that reason, saying he was let go because of his politics. Roy's weakness as a provider added the next link in Pat's lifelong chain of money problems.

While Pat was working on *This Difficult Flowring*, her literary reputation continued to grow. In the summer of 1967 *The Fiddlehead* published Pat's funny and sad poem "History Lessons."[7] The poem retells three episodes in Pat's family history. The first is about her uncle Johnny, who came back from the Klondike gold rush. He had made a fortune all right, but not panning for gold; he had done a brisk business as a barber. The second is the story of Eliza McCain intimidating the RCMP officer, as related in Chapter one. The last is a story of Private O'Day, stationed in Japan during World War II. Spying what he thought were swastikas, he angrily smashed the delicate carvings on a temple. After he had already done the damage, he realized that the age of the temple made it much older than the more recent Nazi symbol.

By now, Pat was getting invitations to read her poetry in public. Her friend Bethoe Shirkoff describes Pat before an audience at the Kitsilano Public Library: "As she smoked her delicate hands lightly moving. As she talked they ... touched her hair, her drink, her cigarette box; plucked at her skirt as she gazed down, speaking with concentration, finding the right word."[8] Fellow poets remember Pat in those days, both what they observed and what they knew about her. What Hilda Thomas remembers most is Pat the poet, but she also remembers her physical presence, especially her "beautiful live long hair."

Poet P.K. Page says that, although she and Pat never became well acquainted, she learned a lot about Pat's character from a simple incident in a cafeteria where a group of about ten poets had met: "I had somehow failed to get a cup of coffee. Suddenly Pat was at my side, cup in hand. She had noticed my lack and unobtrusively righted the matter. This is symbolic of Pat as I knew her —

observant, courteous, modest. Wherever she was, whatever the circumstances, one could not overlook her intent presence. Quiet but always significant, still but unmistakably awake, she was all of a piece with her concerned and memorable poetry."[9] Pat was still the "no fuss" person her mother had described.

If Pat had described the best days of her domestic life in "House," the poem "Toward a Pragmatic Psychology" may well describe the worst days:

> Every night at midnight the house falls.
> Stairs fold like pleated paper.
> The walls slide down
> a straight incline
> like wooden rain.
> Pigeons desert the eaves and fly east.
> The roof is swept away
> a pointed arc
> beaching at last on some intersection
> under trolley wires and pruned trees.
>
> Every morning we have to
> compose the house anew
> paper the walls
> reinvent principles of engineering
> make sure we have elbows,
> mouths, places to sit.
> Every night we lie down
> without prayer. [10]

On July 20, 1967, Pat and Roy moved into a house on 46th Avenue in the East End of Vancouver: the street runs off Fraser, where East Indian women in saris stroll past Chinese stores like the ones Pat describes in her poem "The Chinese Greengrocers."[11] During the years the Lowthers lived in the house, the landlord put stickers for the New Democratic Party on the door, which would have been quite agreeable to Pat and Roy.

The house is still standing today. There is a leaded-glass window in the front door, and a large verandah circling the house. The lawn is well kept. The basement window is a reminder that Milton Acorn once lived in that basement apartment and looked out at the trees from that vantage. There was always a cat in Pat's household, and one can picture their old black cat, Tinker, conducting his watchful life from the kitchen.

In 1987 there were fruit trees, rhubarb and flowers growing in the backyard. Beth remembers her mother turning the rhubarb into pies and crumbles. By March 1996, the house had been painted a light colour and the front door has been sanded down, showing the natural wood. The old fruit trees that stood in the backyard had been replaced by a children's wooden play climber that looks home-built.

It was under this roof that a change took place in Pat and Roy's marriage. Something had to give from the stress of caring for two babies, trying to write and dealing with Roy. According to Roy, he and Pat did not have a sex life after Chris was weaned.[12] There is no information from Pat on this. She may have no longer been attracted to Roy, or she may have been worried about getting pregnant again. Birth-control devices were not Pat's way of relating to nature.

The poems found in the attic trunk show a progression of feelings. At first Pat tried to deal with what she thought were the ordinary problems in a marriage. One, called "Marriage," was written in the early days with Roy. It betrays her innocent hope that the partners in a marriage would fully understand and identify with each other. As time went on, the hopefulness wore thin and was replaced by the restlessness expressed in "Continuing an Argument." As Roy became more difficult, Pat gently chided him with a poem entitled "To a Beloved Zealot."[13]

In spite of Roy's problems, he did give the children attention, although not always of a constructive kind. Virginia Tinmuth remembers what a handful the children became when Roy was around. On one occasion, the family visited the grandparents, and Virginia sat the children down to a snack of bread and jam. The children were old enough to eat with a degree of neatness, but that day one of them spread jam all over the table. Pat said, "Now put your bread on your plate and put your jam on your bread." The child continued as before. It was then that Virginia noticed Roy giving the child signals to continue the behaviour. On another occasion, the children were visiting while the Tinmouth grandparents were repairing their porch railing. Virginia had put a barrier up where the finished railing was to go and the children had been told that it was not safe to lean against the barrier. Beth and Chris were playing on the porch with some neighbourhood children. Virginia stepped out to find that Chris was rocking hard in a rocking chair dangerously close to the edge of the porch. She explained the problem to her granddaughter again. Chris did not pay any attention. After several warnings, Virginia moved close to the child, telling her that she must stop. "Chris said something cheeky and kicked at me twice." Virginia says, adding that she had never had to spank her own children, but felt that this situation called for prompt action. She picked Chris up and gave her four slaps on her bottom. "Chris started screaming her head off and I realized that Roy had been watching from the living room." Only after Chris started screaming did Roy come out to the porch. "He picked the child up and said, 'Oh, Gramma didn't mean to hit you so hard.' He took her into the back room and kept her crying all afternoon. She'd stop crying, we'd hear his voice, and she'd start crying again." Virginia asked Pat, "Does Chris carry on like this often?" Pat answered simply, "Only when he's around."

Roy's behaviour undoubtedly made taking care of the children a difficult task for Pat. Her mother remembers that one of the ways Pat tended to the children's constant needs was to do two things at a time. "She'd be here with her family, she'd be writing while she was talking to the children and doing things for them."[14] What Pat needed desperately was time for herself — and a way to communicate her increasing frustration to Roy.

Pat's friends describe her as soft-spoken and encouraging of others, but she was not one to cower in the corner when Roy got into a rage. Admitting that "memory is a creaky old house with lots of magic wardrobes," Beth testifies: "My mother fought him tooth and nail, and did a good deal of shouting herself. Indeed the arguing was so frequent that it had attained a kind of normalcy ... The memories of my mother's part in these things is elusive, mainly because I always felt she was justified and so I never held on to them."

Among Pat's unpublished poems is an untitled one that opens with "Man you are putting tabasco in my coffee." She tries to coax her partner out of his mood by asking him to "be for me."[15] This poem may mark a new period in Pat's life, when she was still committed to Roy as her man but needed to tell him in strong words that he was making her life hard.

Throughout the late 1960s and early 1970s, Pat continued to act on her political ideas by working with the New Democratic Party and peace groups. "Mum was always speaking at the hall down on Main Street. More than that, she spoke at peace marches," Kathy recalls. Pat also spoke about the environment before it became a household word. As far back as they can remember, Kathy and Alan were taken to peace marches. Kathy liked to draw and she helped her mom make posters. Together they lettered slogans such as "Stop Sending Canadian Arms to Vietnam." Kathy's specialty was decorating the posters with flames.

Kathy and Alan went more or less willingly when they were younger. However, as they got to be teenagers Kathy says, "We used to go kicking and screaming." Alan remembers that the marches were usually held on Saturdays, his day to visit his mother. "It was strange to see your mother stand up and speak in front of hundreds and hundreds of people." Both Alan and Kathy remember with discomfort that she addressed rallies when, as Kathy says, moving her hands from her stomach to a place about two feet in front of it, "she was out to here, nine months pregnant." Alan agrees, "Yes, that's right, and she got herself up [to speak]."

Willing or not, Pat's children also received an education in caring for the planet. Both Pat and Roy were concerned about the environment. When the children went to the beach with their parents, they all picked up the trash left by others. When they left, the beach was more like itself than when they had found it. The Lowthers brought their children to wave goodbye to the first Greenpeace ship to protest atomic testing in the Pacific Ocean. It was on September 15, 1971, that the *Phyllis Cormack* sailed from Vancouver. That is a good memory for Beth.

And then there were two giant trees, over 100-feet tall, growing on the city sidewalk in front of their house. Beth does not remember why, but the city planned to cut them down. Pat and the children took out their crayons, made hand-lettered signs and staged a protest to save the trees. They marched up and down the sidewalk with the placards while the construction workers laughed at them. In spite of Pat's telephone calls to city council, the beloved trees were taken down. Even though their trees were lost, the lesson was not — both Beth and Chris remain active in environmental concerns. Beth believes that regard for the environment is the best gift her parents gave her.

Roy went to peace marches, but his inner life knew no peace. Like other batterers, he became more violent over time. Kathy says that he would fly into terrible rages that often ended with violence against Pat and the children. More bizarre, however, was the violence he inflicted on himself. The ordinary frustrations of everyday life would drive him to bang his head against the wall. Kathy recalls that he did this on a regular basis inside the house, and then he took his self-inflicted pain outside: "One day he did all that and then ran outside in the yard and started banging his head on the outside of the stucco house — in front of all the neighbours — and he didn't stop until he had a big bleeding goose egg on his forehead. I used to be embarrassed to go out of the house, not wanting to meet the neighbours' eyes. I'm sure he must have had high blood pressure because he used to get real red in the face. He was bizarre. Every door in the house was cracked. He'd smash his fist on the door[s] until they splintered and cracked."

Ruth, Roy's daughter from a previous marriage, explains that he was full of fear and it "made him uncontrollably defensive, enraged, attacking like a deranged bear with a bullet in its head."[16] Clearly, Roy Lowther was not a good person for anyone, child or adult, to live with. One of Pat's unpublished poems, "Sleep,"[17] tells of watching her troubled love in his sleep. She fears that his anger can result in killing.

Friends can ease a person through troubles. Lorraine Vernon did that for Pat. She loved Pat deeply and remembers the problems Pat had with everyday management. "She had a hard time finding her way from the back door to the kitchen stove," Vernon contends. This is the sentiment she expresses in the poem she wrote in the wake of Pat's death. She called it "On the Business of Being: A Practical Friend." In the poem, Pat is called the dreamer, while Vernon is "the organizer, indexing / sorrow, recording joy." Grasping the reality of Pat's death, she writes, "There I noticed / petals had fallen / in hideous disarray, / & rushed out / in terror / for a broom, a broom."[18]

Lorraine Vernon and Pat became friends in a roundabout way. Vernon had attended a meeting of the Vancouver Poetry Society. She had several small children and had not had an evening out of her house for some time. She was so hungry to talk about poetry and so happy to be at the meeting that, she said later, "I must have talked a great deal." The next day she received a telephone call from Secretary Roy Lowther. He explained that she could not become a member because he felt that Vernon had tried to dominate the meeting. When the conversation ended, Vernon was sure that Roy saw her as a threat. Although this was a hard pill to swallow, when Vernon later met Pat as Roy's wife, she knew she wanted her for a friend. Because of Pat, she did her best to get along with Roy.

Children were one of the things that Pat and Lorraine Vernon had in common. Pat had four to worry about, and Vernon had five. Although their personalities were quite different, as mothers trying to write poetry, they understood each other's struggles. They also understood each other's message. Vernon wrote of Pat's work, "Whether we like it or not, a woman's life is made up of essential things. Fruit and the flesh."[19] The friendship extended to sharing child care. On many occasions in the late 1960s, Vernon picked Beth and Chris up at school and they spent the afternoon with her children.

Lorraine Vernon believed that the big difference between Pat and her was practicality. Vernon had it and Pat did not. "Pat lived in a world of poetry and ignored the horrific world going on around her." It was as if the intensity of her writing could change reality. Vernon, on the other hand, sees "no connection between life and art." Working on their poetry together, however, was stronger than their differences, and Pat and Vernon often spent evenings at Vernon's house, sharing a bottle of wine and reading poetry to each other. They also shared information about publishers, editors and writing markets. Vernon concludes, "We gave one another the kind of support we needed."

In addition to getting together with Lorraine Vernon to talk, Pat also invited her to informal poetry readings at the Lowther home. Vernon remembers the group fondly. It included bill bissett, Dorothy Livesay, Patrick Lane, Milton Acorn and Pierre Coupe with his yo-yo. Some American poets occasionally joined them. Vernon's husband, Stan Vernon, remembers that they were a swishy lot who got noticed in public. Once they were all at a restaurant and the waiter asked Stan who the two men wearing

capes were. Stan replied, "Don't you recognize them? That's Bat-
man and Robin." Those were the good times.

Above all else, the key difference in the women's lives was that
Lorraine Vernon had a good marriage and Pat didn't. She remem-
bers saying to Pat in the 1960s, "Women are making great strides."
Pat replied, "No, there's still a great deal left to be done."

Throughout 1967 and early 1968, Seymour Mayne and Pat
prepared the manuscript for *This Difficult Flowring*. Because "she
had never had very much editorial response to her work," Mayne
looked at diction and punctuation "more consistent with the forms
that she was attempting to write in."

Since Very Stone House was now running from a single room in
Mayne's apartment, expenses were kept low, and the press had to
be careful not to print more books than it could count on selling.
Steven Slutsky did the cover artwork, which has gossamer insects
overlaying block prints of flowers. Mayne remembers that Pat loved
the artwork. When the book was ready to distribute in June 1968,
Mayne sent out copies to reviewers and to bookstores. They had
standing orders for about 300 copies. He thinks they printed either
800 or 900 books. "And sure enough, bang! in four months, the
book was out of print."

The title, *This Difficult Flowring*, comes from a line in the poem
"Angel." It must have been a soul-wrenching text to write. The poet
is wrestling with her harsh muse and, like the biblical Jacob, will
forever carry the mark. No matter how she tries to banish him, "he
rises out of someone else's poem." Although the poet tries to
compromise with herself, the angel will not. He pursues her with
eyes that are burning holes:

> he damns me for my sin
> of growing lids
> and muscled iris in my eyes
> and jeers me that my Eden was not this
> difficult flowring. [20]

Della Golland, who wrote a thesis on Pat's work, sees this poem as an ironic exorcism of an angel rather than a devil.[21] Another possibility is that poet's unwelcome muse is Satan, the Angel of Darkness.[22]

How did Pat dream up the book title? Mayne explains that the key image of the book is "flow." Pat wanted a suggestion of flowers and growth as well. When they hit upon "this difficult flowring," they feared that people would mistake "flowring" for "flowering," but, they thought, "let's do the unexpected." Mayne says that Pat also liked the pun on the word "flowering." There is another, less famous pun in the poem. It speaks of the "hard labour of changing stone to flower to bread." Caught up in the suggestion of flowering, bill bissett comments that the title says a lot about Pat. It made him think how difficult it is to flower. "Because flower[ing] involves trust and leave taking. It's very difficult." "Flowring" also carries two ideas of time: "flow" is the linear and rational kind, while "ring" is natural time, such as seasons, growing round and having babies.[23]

As Pat and Seymour Mayne expected, many people, even literary reviewers, made the mistake. In Gary Geddes and Phyllis Bruce's compilation *15 Canadian Poets Plus 5*, Pat's short biography at the back of the book lists her first book as *This Difficult Flowering*. Paul Grescoe made the same mistake in his article in the *Canadian Magazine* in 1976. Reviewer Len Gasparini, who almost jumped out of his skin with enthusiasm about the book, managed to make two errors when he reviewed something he called *The Difficult Flowering*.[24] Despite this play on words, there are no anecdotal accounts from Pat's life to show that she enjoyed tripping people up. Mayne says, "The main stream of her psychic moods was a serious one with a few moments of joy, of celebration." Asked if these errors made Pat angry or indignant, Mayne's answer is in two parts. First, "she was always so grateful for being published, for people having interest in her. Pat wasn't like some poets in Canada who would be writing great long tirades to *The Globe and Mail* if someone dared to change a word or two of their text." Second, "she accepted a kind of passive position in regard to the way other people would look at her work." Pat's standing as a poet kept moving slowly upward. Her work was chosen for inclusion in several anthologies. While she was preparing *This Difficult Flowring*, one of her poems, "Amphibia," appeared in a book called *Poet's Market*, a special cloth-bound issue of a literary journal published by the University of British Columbia.[25] The university and Talon collaborated to bring it out for the UBC Festival of Contemporary Arts in 1968.

Poet Al Purdy did not like the anthologies full of stilted language that were used to teach poetry in English-Canadian high schools in the 1960s. His remedy was to put together his own collection, in which he gathered what he felt were the best poems of the previous twenty years and, for spice, added Archibald Lampman and George T. Lanigan from an earlier era. As editor of the anthology *Fifteen Winds*, Purdy set out to engage young adults with poetry that flows easily, the way people speak. From Pat's work he chose "On Reading a Poem Written in Adolescence," a poem that revels in the intensity of Pat's young imagination.[26]

In celebration of Vancouver's growing poetry presence, Jim Brown and David Phillips of Talon Books prepared a collection that was very different. It is a folio-sized book printed on olive-brown paper with abstract artwork by Bob Flick, Walkley and Gordon Fidler. The title page spells "talon books" as two words, with everything in lowercase letters. The print looks as if it has been done on a typewriter. The book was first brought out under the title of *West Coast 68*; it was later changed to *West Coast Seen*. Pat had three poems in that anthology: "Notes from a Far Suburb," "Visit to Olympus" and "Child, Child."[27] Pat was now a benchmark in Vancouver's poetry world as well as being on high-school required-reading lists, but she still did not have any money.

It was probably during the late 1960s that Pat wrote "Woman On / Against Snow."[28] The poem tells of a lone Inuit woman surviving in a bleak landscape. Her physical struggle is matched by the spiritual struggle in which the isolated woman debates with the universe.

"Woman On / Against Snow" became the subject of two scholarly papers after Pat's death. In her 1986 article, "Woman On / Against Snow: A Poem and Its Sources,"[29] Jean Mallinson makes a convincing case that the historic sources of the poem are probably two articles from Gyorgy Kepes' book *Sign, Image, Symbol*. Taken with Mallinson's theory, Della Golland wrote a paper, "Gathering the Light: A Search for Literary Knowing," which explores ways that "Woman On / Against Snow" might be used to teach cultural values to schoolchildren.[30]

The first of the two articles in *Sign, Image, Symbol* that Jean Mallinson looks at is "Image Making in Arctic Art" by Edward Carpenter, which is based on the journals of explorer Samuel Hearne. Writing in the Arctic in 1772, Hearne tells of finding a solitary young Inuit woman, the only survivor of her group after a battle with a hostile band. She had kept her body and soul together for seven months before Hearne's party arrived. Pat's poem paraphrases the journal. Hearne wrote: "It is scarcely possible to conceive that a person in her forlorn situation could be so composed as to contrive, or execute, anything not absolutely essential for her existence. Nevertheless, all her clothing, besides being calculated for real service, showed great taste, and no little variety of ornament."[31] Carpenter is touched by Hearne's words and adds that, although Arctic life must be reduced to barest essentials, poetry and art are among those essentials. In Pat's poem, the woman asks the spirit, Nuliajuk, for bone and blood for her hunger. She goes on to say:

> when I have drunk
> I will save a little
> a thought will come to me
> to help my clothing be beautiful
> in the absence of the people
> I will speak with the world [32]

According to Inuit legend, Nuliajuk was once a young girl. One day when she went out fishing, a man (in some versions, her father) threw her overboard. As she tried to cling to the side of the kayak, he cut off her fingers. As each finger fell into the water, it became a certain species of animal. Nuliajuk then disappeared into the water and became a sea spirit. Nuliajuk is the spirit of the people, and her fingers, turned animals, are their food.

Carpenter explains that there is no Inuit word meaning "to make" or "to create." Instead, the Inuit poet says, "Let me breathe of it ... One has put his poem in order on the threshold of his tongue."[33] Pat's poem says:

> Song arranges itself
> at the door
> of one's mouth
> One is abraded by grief
> like snow with many teeth
> The walls drip water
> and glaze
> Words name the dead
> For a time breathing song
> one is not alone [34]

The second article Mallinson considers is "The Eskimo Discovery of Man's Place in the Universe" by Paul Riesman.[35] Riesman tries to understand the Inuit view of how the human fits into the universe. Looking again at the Nuliajuk story, he says that the destruction of the girl Nuliajuk makes the people take responsibility for their lives, the lives of others and even the universe. They are in a constant debate with the universe, whose harshness seems to tell them that they have no place. This debate is their spiritual task. Pat takes up this idea, which is perfectly in tune with her own poetry, saying:

> The first/last human is
> poet
> shaman
> debater
>   with the universe [36]

In Pat's poem, the abandoned woman calls upon Nuliajuk and perhaps is transformed into her. Della Golland found that Pat and her ideas settled into her own mind in a powerful way. After doing the paper, she wrote her master's thesis on Pat's way of seeing. Partly based on "Woman On / Against Snow," her thesis asserts that myth and art are redeeming.[37] Pat grapples with survival against great odds and finds answers in the culture of the Arctic people. Nuliajuk gives birth to the animals. Pat's solitary woman "must shape the world by being alive." And the poet breathes poems into the vast emptiness.

CHAPTER 6

Victories in the Mire

Mum's lips were always chapped. As a child,
I liked to run my finger across her lips.

— Beth Lowther[1]

IN DECEMBER 1968, PAT WROTE A LETTER to Dorothy Livesay that contained strong hints of her problems at home. She apologizes for taking a long time to write to Livesay, and even calls the gap an "inexcusably churlish silence." Pat seems to have felt the need to write sooner to thank Livesay for giving high recommendation to her work: "Shortly after our last conversation, problems began erupting in my family — some of them foreseeable, but others completely unanticipated. They kept coming one after another, and just seemed to heap up and overwhelm me. I've really been so distraught these last several weeks that at one point I felt in danger of losing my ability to function at all. Certainly I've been functioning on a minimal level."[2]

People such as Seymour Mayne began to hear through the grapevine that Roy was "getting violent, either in a self-immolating way or toward her, that she was getting increasingly fed up with it."

Mayne and his friends were students and young writers; no one had any extra money. However, one member of Very Stone House had a friend with a truck. He offered to organize a group of people to load Pat, the children and the furniture into that borrowed truck and spirit them away. They were just waiting for Pat to say when. Mayne tells that story sadly and adds: "She never ... made the move, which is the great tragic decision of her life." He, like many people who have no experience of family violence, made the error of believing that getting away from a violent husband ends the violence.

How did Pat Lowther get pulled into the quagmire? After all, she had figured out how to get a job as a keypunch operator when she was a teenager. She had figured out how to get out of her first marriage. She had supported herself and Kathy when that marriage ended. Why in the world did she put up with Roy's abuse? In spite of Pat's gift with words, she had things in common with other battered women. Although each woman is different, any study of the problem will show similarities among individuals. Beyond the physical violence, there is always an emotional punch. Threats are as effective as actions; they are like an emotional leash. They let the abuser push, pull, lead and sometimes slightly choke his victim. Every battered woman I have met has been threatened with even worse than she experienced. There is no evidence that Roy threatened Pat with murder. He did, however, threaten suicide — often. When that happened, Pat dropped everything and paid attention to him.

An abusive partner also finds the places where a person is unsure of herself and works to break her down with ridicule, sarcasm or threats. Unfortunately, if a person is told often enough that she is crazy, she does begin to feel that way. Roy's emotional attacks on Pat had made her feel that she could not manage the children on her own.

Counsellors today have worked with enough abusive men to tell about some things they have in common.[3] It's as if the abusive person carries a sack filled with characteristics that are the same for very different people. One parcel in the sack is shirking responsibility for behaviour. The abuser usually denies hitting his partner. If he does admit to anything, he minimizes what he did or says she provoked the attack. Roy Lowther's life and journals show a man bent on shifting responsibility away from himself. Restating the blame he parcelled out in his journals would take several hundred pages. Another parcel in the sack is emotional dependence complicated by a fear that his partner will control him. The normal desire to open his heart to her is met by fear, which turns to anger. Roy's dependence upon his family is amply documented in his papers.[4]

For an abusive person, the idea of a relationship is to have control. Some of the ways to gain this control may sound harmless, but they add up to an unfair relationship. A man may tell his partner how to dress or wear her hair. Next, the man becomes the only one who can decide whether or not she should take a job. Even though she may have been self-supporting before marriage, he makes all the financial decisions. It does not matter if the family has very little or a very large amount of money, the script is the same. Only the numbers change. The abuser often monitors his partner's time. Such a man may telephone his wife many times a day to check up on her. Lorraine Vernon gave a statement to police saying that Roy did just that.[5]

Although the abusive person works to control the person he loves, he himself has never developed impulse control. In his growing years, he has never learned which impulses are okay to follow and which ones are not. The result is a thirty-year-old with the emotional control of a five-year-old and the physical strength of an adult. When such a person says, "I wanna," his large infant hand can do great damage. Violence often follows. It may begin small, with a shove or a slap. But that first slap makes physical control of a wife thinkable. The violence tends to get worse over time and can end in permanent injury or death.[6]

It is common for battered women to cut themselves off from friends and family.[7] Pat was lucky enough to keep her friends, and Roy was not able to drive a wedge between her and her family, although he did make Kathy unhappy enough to leave home at age fifteen. While he could not cut Pat off completely, he was successful in making her feel uneasy about inviting friends to their house. Roy's papers show that he served Pat's friends and family generous portions of criticism, and the person who bore the brunt of this criticism was Pat's mother, Virginia. Until a woman's marriage, the person who knows her best is probably her mother. If a woman develops a health problem, loses or gains weight, or increases her smoking — all common problems for battered women — her mother will be the first to notice. Most uncomfortable for an abusing man, Mother will ask why. How does an abuser counter this? Ridicule is a good weapon. He'll make light of the mother's concerns and paint her as a buffoon.

The thing that leads abusers to do the most damage to others is that stick of dynamite called "feelings." A battering man has never learned to sort out and deal with his own feelings. He cannot tell feelings of fear from feelings of insecurity or frustration. As a result, he certainly does not understand other people's feelings. When such a troubled person marries, the best partner in the world cannot change what he feels. Ruth Lowther Lalonde thinks that her father was consumed by "his fear-anger-cycle illness." She imagines the words that would enter her father's head when the feeling got hold of him and he would bash his head against a wall, "to get that frenzy out of my brain ... If that doesn't work, I try to get that Fear Monster out of my body by grabbing the nearest person as a vent ... If they really do love me, they might understand that it's not me that is hurting them, rather it is the Fear-Anger Illness controlling my brain."

Inevitably the loved one could not take away the illness, so Roy felt abandoned and would go into the next level of attack. Ruth hears her father saying to Pat: "What do you mean, Pat, that you're going east to read poetry? And leave me alone with this Sickness? And not be a victim of it with me? ... That Fear-Anger might take over ... That means you want to hurt me, too. That means you have joined against me, too! You don't want to help me cure myself of this Fear-Anger Sickness; you want to perpetuate it, increase it! And like this Sickness, you want to control me, too! I won't let you! You can't leave me here alone with it! ... You can't get other people to scorn me! You can't turn all of Canada against me, laughing at me! I won't let you! I must STOP YOU!" Ruth continues: "I heard my father screaming many of the above words at my own mom over and over again, so many times in the short time that he lived with me. I will never forget, in particular, the raging rant in my bedroom while he was strangling her. This came out of the father I adored."

Ruth explains her father's twisted logic: "He let himself be enraged, because it felt strong, but it wasn't possible, logically you see, to be violent because 'I am a poet. Poets aren't violent. Poets don't kill.'"

An unpublished poem among Pat's papers entitled "To a Husband" catches Roy's feelings of sadness, frustration and insecurity that, once denied, festered inside him to be manifest in anger:

> Dying against the blank wall of your breast
> Baffled, blocked by your ripely latent wrath
> Until the last lines, the pity and the hope,
> Ran out at the end like an old and frayed thin rope,
> Gave you at last, all-murderous and mighty,
> Hatred — the one safe passion you finally found. [8]

Every decent person wants to see abused women leave their place of torment. Many do, but that does not end the danger. If ever there was a choice between being cooked in the frying pan or directly in the fire, this is it. Murder statistics show that women who have recently left, or who are trying to leave an abusive husband or lover are five times more likely to be murdered than other women. [9]

Pat was lucky in that she had a lot of people who cared about her. First there was the Tinmouth family, who suspected that Pat was being battered. Although the adults never witnessed physical abuse, they have many stories of strange behaviour by Roy. Pat's son, Alan, tells of seeing Roy hit Pat. On one occasion, Alan saw her knocked across the kitchen. Pat's brother Arden spent more time visiting Pat than other family members and told the others of continuing abuse. Since Pat never told her family outright about the battering, it was easy to minimize Arden's account. Many of Pat's friends shared her family's suspicions. Her close friend Lorraine Vernon desperately wanted Pat's life to be different. She saw Pat trying to work out the problem in poetry and concluded that she was using her poetry to escape from life.

In the early years of their marriage, Pat seems to have felt that managing Roy's temper was her responsibility. Although she eventually realized otherwise, it took her time to come to that understanding. Two unpublished poems could be taken as testimony of her struggle to find a way to cope with Roy. "Metamorphosis" addresses something Pat called "the sweet pain of love," a subject well covered in popular music. The other poem, "Primrose Room," probes the place where beauty and pain coincide.[10] If only she could find a way to balance the good and bad in the relationship, she could keep on loving Roy.

And how did Pat's children view her as she tried so hard to hold her life together, balancing her burning need to write and her need to provide for her family? Kathy confesses: "We didn't understand Mum's poetry. We knew that she wrote poetry because our house was bookcases and bookcases full of paper. And she was forever rat-a-tat-tat on the old Remington. I didn't understand it … I hate to say, we probably didn't show a lot of interest in it." Although Pat and some others believed she was hopeless as a homemaker, Beth has memories of home-cooked meals and fresh coffee perking. Beth says her mother did a wonderful casserole of hamburger, spinach and mushrooms. Tomato aspic salad was another favourite. She also remembers ordering in Chinese food. Perhaps that happened when Pat was doing a final preparation of a manuscript or suffering from a migraine. It may have been by the skin of her teeth, but Pat did make a home for her children.

In that home, there is no question that the children also had to do a certain amount of looking after themselves. Beth tells of coming home from school one day to find the house empty and the door locked. As the elder child, Beth knocked on the neighbour's door and told her that their parents were not home. The woman welcomed the girls in without hesitation and fed them "really good cabbage rolls." That day, fate had sent Beth and Chris a kindly protector. Unrealistic virtues are often heaped upon people after they die. Allan Safarik wrote to Chris Lowther, saying "Your mother was the closest thing to a saint."[11] Beth thinks about that statement and then responds, "I think that does her a disservice." Beth wants to remember her mother as a fully human woman, with flaws as well as strengths. She says, for example: "She put down Gramma's painting. Mum used to call it candy-box art."

Pat's health had always been borderline. One thing that may have contributed to her problems was the poor condition of her teeth. Seymour Mayne describes her teeth as ungainly. Although some writers "use a blatant public persona" to get media attention, Pat Lowther had trouble presenting a calculated image, perhaps because of the way her teeth affected her appearance. Mayne observes that some writers' faces "read like signatures of egotism; not her face at all." Rather, she was genuine and authentic; a person "given to the verities and the versities of the spirit rather than to ostentatious and superficial behaviour. When she smiled, there was a winsome quality; you sensed that there was a real person there."

Hilda Thomas tells of a particular health problem. She and Pat got to know each other in their work with the New Democratic Party. Thomas had carried the NDP banner in four unsuccessful election bids for the British Columbia Legislative Assembly. She recalls walking a picket line with Pat in support of women workers trying to form a union at a restaurant chain. This was shortly after the junta had seized power in Chile, and Pat was to read a tribute to Neruda at a convention. Pat quietly asked Thomas if she would read the work for her. Thomas protested, saying Pat was the obvious one to do it. To Thomas's alarm, Pat explained that she had just come from a medical appointment where she learned the cause of a pain in her chest. Her doctor had found a small hole in her lung. Pat said that she was going to try to get more rest. As a result, Pat did cut down on her smoking. She wrote in a letter to Dorothy Livesay: "Nobody has even noticed."[12]

How was Pat keeping body and soul together? The biography in the back of Roy's journal reads that in 1968 and 1969 he taught seventh- and eighth-grade music at the Porter School in Coquitlam. In his words, he was "bounced before tenure for striving to increase concerts, i.e. change routine."[13] The official reason was a poor inspection report by the principal. Hoping to get support from the Teachers' Union, Roy appealed the report. Unfortunately for him, an inspector from the union concluded that he indeed had "DIFFICULTIES WITH STAFF AND ADMINISTRATION." When he had lost his job with the Maple Ridge School Board the previous year, he had also disagreed with the official reason. Except for the odd day of substitute work, Roy was not employed after June 1969.

The loss of Roy's job meant that Pat and her family lived largely on welfare, broken only by small royalties from Pat's book and anthologies, which could not have supported the thriftiest family. Pat desperately needed to earn some money. In September 1968, she wrote to the Canada Council, asking for an application for a bursary. Now that her first book was out, she had the status of a published writer and could ask for money to do her work. She wrote: "Recently the demands placed on my time and energy by my young family have made writing itself very difficult."[14] She had some new poems that she wanted to prepare for a collection and suggested that a grant would make it possible for her to hire clerical help to prepare the manuscript. Clerical help! Money for rent and food is what she needed. Maybe she thought that the folks at the Council used their extra money for office workers and would sympathize with the request.

The Council sent her the form, and Pat returned the completed application in October. She asked for $3500 so that she could prepare the manuscript for a second collection of poems. Question fifteen on the application asked: What is your occupation now? Pat did not answer "poet." No indeed; she said, "housewife." This simply reflected the truth, since she probably spent more hours of her day as mother and homemaker than as poet. Furthermore, her income from poetry was negligible. Since the family was living mainly on social assistance, her finances were set by being the mother of three minor children.

According to Canada Council records, her application for $3500 was approved. Roy recorded bitterly in his journal that the grant did Pat and her family absolutely no financial good.[15] In his account, a Canada Council cheque for $2000 arrived in May 1969, on the very same day that he lost his temporary position teaching seventh- and eighth-grade music at the Porter School. (In fact, the cheque arrived in April, weeks before Roy was let go.) Since they had no means of support, the family would have to go on social assistance. Pat's grant would have to be reported to their social worker and most of it would be deducted from their allotment. His account continues: "So these two things happened the same day, and she went downstairs in tears."

The rules for a family receiving social assistance in British Columbia allowed earnings up to $100 a month. Pat knew that she would lose 75 cents of every dollar over $100 as a deduction from her cheque. Pat's Canada Council file shows that the grant was sent in three instalments. The first, on April 15, was for $1500 and was to cover three months of the year. This probably meant that she lost 75 percent of $1400. Even if social assistance had been willing to consider that cheque the three-month allotment that it was, she would still have lost 75 percent of $1200. The second instalment, sent on August 1, 1969, and the last, on December 9, 1969, each for $1000, would suffer the same fate.

Roy may have been wrong about the date and the amount, but he was probably right about Pat's tears. If Roy had been able to keep his part-time work, the family might have managed on his salary, together with the grant. As it was, although the artistic world represented by the Canada Council had recognized that Pat deserved to be paid for her work, circumstances turned the award upside down, and she was once again reduced to living on the barest necessities.

On April 23, 1969, Pat wrote to Dorothy Livesay, thanking her for the support she had given to her Canada Council application. She told Livesay: "I have the first cheque already, but so far I'm hoarding and mumbling over it." She went on to say that she did have several projects planned for the money. She also explained: "I've been plagued by a series of minor illnesses ... I think I've been in considerable danger of becoming a useless neurotic, and simply the freedom that this grant makes possible is bound to make a difference in that."[16]

The letter ended with Pat saying that Livesay's book *The Unquiet Bed*, together with a book on gardening, had inspired her to write a poem, most probably the one that Pat later dedicated to Dorothy Livesay: "Growing Seasons." Pat describes herself in this poem as "blinded by migraine" while Livesay is a Hazel woman, suggesting she is witch-like, with "fifty summers of nasturtiums." The poem was first published under that name in the literary journal *Quarry*. It later appeared in Pat's book *Milk Stone*, titled "Growing the Seasons."[17]

While Pat was writing about Livesay's "summers of nasturtiums," there was apparently no romantic bloom left in her own life. She wrote a poem, compassionate but without hope, a poem that has never been published. "I Feel I Am Watching at Your Dying" probably describes Roy's deterioration. It opens with: "I feel I am watching at your dying, / seeing the poison spread from the central wound / into all your members; / a skin prick will burst it someday."[18]

Allan Safarik says that Pat used the 1969 Canada Council grant to "buy her kids shoes and pay her kids' dental bills. She had to use eighty percent of her Canada Council money just keeping her act together." Safarik says he once queried her: "Pat, for God's sake, why don't you get your teeth fixed?" She answered simply, "I can't afford it."

Just a few months later, Pat wrote another apology to Dorothy Livesay. This letter says that she suffered "certain paralyses of will" about writing letters: "So this is not a letter, but a symbolic representation of a letter." The big news was acceptance from *Quarry* of "Growing the Seasons" for publication.[19]

If the stresses in her life were making it impossible for Pat to write letters to friends, why did she not change her life and leave her marriage? After all, had she not pulled out of a marriage once before? The sad truth is that Pat did try to leave. On several occasions in 1970 and 1971, Lorraine and Stan Vernon drove her around, helping her look for a place where she and the children could live. Pat never found anything suitable. Lorraine related one specific incident in her police statement after Pat's death: "I went to her house on East 46th Street, where she had packed her belongings into cardboard boxes, and I swept and tidied the house to help her in her intention to leave. Roy was on a canoeing trip in Howe Sound, and it was her intention to leave before he returned."[20] Pat never left.

When Lorraine Vernon asked Pat why she could not make a life for herself, Pat replied that Roy would follow her; that there was no way; that he would come after her, especially if she had the children; that the only way she could escape would be to leave the city entirely.[21] Vernon says: "Pat could not see her way out of the relationship, although she had a foreboding, almost to the point of desperation at the end." Hilda Woolnough, another friend, confirms the dilemma: "Pat believed she did not have the psychic strength to raise the kids alone." She also said that if Roy discovered she was planning to leave, "he'd get pretty rough." Pat may not have known the murder statistics on women leaving violent men, but she knew what set off Roy's rages.

The only written answer to the question "Why don't you leave?" is in a letter Pat wrote to Patrick Lane in the spring of 1973: "As for leaving Roy, I see no way out of continuing to live with him. I finally escaped the emotional bondage, much, much too late, but leaving would mean having to be a full-time mother with no time or energy for writing or simply being the person I have to be. Some people could do it, but I know my limits ... It's the kind of situation psychologists devise to drive white rats crazy ... Oh well, nothing lasts forever and it's objectively spring, which helps."[22]

While Pat was trying to relate to two sets of children and a stressed husband, as well as writing emotionally demanding poetry, Mayne Island continued to be a reprieve for the family. Even Roy seemed to find a degree of peace there. Probably the happiest times that Pat, Roy and the children spent were in the cabin that the Wilkses called Sleepy Hollow. Sleepy Hollow sits at the foot of a steep embankment. As you walk into the main room, there is a window on your right. You enter a second room through a doorway where a curtain of beads serves as a door. At first there was no electricity. Later an electric bulb, covered with a Japanese paper lantern, hung from the ceiling. The furniture consisted of a table, chairs, a wood stove, a wooden chest of drawers with a mirror, and two double mattresses on the floor. There was an old washboard. The food was kept in a cooler attached to the outside of the house.

It was made of wood and covered with wire mesh to keep animals out.

Beth remembers Mayne Island as being "full of leaves." She says, "There is always a crackling sound." Pat's elder children, Alan and Kathy, also speak with fondness of Mayne Island, Aunt Elsie and Uncle Bill. They remember particularly Uncle Bill's skills as a diviner. Bill Wilks spent years doing experiments in electromagnetism and wrote a book about his research. His title, *Science of a Witch's Brew*, dares to utter the words "science" and "witch" in the same breath.[23] There are no tricks here, and in the book he asserts that there is a scientific basis for divining. The book documents observations he made doing experiments that he invites his readers to repeat. He maintains that plants and animals, water and minerals all give off electrical impulses and have magnetic ranges. He and witnesses say that, in his hands, a divining rod will locate the "vital centre" of a desired object and point toward it. Bill used either a carpenter's roll-up measuring tape or a straightened-out clothes hanger for his experiments because he believed metal tools are better for picking up electromagnetism than the forked willow branches diviners traditionally use.

It is clear from reading *Science of a Witch's Brew* that Bill Wilks is not a man writing about his hobby. He is a plain man asking great questions about nature and about humans' relationship to the cosmos. He is convinced that the elements and all living things are connected. Injury to one part injures the whole. He cautions that human greed, which destroys both the environment and people, will break the delicate electromagnetic relationships that connect everything.

Pat's poetry also seeks to make connections between things. Several of her poems look at injustice or violence and see it spreading injury on a grand scale. "The Earth Sings Mi-Fa-Mi" is about the misery of the Vietnamese people during the war.[24] People who care about their pain chant in support of Ho Chi Minh, and the screaming wind carries their chant to the centre of the earth. In

Pat, at 35. (1970)

"Chacabuco, the Pit," she writes of tortured Chilean prisoners, insisting that everything is connected and that even the most wretched remain part of the body of humanity.

> they are the fingers sliced off
> when the wood was cut,
> the abortions born living;
> they are the mangled
> parts of our bodies
> screaming to be
> reunited. [25]

Pat's notebook has an entry called "O Sybarians," which has not been worked into a poem. The notes are about Sybaries, a destroyed city in southern Italy. Archeologists discovered the city "by instruments that measure disturbances in the earth's magnetic field." Pat writes that the "former human occupants left their magnetism."[26]

Pat's poetry continued to receive public acclaim. Once again, in 1970, her work was selected by the Borestone Mountain Awards for the *Best Poems of 1970*. They chose "The Chinese Greengrocers" and "Penelopes," which had first appeared in *The Fiddlehead*.[27] That same year, Pat was included in the collection *Contemporary Poetry of British Columbia*. Editor Michael Yates, working with the creative writing department of the University of British Columbia, had chosen "Prometheus" from *This Difficult Flowring*.[28]

It was also in 1970 that Pat met George McWhirter, head of the creative writing department at the University of British Columbia. Before they met, Lorraine Vernon had told him about Pat as a poet to watch. It was an acquaintance that would help Pat in the future.

CHAPTER 7

Moving Mountains

The uncontested number one
woman poet in the city.

— Andreas Schroeder[1]

PAT LOWTHER STARTED HER LIFE in an era that taught women that they were made to bear, to give and maybe to suffer. In the 1970s, the women's movement came upon Pat and caused her, along with many others, to rethink all this. That rethinking shows in the introduction Pat wrote to her poems in the multi-author anthology *Mountain Moving Day*.[2] The title of the book bears witness to the courage and optimism that marked those years. Women, pacifists and human-rights activists were doing and saying things that ran counter to the powers of the day. If people in the street could contradict the mayor, the preacher and Sigmund Freud, then moving mountains was thinkable. The anthology was the inspiration of Elaine Gill of Trumansburg, New York, who had an interest in Canada, and it features both Canadian and American women poets, giving Pat another international publication to her credit.

Pat introduces her five poems by linking a new consciousness, women and evolution: "I see the women's revolution as part of a new outreach of consciousness. The liberation of women from imposed self-images is happening. Even the most hostile and fearful women are absorbing it subliminally right along with the cream depilatory commercials. New assumptions are being accepted below the level of consciousness. Then maybe our poems, maybe some of the poems in this book, provide the 'shock of recognition.'

"At one time I believed we humans were coming to the end of our evolutionary cycle — devolving like dandelions. Now I see the half-breeds of the future passing like migrating birds, and I begin to have a kind of tentative hope. Maybe they'll find some clear space for consciousness, for going on. Not that I wholly trust them to be right. It's too easy to be wrong when you've grown in a culture that functions basically by mind-manipulation. Maybe we have to go through the whole trial-and-error thing again. After all, that's how we got here in the first place."[3]

The poems Pat chose for that book are "Morality Play," "The Piercing," "Remembering How," "The Earth Sings Mi-Fa-Mi" and "Regard to Neruda." The poem "Morality Play" looks at the "light people" who have casual love affairs without entanglements. She thinks that might be fun, but knows it is not for her. If she tried it, she would get into a "jumbled knot." She ends by asking:

> Is it some
> consolation that
> I'm a woman
> no one has
> ever taken
> lightly? [4]

More and more, discussion of women's issues and how they touch poetry were pushing their way into Pat's thinking. Among her papers is an essay by Daphne Marlatt, "Musing with Mothertongue."

Marlatt insists that, for poets, language is life: "Putting the living body of language together is putting the world together."[5] This is exactly what Pat's character in "Woman On / Against Snow" struggles to do.

Pat's total devotion to poetry caused Réshard Gool to join the friends who worried about her. He feared that she was becoming "exclusively poetic" and that this might immobilize her. Gool further believed that, if Pat were "mobile," she'd be able to leave her bad marriage. He didn't understand that her immobility was not inside herself. It was something outside. Pat knew what Roy could do.

Although Gool had cause to worry about Pat, he worried for the wrong reason, for she did see the limits of language. Bethoe Shirkoff tells of a time when Pat put writing on the back burner for something she felt was more important. Before they became friends, Shirkoff had seen Pat at a New Democratic Party Area Council meeting. She remembers Pat rising and saying, "in her level carrying voice," that the NDP should do more and write less. Instead of complaining that the press was biased because they did not print the NDP's press releases, Pat suggested thinking of other ways for "the dispossessed" to get their stories to the public. "'What a surprising, original woman,' the stranger beside me said. 'Sure,' said someone else, 'you can always count on Pat.' Pat said that she was stating the obvious, but that the ways of implementing the solutions were the hard problems. I had no idea she was a poet, that her writing was life and breath to her."[6]

After they became better acquainted, Shirkoff told Pat that she did not know she was a poet. No one had mentioned it. Although by that time Pat had a body of published work, her response had no anger or self-pity. She simply said: "That's because I'm a woman."[7] Was this a fatalistic view, accepting fate instead of wrestling with the gods? Elizabeth Gourlay believes that Pat, like herself, was a fatalist. Seymour Mayne is inclined to say both yes and no to that. "She took the blows. Defended herself from some of them, but took them and kept taking them ... To some degree, she let herself go down that road ... Among the poets ... we just sensed in her, that reticence to turn a corner in her life ... We all felt that she had to save herself." When Seymour Mayne was grieving over Pat's death, he wrote a poem called "For Pat Lowther (1935 — 1975)," in which he compared her to a lamb led to slaughter. The poem says: "Sheepishly you bruised / yourself against sharp / sticks and thorns ... with that vulnerable / and unfinished / rhythm."[8] Nearly ten years later, "vulnerability" was the word he used: "Speaking of her poetry, I always felt it had that vulnerable and unfinished rhythm. Because, in a sense, I think there was something vulnerable and unfinished in her life."

Did Pat accept bad things without resistance? Mayne says that Roy was: "... poison to her, her kids, and especially to her muse ... And it could be that she had a failure wish within her. And she stayed until the worst possible scenario was played out ... I don't believe that people who have poetic temperaments do things simply, in a gratuitous way. I think, in some way, they work out their own destiny ... In a sense, she was ... testing fate. Or she didn't want to take that difficult step of independence, a new road, a new line of growth in herself."

Mayne hastens to add that there was also another side to Pat's character. It was "a quiet, strong side. Without that capacity, she never could have done what she did." He lists her problems as "vexing psychic, physical, economic and social" and marvels that she had the psychic and creative strength to manage her life and to write.

Mayne did not know just how much Pat was managing. Kathy lived with Pat and Roy through her early teen years. She remembers Pat with bruises and black eyes after Roy's outbursts. Kathy, as well, was often in the path of his anger. "Most of the time, it was grabbing me and shoving me and dragging." Here is the worst encounter. One day she was being a typical teen, and annoying her mother: "I was running a bath. Mum said, 'Oh, Katherine.' I mimicked her back and said, 'Oh, Katherine.' I could hear him squeaking down the hall. He came into the bathroom and punched me squarely in the face. And I ran down the stairs, or tried to run down the stairs, and he grabbed me by my hair and dragged me back up and then down the stairs again. For years I had scars all the way down my backbone from going down those stairs."

For many years, until Chris released a book detailing her childhood experiences, Alan did not think that Roy ever beat his half-sisters, "but the emotional abuse was just unbelievable. He treated them like they could do no wrong. But when they did wrong, he made them feel they should never have been born." Kathy concurs, "He wouldn't let anyone else give them hell. Not even Mum … They would not listen to anything Mum said." Kathy feels that Roy's treatment of Beth was particularly bad. "He would be in her bedroom with her for hours and I'm sure he was dragging these traumatic things out to the bitter end … Somehow, he would make out that it was Mum's fault." In spite of the mistreatment, Beth was able to tell her parents what she wanted. One day she marched home with an old male cat the neighbours were trying to evict. Beth announced to her parents, "His name is Junior and I'm keeping him," and that was the day Junior joined Tinker in directing the affairs of the kitchen.

In the early 1970s, Pat also had to cope with her father's death. Arthur Tinmouth was happy-go-lucky to a fault. Pat had written:

> My father was a confirmed
> lampshade-on-the-head man.
>
> Legends are told
> of his dancing,
> his ukulele solos;
> …
> or instruct grandchildren
> in the art of showing off [9]

He loved jovial people and he enjoyed celebrations. Christmas, the arrival of a new grandchild, family birthdays were all reasons to gather with friends, make music and hail the event.

Arthur's own sixty-second birthday was no exception. On April 25, 1970, after drinking a cup or two of cheer with his friends, he joined them for a walk and climbed a steep hill. As a result, Arthur suffered a fatal heart attack. Given a choice, he probably would have liked to end his days in the company of friends, celebrating happiness. If such choices were given, he probably would also have asked for a few more years.

It was Pat who prepared the obituary notice for her family. She told her sister, Brenda, that it was not until a few days later, when she read her notice in the newspaper, that she really believed her father had died. For Pat, the written word made it real. Later that year, she wrote a poem — found among Roy's papers — called "Christmas Eve 1970." The poem is typewritten and the word "posthumous" is handwritten above the title. It says: "My father with his Christmas-red vest / and braggart's moustache / is boycotting the party." The family tries to celebrate Christmas, but "My father's a cold / sulk of absence / in the corners / planted with odourless poinsettias / red as his vest."[10] The words "City Slides" are also handwritten on the page. "City Slides" is the name of a group of poems in her book *A Stone Diary*, but "Christmas Eve 1970" is not among them. It is likely that Pat had intended to include it, and either was not satisfied with the poem or was not ready to make her feelings about her father public. The last line in the published "City Slides" reads: " — Christ O Christ, no one lives long."[11] All these poems were most probably written while Pat was grieving over her father's death.

Living with a violent man, worrying about her children and grieving for her father: it is not surprising that Pat told bill bissett that she was "falling into a hole." During a telephone conversation in early the 1970s, when bissett asked her how she was, she responded that she was "falling down a black hole"; when he asked her if she could get out, she replied: "I don't think so." Bissett believes that Pat was one of the people who "don't escape oppression because they're not capable of fighting back. And sometimes murder is the only way of fighting back ... For her to kick back, scream at him, and take a knife at him, it would give up her belief." He wonders whether or not, personally, Pat had any hope that men and women could understand each other. He counters that thought with "in the poetry, it doesn't seem as if she lost hope ... I want life to be softer, and I don't want it to be so strict. I don't like life when it's like that. And I don't think she did either."

Beth has a memory of one of the good times that relieved her mother's life. Her parents had come home from the movie *Stairway to Heaven* in high spirits and told the children about it with laughter. Although the film was not billed as a comedy, Roy and Pat found it humorous. Pat's response could well reveal her feelings about power. *Stairway to Heaven* is the story of a poetry-writing aviator who is critically injured in a plane crash. While the best neurologists in England perform surgery on him, the woman he loves fights for his survival. At the first stage of the operation, things go badly and the hero approaches Heaven, which is a colourless, humourless, regimented place. When the heroine sees that the patient has no pulse and no heartbeat, she grapples with the circumstance. Taking a tear from her cheek, she places it on a rose and sends it to Heaven. It works: the pulse throbs, the eyelids flicker. This reversal causes great distress in Heaven, which, after all, is an orderly place. The distress in Heaven delighted Pat. Beth remembers her mother telling the children, amidst gales of laughter, that "all Heaven was in an uproar." Pat found it hilarious that Heaven could make a mistake. Heaven had not dealt Pat the best hand at the card table. Maybe the fault was in the dealer.

By 1971 bad things and good things were chasing each other across Pat's life. She was included in an anthology of women poets brought out by a new Montreal house called Ingluvin. It was entitled *40 Women Poets* of Canada and was edited by Dorothy Livesay with Seymour Mayne's assistance.[12] The book was well received and was shortly out of print. Pat had four poems in the anthology: "tv," "Mr. Happyman Is Coming," "Killing the Bear" and "Woman." All these poems were eventually included in *Milk Stone*. The work "Killing the Bear" is part of her longer poem "In the Continent Behind My Eyes." In the later version it is written in italics, but here it is not. "Killing the Bear" is one of Pat's meditations on the rituals of early people and shows her effort to enter their way of feeling.[13]

Literary biography depends upon documents, memories of people who knew the writer, and clues in the writer's work itself. Among Pat's papers are fascinating letters with missing pages and no dates. Were these just ideas she wrote down or first drafts of letters that were later completed? The papers show that her mind was busy with ideas about community projects and politics, as well as about poetry and art. There are also clues that she was distancing herself emotionally from Roy. In 1971, Pat received a gift copy of *Outerings*, a chapbook published in 1971 at the University of Windsor. It was among the magazines stored in the trunk in Alan's attic, along with several journals with the work of other poets, inscribed either to Pat alone or else to Pat and Roy as valued colleagues. This one is simply inscribed, "For Pat Lowther with deep admiration of your work." It is signed by Eugene McNamara.

Pat had no office or filing cabinet for her work, and Roy noted in his journal that she kept her files and letters on the kitchen table.[14] She also had the dangerous habit of carrying work in progress around in her briefcase. Perhaps bus stops and waiting rooms were more peaceful for writing than her home was.

There are many stories of lost or destroyed poems. The loss that became legendary was the misplaced poetry for a reading in

Charlottetown, Prince Edward Island. But that calamity, as we shall see later, had a happy ending. Other losses could not be remedied. Allan Safarik tells of a mishap at Simon Fraser University. Pat had been invited to be one of the poetry readers at an arts-access conference sponsored by Simon Fraser's English department. During the morning session, she carried her poems in an attractive new briefcase, which held about a year's work. At the lunch break, everyone left the room and Pat left her briefcase on a table. When they returned from lunch, to Pat's horror her briefcase was gone. She had lost the only copies of some of her poems. The group scoured the room, adjoining rooms, the lunchroom — with no success. They were all hoping that someone had stolen it for the value of the briefcase itself and maybe had thrown out what looked like handwritten sheets of paper with no dollar value. The university security staff looked too — with no results. The following day they got the building custodian to allow them to look through the garbage dumpster. At the end of the frantic search, Pat's devoted friends had smelly hands and no poems. They even posted ads for the poems, but they were not to be found.

It was now June 1971. Pat's Canada Council grant had ended in December 1969. Her final report was expected shortly after that. But her report was late; it was over a year late. She wrote to the Canada Council to explain: "By the spring of 1970 I had produced a book length manuscript. However, I was not satisfied with it, didn't send it to any publisher and eventually discarded much of it. This happened again with a subsequent manuscript, so that in fact, it has taken me two years instead of one to complete a second book of poems, which is as yet untitled; but will be published by Very Stone House in 1972."[15]

This was an explanation, not an apology. Pat knew what she was doing with her writing. If she had to stretch the patience of funders, so be it. She confidently ended her letter to the Canada Council by saying: "I feel very sure now that it was the right thing to do, and that my forthcoming book is far stronger than it would otherwise have been."

The report lists poems published in 1969 and 1970 and adds, almost as an afterthought: "Two poems in Borestone Mountain's *Best Poems of 1970.*" Here was a combination of qualities. Although Pat spoke confidently about her reason for needing more time, she almost missed an opportunity to call attention to being chosen for *Best Poems of 1970.* Pat Lowther never would have structured a poem with so little thought to strategy.

Allan Safarik was part of Seymour Mayne's network and he quickly picked up Mayne's enthusiasm for Pat's poetry. When Safarik and Pat met in 1970, he was in his early twenties. "I was just coming out of the stage of mimeograph magazines. I learned something about publishing by putting out a mimeographed journal." In 1971 he and Brian Brett had started *Blackfish,* a literary magazine and publishing house. The second issue in the fall of 1971 had twelve of Pat's poems, almost half the magazine. In 1972 *Blackfish* did an artistic folio series. One number in the series is Pat's long poem "The Age of the Bird," done as a broadsheet. The folios are a delight to the eye, printed on parchment paper and placed in Spanish-weave paper folders. Each one was hand-numbered and signed and had the author's name hand-painted on the outside. "The Age of the Bird" is about Che Guevara's attempts to rally people in remote villages to the Cuban revolution. The work ends with the poem "Regard to Neruda," which was later published as a separate poem in her next book, *Milk Stone.*[16]

Pat's folio was especially striking because it was illustrated with South American Indian artwork. The way she came about the artwork is another matter. It was cut out of a book that Roy owned. Safarik remembers being at Pat's house and looking through the books for the design. He was sitting at the table when he suddenly looked up and saw Roy's face peering at him through the bookshelf. "It was the eeriest feeling." Roy's lack of social grace is what Safarik remembers. He did not say whether or not Roy agreed to have his book cut up. Likewise, the artist and publisher were not asked if *Blackfish* could harvest their work. When it comes to artistic property rights, this was not Pat's finest hour. The broadsheets sold for $5 each and *Blackfish* "split the proceeds with each poet."[17] At $2.50 per copy, Pat did get a few hundred dollars as her share. Because only 200 copies of most of the folios were produced, the only sure way to see them now is in the rare manuscript rooms of libraries.

For a time Milton Acorn, another political poet, lived with the Lowthers. Chris Gudgeon, Acorn's biographer, thinks this was probably in 1971, but no one knows for sure. "Milt was always moving on." Patrick Lane, who wrote an article titled "Lives of the Poets" in *Geist*, said it was about 1973.[18] Poet Judith Copithorne thinks that Acorn may not have actually lived there, but "crashed" when he needed a place.

Kathy remembers being afraid of Acorn when she first saw him. "He was a big guy with big bulbous eyes and wild hair. He had a big voice too." Alan admits that, even though he was the elder brother, he was scared too. Gudgeon writes that most people were afraid of Acorn. Pat's children recall that once they got to know him, they really liked him, as did Pat. Kathy remembers the time they were all sitting at the dinner table. "Milton was talking in his booming voice as he sprinkled salt on his food. The top came off the salt shaker and a bunch of salt fell in his plate. Well, if his eyes were bulbous before, they really popped open then." After Acorn got over the shock, he joined the whole table in laughter.

Pat wrote a poem to Acorn, called, simply, "Milton Acorn." There is no date on it. It's an affectionate poem showing that one of the things they shared was a love of islands and the ocean. The poem shows that Pat understood the tender parts of this often bombastic "poet man." As Pat writes, she says her cigarette burns to ashes "purposefully." She pictures Milton's cigar, likewise burning to ashes. Companionable smoking, like breaking bread, fosters a kind of kinship. Pat signed the poem with a fine black crayon, "With all my love, Pat."[19]

After Pat's death, Acorn reminisced about a continuing joke he had with Pat. Perhaps he was trying to test her approachability when he asserted that "ten lovers in a lifetime is about average." Pat's response was "ten lovers isn't nearly average." They spoke again ten years later and Pat told him she believed "ten lovers is somewhat above average." Acorn added with a great guffaw, "I doubled the score!"[20] According to Allan Safarik, Acorn had more than a comradely interest in Pat. One day when they were visiting, Acorn confidentially asked Safarik to leave him alone with Pat. When Safarik returned about half an hour later, he found Pat breathlessly saying, "Get me out of here!"

In those years Allan Safarik drove an old truck, a rare find in that crowd of threadbare writers. He and Brian Brett usually ended up driving Pat home from readings. Safarik remembers: "Pat was always getting on the wrong bus: If you didn't drive her home, how was she going to get home? She was always wandering around the building, looking for the entrance, going in the back way and it was locked and standing outside. So we always ended up at all-night restaurants, having a sandwich or something and then dropping her off at that house off Fraser Street, there. She was almost a space case, interested in everything. She'd talk in tangents ... It was obvious that her home life was having an effect on her."

Safarik says that, in spite of Pat's ineptness in the practical world, she knew that she was a good writer. "That's what contributed to her laid-back nature." He explains that the core of Pat's nature was calm. Réshard Gool also raised the question in a radio script about Pat's visit to Charlottetown. He comments: "It was only a few weeks later, when she arrived in Charlottetown, having lost en route her baggage, that I realized how lacking in confidence she was. Was this a necessary defense, a refuge, like Auguste Renoir's invalidism?"[21]

Along the same line, Safarik maintains that Pat could not deal with the banks. "They wouldn't cash her cheques and her account was always funny." Most people learn to conduct their personal affairs as young adults. When they are in their twenties or thirties, they learn the consequences of overdrawing their chequing accounts. If they do not have children to feed, their mistakes are not a disaster. However, there were no such grace periods in Pat's life. Before she knew it, she had the responsibility of young children. As a result, in her thirties, she continued to tussle with matters that others conquer earlier — such as knowing that the best way to get money from a bank is to appear not to need it. Pat had no occasion to practise that strategy.

Pat could pull her head out of the clouds when she saw the need to. She had, after all, been an office supervisor at the Burrard Shipyards. It is clear that Pat had problems doing practical things if they seemed pointless to her. It is also clear that when something was important to her, such as working for her political views or organizing poets, she could take matters in hand. Picture young Brenda lacing up her older sister's skates — perhaps avoiding daily concerns allowed Pat's mind to dig in her own secret gardens.

In November 1972, Pat shared the stage with Margaret Atwood at a Simon Fraser University poetry reading. The campus newspaper reported that she had read her Che Guevara poem, "The Age of the Bird," and several poems in a series that might be called the iris poems. The reviewer wrote, "Pat Lowther is not the most emphatic reader. One is rather more struck by something in herself, something which has suffered heavily. Her softness and smaller reputation kept her in an odd sort of supporting role."[22] Margaret Atwood is described as a silver bullet in contrast to Pat, the iris. The article has photos of both poets. Pat is looking directly into the camera and smiling over her cigarette.

Allan Safarik had arranged for Pat to drive to the airport with Atwood after the reading. That brief acquaintance was the basis for Atwood's poem about Pat: "Another Night Visit."

The height of
moon, cat
against my heart, heart
that feels like luck
so far, the house
floating on wind

Which stone
are you in?

       This is your voice I hold,
       it came in the mail,
       this white pebble
       face with the high bones
       taut, in shadow, this tight smile

That mouth is gone,
sealed over, like a jar
closed, no, broken, skull a cave no
longer. Blood, your
fire on the wall & floor,
smouldering there weeks after.

It was not bad luck

and he put you somewhere
after that, it was in
water.   Then they found you, consigned
you, smoothed you over.

       Goodbye, or anyway
       it was on a plane
       we talked last time.
       I remember
       a plastic stick, ice, your long
       dark hair, sunlight, uncertain
       fingers, not

what we said.

Is that you, in the wind or
as you said, in stone

But this is not a stone,
it is your voice,

alive still, moving
around each word like
wind, these words un-
earth you. [23]

Atwood also agreed to look at the manuscript of *A Stone Diary* and evaluate it for Oxford University Press.

The audience at the reading had no way of knowing that yet another stress had recently entered Pat's life. This was the year that Kathy left home. Neither Kathy nor Roy could stand to be around the other any longer. When Roy knew Kathy was coming home, he would go out and sit in the car until he thought that she had gone to bed. According to Kathy, Roy actually gave her an ultimatum: "'Either you go or I go.' Being a teenager, I wanted out in the worst way." Roy's side of the story is recorded in his journal. His attack on Kathy runs through more than 200 pages like a leitmotif.

Roy seems to have needed to be in control of his little kingdom. Pat was bound to him in marriage. For over eight years he had managed emotional control over his own two little girls. Kathy was the only one under his roof with an objective eye and that eye was a threat to Roy's version of reality. She could see what was going on and report it with a young person's candour. When the time came, she did just that.

Years later Kathy second-guesses her decision: "Now that I think about it, I kick myself. I should have stuck around. Although I doubt he would have left." By the time she was fifteen, she had left home permanently and made a life with friends as best she could. Worry over Kathy facing the world on her own heaped even more stress and guilt upon Pat. No one gave Kathy money. No one protected her sexually. No one fussed over her education. Her mother kept on loving her. That was all Pat had to give.

The writing for Pat's second book, *Milk Stone*, was finished by 1971, but, with her usual bad luck, it was not published until 1974. The words "milk stone" pun on "moonstone," the common name for selenite. Legend attributes to moonstone magical qualities because, as it glows, its colours change as though a message were coming from within it. Pat makes moonstone into a touchstone and stretches it to "milk stone," which is fitting because many of the poems in the collection are about women and birth.

Unfortunately, by the time the book was ready to be published, Very Stone House had folded. Seymour Mayne continued to support Pat's work and so took the manuscript with him when he moved to Ottawa in 1971. He thought that Ingluvin, the publishing house in Montreal that brought out *40 Women Poets* that year, might accept it. One of the important things that Mayne did for Ingluvin, and for Canadian literature in general, was to alert people in the East to the existence of significant West Coast writers. Ingluvin agreed to publish the manuscript that was to become *Milk Stone*.

On December 31, 1972, Seymour Mayne wrote to Pat enthusiastically, saying that there was a good chance that *Milk Stone* would be out by spring. He went on to tell her that the books which Ingluvin had printed the previous year were almost out of print. He added that the copyright and a percentage of the royalties would be hers. He also suggested that she apply for a Canada Council senior grant.

Pat's answer to that letter followed quickly on January 5. Pat explained that royalties were "not a major concern." Her goal was getting the book out and getting it distributed. It was now early 1973 and she reminded him that he had had the manuscript since 1971. Softening her words by saying, "I'm not blaming you directly," she explained her position: "I'm thirty-seven years old and have only one book out. I'm chronically broke. I haven't a hope in hell of getting even a junior grant from the Canada Council without at least one more book. Another well distributed book will yield more readings. My career is hanging on this."[24] Pat did speak up for herself when she saw the need.

The British Columbia election of 1972 brought Dave Barrett's New Democratic Party to power. After the election Robert Harlow, a professor in the English department at the University of British Columbia, asked Pat how she liked being in power. He remembers her looking at him sadly and answering, "It's a shitty government, but it's ours." Phyllis Young was the member of the B.C. Legislative Assembly for the area of Little Mountain that year, and Rita Lalik was her executive assistant. In June 1973, Young was appointed Minister of Consumer Affairs. For Lalik that meant moving from Vancouver to the provincial capital, Victoria. Because of this, Phyllis Young needed someone to run her riding office. Pat was hired on a part-time basis to do just that. A part-time job did not yield her a large salary, but it was something. Pat's job was to respond to problems that constituents encountered in their dealings with the province. If a person had a problem with a pension or health coverage, Pat would straighten it out. In a letter to a friend, Pat described the job as "mostly social work."[25]

Pat was also in charge of the constituency newsletter, and she encouraged full discussions of ideas, including criticism of the NDP. In the eyes of some, this was too much for a partisan organization and so, in Hilda's Thomas's words, after a few months "she was essentially fired." Bethoe Shirkoff sees it much the same way.[26] Rita Lalik's memory of the parting is different: "Pat was very good, not gossipy. There is no reason we would have let her go." In her memory the riding office needed a full-time person, which would have been hard for Pat, as a mother of young children. Whatever the reason for the parting, there is no evidence that Pat was resentful about having to leave. It is more likely that the searing vision of a poet and the practical manoeuvring that is needed for politics were in collision with each other.

In Pat's life as a mother she watched Beth grow into a child with an imagination who wanted to have an adventure. One day, at about age eight, Beth decided to run away from home. Running away was not about feeling unloved or unwanted. It was about a picture that Beth had in her mind of a sack tied to a stick carried on the shoulder of a traveller. It seemed like a great activity, like going swimming. She tied her sack firmly to her chosen stick and told her mother she was going to run away. Pat knew what was going on inside Beth. She responded: "'Bye, be home for dinner." In the style of a storybook adventurer, Beth set off on her journey. The neighbourhood children were too literal to understand that this was a game. Commandeered by a little girl named Deborah, they organized a posse and chased her down the street hollering, "Don't go!" A terrified Beth fled home into her mother's arms.

CHAPTER 8

Pat's Vision and *Realpolitik*

*Poetry — if it doesn't open the body and the body
politic, it doesn't address the central thing.*

— bill bissett[1]

PAT'S PATERNAL GRANDFATHER HAD DIED in an industrial accident
and she had a brother born with a disability. She had been a single
mother and later the wife of an unemployed man. Her poetry and
her political involvement demonstrate her understanding that
what happens to housewives is also political. Her own conclusions
were founded on and strengthened by her family's history of
political activism.

Having had a grandfather who was a labour organizer and
parents who worked in neighbourhood politics, Pat was able to
put her beliefs into action easily. Like her parents, Pat believed
in social democracy and supported the New Democratic Party.
Critic Robert Fulford discerned, "Hers is a resentful socialism
that has suffered too many defeats already and expects to suffer
many more."[2] Ed Livingston served on the NDP Provincial

Council with Pat. He notes with admiration: "She was a real political animal."

On one occasion Pat worked with Bethoe Shirkoff in an NDP women's group, planning a conference on poverty. The woman chairing that committee was an unforgettable person. Sturdily raising her seven children by herself on welfare, she looked at her hard life and said that her seven children were "the best string-a luck I ever had." The women were working together well and had their conference program set. Ian Adams, author of *The Poverty Wall*, had come in from Toronto and was to be the main speaker.

As the evening wore on, Shirkoff looked at her slim purse and hoped that someone would offer her a lift home so that she could save the bus fare. She writes: "Complications arose with the arrival of two vigorous young men, heavy thinkers in the NDP at that time, who scrapped half of our carefully laid plans which they said exceeded the terms of reference with which we had been entrusted. Pat made no objection, though I learned later that she valued her time as much as any of us. I was angry that we should not be given *carte blanche* but needed paternal correction, and mumbled resentfully that although we were only women and had not spoken to Ian Adams we knew about poverty first hand."[3] No, Pat did not raise a ruckus. She quietly borrowed money for her bus fare home and left the meeting.

In September 1970, both Pat and Roy ran for office in the NDP Area Council. Roy wanted to develop a plan within the local council for contesting civic elections. He ran for vice-president and lost badly, getting only three votes. Pat ran for second vice-president and won. People present at the meeting remember that Roy walked out. We may never know what happened in their relationship after his defeat alongside her victory, but we can guess that it increased his feeling that Pat was surpassing him, and not just at writing. The only public office he ever ran for after that was member of the Parks Board. He was not elected. By contrast, Pat, instead of actively seeking office, was asked to stand for the nomination of Member of the Legislative Assembly for the riding of Little Mountain. In her usual "no-fuss" way, she almost got that nomination.

Some critics condemn art that has a political message; others believe that artists must be rooted in the real world to be able to comment on it. Professor Réshard Gool believes that Pat's political poems do work as poems. "It is not propaganda art ... She is trying to very intelligently, very sensitively ... hold a very complex universe together. Part of that universe is political." Poet bill bissett says simply: "I think there's a place where poetry and politics are the same. And I think she was defending that place."

Seymour Mayne believes that: "she felt a possibility of a bridge between the words of a poet and the vision of a poet ... translating that vision into justice and social democracy, into the everyday lives of British Columbians, ... that everyday life was not just a matter of coping, but it also had to have, underpinning it, a vision of what life really should be ... helping human beings, concern with justice and ethics and trying to create a more harmonious society."

Mayne grants that these are "the clichés of social democracy," and that the other school of thought of the poets of our age, led by Anglo-Americans such as T.S. Eliot or Ezra Pound, is a poetry of alienation and cynicism, with no hope for humanity. That view has led them to right-wing political stands and, in Pound's case, to fascism. Mayne concedes that although socialist and communist societies have not always turned out as they were initially envisioned, at least they have had the goal of making life better for people.

Bill bissett states that on some political issues — the Vietnam War, the overthrow of the social democratic president of Chile, Salvadore Allende, the mourning for the students killed by state police and the National Guard at Jackson and Kent State Universities — Pat and Roy would have agreed, but for different reasons. Bissett says that, for Roy, communist ideology came first; for Pat, it was individual freedom. He continues: "She was interested in essence and she was interested in being." He remembers Roy being critical of people who put literature above politics.

Bill's group of writer friends in those years included Patrick Lane, Maxine Gadd, Judith Copithorne and Milton Acorn. They were certainly not elitist and did not reject Roy's writing. "But he had a lot of problems with us," bissett explains. Roy did not have a feeling for contemporary language and carried his preference for structured rhyming verse over to criticism of free verse and other experimental poetry. "Roy was what we used to call straight … And it was clear to me that he didn't really approve of any of us." Bissett was part of the downtown LSD culture, which was — in location and feeling — far away from the life that Roy and Pat led in their working-class neighbourhood on East 46th Avenue.

Bissett recalls that the collapse of democracy in Chile in 1973 meant the loss of hope for a lot of people in Canada who were left of centre. "And it became hard to talk politically. Because, since that had happened, it meant the empire had gained an incredible foothold in our mind, which is what we were trying to resist." When bissett says "the empire," he is speaking of the United States, which helped to overthrow Allende and imposed a military junta.[4]

Humane political values are what drew Pat to the poetry of Chilean poet Pablo Neruda. He wrote numerous poems, published in his now-famous *Canto General*, about the collaboration between the American government and certain multinational companies such as the Anaconda Copper Mining Company and the United Fruit Company.[5] His voice appears to have given Pat broader evidence for the political realities that she saw around her:

> For I have bowed to stone
> since my great brother is dead
> who feasted me after hunger,
> who taught me art
> and adoration [6]

Pablo Neruda held a special attraction for American and Canadian West Coast poets. This was partly due to the location of Chile on the west coast of South America and to the mountains that run along the coasts of both continents. It was also due to Neruda's commitment to justice for the earth and its peoples.

Neruda's life spanned the years from 1904 to 1973. His work explores human life as it relates to the cosmos. He uses simple, elegant language because he believed that "we are nations made up of simple people who are learning to read. It is for them we must write."[7] He did succeed in writing for everyone. As a holder of the Nobel Prize for Literature, he was admired by international intellectuals, but he was also read and loved by the common people of Latin America. His work ponders stone, earth, water, air and sensuality, and explores human life as it relates to the universe.

"Ode to a Lemon" is part of the series "Elemental Odes."

> So, while the hand
> holds the cut of the lemon,
> half a world
> on a trencher,
> the gold of the universe
> wells
> to your touch:
> a cup yellow
> with miracles,
> a breast and a nipple
> perfuming the earth;
> a flashing made fruitage,
> the diminutive fire of the planet.[8]

Neruda's poetry rolls our modern minds in just enough myth to show us the lights and darks of the earth. In the poem "Some Beasts," he tells us that the animals are "drenched in the ritual mud, / rapacious, religious, / gigantic, the coiled anaconda."[9] This union of the rational with the mythic leads some of his readers to consider him a magician.

Born into a working-class family in 1904, Neruda identified with the common person throughout his life. Poetry was his weapon to attack injustice. "La United Fruit Co" denounces the control over, and exploitation of, his beloved Chile by a foreign company.[10] Neruda was also a man of action and, for the last half of his life, a communist. Several Latin American countries have a novel way of financing writers. They make them ambassadors. Neruda was Chile's ambassador to Spain during the Spanish Civil War and unilaterally declared Chile to be on the side of the Republicans. Predictably, this ended his diplomatic career, and he returned to Chile. Once in Chile, he criticized President Gonzales Videla. Videla had little patience with dissent and tried to have Neruda arrested. The poet managed to escape Chile and lived in Mexico and Paris until Videla's government fell in 1953.[11]

Pat was drawn to Neruda's study of everyday objects — tools, seeds, mud — and the way he used them to reach the unknowable. Brian Brett says: "Like Neruda ... she was equally able to encompass the love life of snails and the politics of a country."[12] In her poem "Last Letter to Pablo," Pat writes:

> our planet carries Neruda
> bloodstone
> dark jewel of history
> the planet carries you
> a seed patient as time. [13]

In 1973 the elected government of Chile was overthrown by the army. In September 1973, Pat wrote, in a letter to a friend: "I'm worried about Neruda. He may have been out of the country during the junta."[14] (Although the Spanish word *junta* means group or council, Pat was using it the way many English-speaking people do to mean a military takeover of a state.) In fact, Neruda was in Chile, and at age sixty-nine was seriously ill. The junta knew that jailing a Nobel Prize winner would hurt their international standing. He was not arrested, but he was denied medicine, and he died at his home on Isla Negra on September 23, twelve days after the coup.[15]

On December 31, 1973, Pat was working on one of her most important poems. On that date she wrote another letter to a friend, saying "I'm writing a poem about Chileans imprisoned in an old nitrates mine mixed up with Bach's Easter Cantata."[16] From the blend of the day's news and Bach's cantata came "Chacabuco, the Pit,"[17] which some critics call Pat's best work. Perhaps Pat felt she was paying a literary debt to Neruda in writing it.

A few facts about Chilean history help in reading "Chacabuco, the Pit." In 1970, Salvador Allende was elected president as head of a social-democratic government. In Pat's eyes Allende's election was good news. Now the common person might have a chance for a good material life and live free from political fear. But in 1973, the Chilean army toppled the government and, in effect, assassinated Allende.[18] Opponents of the junta were arrested and tortured; many were killed. Elections and comparative freedom did not return to Chile until 1987.

In "Chacabuco," Pat becomes the voice of a Hebrew prophet, warning the people that moral lapses have consequences. She calls upon the powers of the universe as she tries to stop great evil. The evil is the torture and murder of prisoners held in the abandoned nitrate mine Chacabuco. She points a finger at American support for the junta by quoting a plan sent by the International Telephone and Telegraph Company to the White House. Then she goads her readers to stop the torture. She reminds us that "... here as in all human places / prayer has been uttered." Finally, she weaves together ancient Mayan, Jewish and

Christian devotions to summon the powers of the universe. In so doing, this passionate poem becomes a prayer.

Pat countered the effects of the junta having chosen an abandoned nitrate mine for a prison by stirring up Neruda's images of mineral elements giving sustenance. She has the prisoners dream of "… sucking juice from it / pissing nitrate dust." It may seem hopeless to be forced to get nourishment from dust, but Pat, like Neruda, reminds us that the earth is made from dust and we are creatures of our earth.

Throughout the poem we are made physically uncomfortable by images of blinding sunlight. The poet asks: "is God blinking? are you / shuttering your eyes, turista?" Pat worked with the feeling of glare because Chacabuco is located in Chile's fearsome Atacama Desert, located in the extreme north. Its intense heat and blinding glare have sparked a store of legends attaching mystic powers to it.[19] Even before Pat wrote about the Atacama, it had been the subject of several important Chilean poems. In addition, Chacabuco was the site of the decisive battle in 1817, in which San Martin defeated the Spanish colonial forces, thus bringing about the independence of Chile and most of the rest of Latin America.[20] The Atacama Desert is one of the most arid places in the world. As Pat walks us through the heat of the land and the suffering of the prisoners, the desert stories hover.

The Atacama Desert is the first strand of an otherworldly web Pat weaves by invoking rituals. An early line of the poem harks back to an ancient Mayan prayer: "*I shall speak to the Lord of Heaven where he sits asleep.*" Itzamna was the Mayan god of heaven and the creator of the world. He seldom took an interest in the lives of his people, but they did pray to him, especially on the new year, hoping to avert calamities. Itzamna is sometimes shown as a two-headed serpent, with one head and one hand facing east to symbolize the rising sun and life, and the other head and hand facing west to symbolize the setting sun and death. We are facing an indifferent god who permits good and bad events.[21]

In Pat's poem, there is also a harnessing of the power of the Jewish psalm 137, verses 5 and 6, which says: "If I forget thee, O Zion / Let my right hand fail / Let my tongue cleave to the roof of my mouth." The poem paraphrases:

> Let statesmen's tongues lock
> between their jaws,
> let businessmen's cheque hands
> be paralyzed,
> let musicians stop building
> towers of sound,
> let commerce fall
> in convulsions:
> we have deserved this.

The prisoners kept in places like Chacabuco were people seen by the junta as agitators. Among them was Victor Jara, a musician and teacher. Jara was a target because he had used his music to support Allende and was probably one of the "patriots … forgetting to bribe generals … organizing anti-Fascist song festivals."

Jara was arrested in the presence of his students and was to become one of thousands of political prisoners held under terrible conditions in the National Stadium. When the stadium became too small to hold them all, prisoners were moved to places such as abandoned mines, including Chacabuco. Jara's captors did not know what to do when he responded to their routine beatings by singing. Infuriated, the military publicly mutilated his hands. Jara then raised his bloody arms like a badge of honour and led the crowd in song. He died from these and other wounds in September 1973. Joan Jara, his wife, wrote of his life and death in her book, *Victor: An Unfinished Song*. Remembering when she was summoned to identify his body, she writes, "His hands seemed to be hanging from his arms at a strange angle as though his wrists were broken." One of his friends smuggled this unfinished poem out of the National Stadium and gave it to her:

> How hard it is to sing
> when I must sing of horror.
> Horror which I am living,
> horror which I am dying. [22]

The martyring of Victor Jara has an amazing parallel in Jewish lore. During the twelfth century, the scholarly Rabbi Amnon lived in Mayence, Germany. He was repeatedly hounded by the local archbishop to adopt Christianity. One day, weary of the harangue, Rabbi Amnon asked for three days' respite to consider the question. When he went home, the rabbi fell into a depression and did not appear on the third day. The archbishop had him arrested and forced him to plead guilty to the crime of failing to appear before him on the third day. The rabbi was punished by having his hands and feet cut off. In his misery he composed the "U'Nethanneh Tokef," a prayer-poem that would become part of Jewish liturgy. Although mortally wounded, he asked to be taken to the synagogue for the Jewish New Year. Rabbi Amnon recited the following prayer and died: "How many shall leave this world and how many shall be born into it, who shall live and who shall die, who shall live out the limit of his days and who shall not, who shall perish by fire and who by water, who by sword and who by beast, who by hunger and who by thirst, who by earthquake and who by plague, who by strangling and who by stoning, who shall rest and who shall wander, who shall be at peace and who shall be tormented, who shall be poor and who shall be rich, who shall be humbled and who shall be exalted."[23]

Pat had no special religious training, and she likely did not know Rabbi Amnon's story, yet she must have come upon the prayer and seen its power as a model for "Chacabuco, the Pit." Using the form of the "U'Nethanneh Tokef," she wrote:

> Some one decides
> who shall eat
> who shall not eat

> who shall be beaten
> and on which
> parts of his body
>
> Some one decides
> who shall be starved
> who shall be fed
> enough to sustain
> another day's torture
>
> A man decides.
> That man does not breathe dust:
> He is dust.

Is she saying that the torturer is "dirt"? Is she reminding him that he is made of the same clay as others? Is she warning him that it is a perversion for one man to decree another's fate? Most likely, all three.

After describing the agony, Pat echoes the Christian apostle Paul in Corinthians 15:32: "And the dead shall be raised incorruptible." Her message of hope follows and she insists:

> For I tell you the earth
> itself is a mystery
> which we penetrate constantly
> and our people a holy mystery
> beyond refusal

She marvels at the mystery of the earth and the mysterious human capacity for both good and evil. The rock and glare of the Atacama Desert can lead to light and life or to heat and death. Pat Lowther, the entreating prophet, has shown us the wilderness. We are left to choose:

> ... what we determine shall be
> made truly among us. Amen.

Poets force us to look squarely at the chances of life and death. Poets can also be troublesome. They "forget" to give the powerful their due. Instead, they remember their dreams and try to bring them to life. Pat Lowther, Victor Jara and Rabbi Amnon, so far away from one another in time and place, share a refusal to live by the rules of the powerful.

In 1971, Bethoe Shirkoff heard Pat read some of her poems about Neruda at the Kitsilano Public Library. She wrote: "[Pat] talked briefly and assuredly about each poem before she read, each time, to let the listener in on her intent when she wrote it: that this one was in response to the poet Pablo Neruda running for the office of president of his country, or that this one reflected her situation as a woman; or that this one was going to be more intricate because she had been trying to catch the wind's sound. It seemed as though we were in a smaller room and she was showing us clear images of her inner life, places in her mind she wanted us to share.

"She read one perfect poem after another and it was exciting to be listening to her read those poems in that strange lilting voice, the way poets read their own work. The words pierced through the voice and landed on us and a strange thing happened to us all. When a cold trembling took hold of me I furtively looked around to see if others were affected the same way and really it was impossible to tell except that there was not a sound, not a cough, not a rustle, just Pat's voice. The words were carefully, sparingly chosen. Surprising, startling, fine. We held our breath at her craft. I waited for a poem that would not be as fine as the others. None came."[24]

Some readers look at Pat's work and conclude that she was fascinated with violence or advocated masochism. Then, when the same readers learn that Pat was a battered woman, they become convinced of it. Some people even ask if Pat had a death wish. Perhaps these questions are asked by those who have not looked at the suffering and death that surround us. Much of Pat's writing urges us to look.

In her poems, Pat recorded the violence she saw around her, bringing it to the reader's attention. This is strong medicine for sensitive readers; some may dismiss the work rather than enduring the details. As Len Gasparini says, "She offers no easy exits for tailor-made sensibilities."[25] However, to conclude that recording violence equals promoting it is tantamount to blaming the messenger. It is reasonable to say that children who are surrounded by violent television and comics will get the mistaken message that violence is exciting. Cartoon characters get hit on the head and are fun to watch; the characters do not seem to feel pain. Pat, however, never stands outside the pain.

A major thrust of Pat's poetry is trying to understand feelings, feelings that are not often expressed anywhere else. She even tries to figure out the sentient qualities of stone, bone and ice. In violent entertainment, one person always benefits from the hurt given to another, even if the benefit is only the bad guy chortling with evil laughter. Pat did not record anyone's pleasure from violence; when she does record individual hurt in her poetry, she turns it into a pain that hurts the whole universe. Writing about the torture of Chilean prisoners, she says: "For I tell you the earth / itself is a mystery / which we penetrate constantly / and our people a holy mystery / beyond refusal."

Perhaps it was living with a violent man for over a decade that gave Pat the insight to write a poem with the sickening title "To a Woman Who Died of 34 Stab Wounds."[26] When Pat read the poem in Charlottetown, she prefaced it by saying it was her "contribution to survival," presumably to the survival of the woman's memory, for it was based on the story of a woman she knew. This woman was in her sixties and had been on vacation in Hawaii. She was a friendly person who trusted people. Pat said she could picture the woman befriending someone in her usual open way. But, unfortunately, violence attached to sex is part of the world in which we live. Pat's poem reminds us of the woman's humanity, her pride, her genuine liking for people. This openness to all people, set in a place where beer is poured and where "glances would cross behind your back," proved to be a fatal mistake. We have no reason to think that the woman invited the violence that led to her death.

> I can see it as though I'd been there,
> you pouring beer and talking,
> your heavy scarlet smile
> held out like a credit card.
> …
> They wouldn't know
> that milky velvet you affected
> was your true face.
> …
> Your murderer couldn't believe
> so much pride could survive
> in flesh gone soft.
> At the end, coiling, striking,
> his rage was for himself,
> for his fine body failing
> to humble your sagging sixty. [27]

Pat's words to us here are evidence that she understood fully the unquenchable rage of violent people. Another woman writer has said: "After the blows are over, the one who strikes hates more than the one who is struck."[28]

"Vulnerability" is a key word. Vulnerability runs through Pat's poetry as it did through her whole life. The only way to be completely invulnerable is to withdraw. That was not Pat's way. Pat refused to let herself or us forget this. Trusting people is sometimes inadvisable, but it does not, by itself, equate flirting with violence. Pat's refusal to withdraw set her apart. As for the vulnerability, women's psychic and sexual need for men makes them vulnerable to men, some of whom are violent. Pat's need to understand things left her open on a grand scale.

Pat believed in the power of words to change people. In the work titled "Poetry," she plays with images of violence in the same way that we say we'll *beat* an illness or *kill* a problem. She invites the reader to walk with her through land mines; fire bombs are planted in the mind; and Pat confesses that, in her craft, she does "practice / love and war."[29] She is confessing that she wants, somehow, to change the reader. Few of us submit willingly to being changed, so her methods must be strong ones. This guide who walks us through the land mines warns the reader that they "go off at the first footfall of perception." Passion to have people understand leads the poet to coax: "But come / the view is worth the danger." The greatest obstacle to her efforts is the protective shell we grow over our feelings. She continues: "Or if you fear / bring winter, lay a crust of snow / to guard your senses."[30] Fixing attention on the shells that we put around sex, she asks: "Why is the shell more dear / than those rich minglings?"[31] Pat's solution is to abandon the shell, but the choice she makes entails risk. In the poem "Wanting," she fears she "may be broken / utterly open / and he not see / the flower shape of me."[32]

Poets take on the job of worrying about the great questions: justice, love, birth and, yes, death. Pat did think and write about death, looking at more faces of death than most people can imagine. Her overarching view seemed to be that if death must come, let it be a worthy one. The preliminary manuscript for *Milk Stone* contains "Socrates for Mayor," a poem in which Socrates chose death rather than deny his beliefs. The poem says, "I'll drink to the exquisitely correct curve of Socrates' finger / on his cup."[33] Here is evidence that, for Pat, there are real principles to guide both life and death.

In her poetry, Pat forces her readers to think about blameworthy deaths such as that of the woman who died of thirty-four stab wounds and those of political prisoners in Chile. In "It Happens Every Day," she also meditates on needless deaths, such as those of children who end up suffocated in dumped refrigerators while playing hide-and-seek and housewives who, without wanting to, wipe out whole families with contaminated preserves. The one sexually coloured example is joined to these others in a way that is not at all titillating, and, in fact, the grouping of these tragic deaths together emphasizes that they are all the result of unnecessary ignorance. Despite the lines "Women court dangerous men / who will beat them to death," the total poem is, once again, a map of vulnerability, not a map of flirtation with danger or violence.[34]

It is not clear that Pat had any idea of what Roy would do to her. Brian Brett laments that her "eerie intelligence and premonitions are devastating" and cites four poems that show her thoughts about violence. Brett, however, admits: "It's easy to second guess now, asking why she remained in a situation where she could smell her own death. But then it was not so easy."[35] Peter Gzowski suggests she had an "eerie premonition of a violent death,"[36] and Seymour Mayne wonders if she was only "testing fate." Réshard Gool considers the question and follows it with more questions, "What is poetry about if not love and birth and death? So what could be more real than to play with your own death?"

Pat's daughter Beth comments, "Perhaps, inasmuch as all women living with a violent spouse carry, like a virus, the possibility of their own deaths inside them, she knew and subconsciously began making preparations."[37] Pat told Hilda Woolnough that if she tried to leave Roy and take the children, "he would get pretty rough about it." It is no secret that the surest way for a woman to be murdered is to try to leave a violent and controlling man. Murder statistics for women bear this out. And if it does not happen while she is trying to leave, she will often be stalked by him afterward. Pat knew Roy's tender spots.

"The Egg of Death," though not often quoted, may be Pat's deepest meditation on death, that "faint-ticking time bomb." Full of caution about the fragile egg, she is one who moves "softly softly not to jar it." At the same time, she is baffled by other humans who casually "devise the detonators for a swarm of deadly eggs,"[38] presumably nuclear bombs. Like it or not, death abides with us all through life. Pat seemed acutely aware of this. In "A Simple Song of Love," she wrote about "one foot poised over the grave."[39] But she dares a defiance of death by saying, "but I've noticed some people / don't lie down / when their number's called. / I intend to be / one of them."[40]

Lorraine Vernon has called Pat "incredibly passive, warm and beautiful, but passive." Paul Grescoe's article in *Canadian Magazine*, with its subtitle "Pat Lowther lived passively, wrote lyrically and died violently," emphasizes this same point.[41] These opinions are shrugged off by Margaret Atwood, who asked the magazine *Ms.* to do an article on Pat. She sent the Grescoe article to them with the added comment: "I didn't think she was that passive."[42] Like Atwood, Bethoe Shirkoff is also bothered by the emphasis in the title of Grescoe's article. She responds: "It seems to me that human beings make serious mistakes and bad choices more often than they deliberately choose to be victims." Stephen Michael Bersensky puts it this way: "Pat was a genuinely caring person ... I think the extent to which she cared was a factor in her death. She did not totally protect herself, because she loved her children."

There are those who will still point to the attention that Pat gave to violence and say that she was attracted to it. They might wonder if her choice of Roy Lowther as a husband shows that she wanted to take risks. Perhaps, but reporter Scott Lawrence has read "Coast Range" and says that "the mountains ... are like her heroes; they are humble, embracing the violence of highway blasting crews; they are survivors, enduring; they are irreducible, mind shattering in their purity."[43]

You can gut them
blast them
to slag
the shapes they've made in the sky
cannot be reduced [44]

The poem "Baby You Tell Me" gives further clues. It was written as a reply to a man who had said that he found her poems "indigestible." He requested that she grow teeth in her brain so that she would be easier to digest. The poem addresses the affront to her mind and her feelings. In it Pat declares: "Anybody's going to eat me / he's going to know / he's had a meal."[45] At no point in the poem does she attack her attacker. She plays fair and focuses on the insult. This is not the work of a woman who loves to be beaten.

Behind all the allusions to violence and death in Pat's poetry is the feeling that she in some way felt the future coming. In spite of the reasonable explanations for possible premonitions, one has to ask if Pat had a kind of second sight. Chris believes that her mother was working at "a different level of consciousness." Consciousness does not have to mean that Pat was able to see into the future; it could simply mean that she had more finely tuned perceptions than most of us. Ward Carson says that years before Pat met Roy she "had bad premonitions of the future — dark premonitions." Pat wrote two poems that support Carson's statement. She may have written them only for herself, not for publication. One is entitled "Out of the Mouths of Teacups." It lists catastrophes, such as drowning and "bloody war," and ends with the line "And WHO wrote / in the dust on my mantel: / YOU'RE NEXT?"[46] The other is handwritten and untitled. It is about a darkness tree that "rears its absolute to me." The tree kept reappearing and waving its laughing leaves at her.[47] This poem has a rhyme and rhythm that stay stubbornly in the mind.

If Pat had dark premonitions, her poetry also fights this awareness. Her poetic struggle was to connect death, birth and creativity with the universe. Her poems do not dwell on violence and death, instead they search for solutions, such as new births and the solace of the seasons. Writing of Pablo Neruda's death, she sees his body blend with the earth while his spirit soars through the universe. Patricia Lowther was not a poet who willingly embraced darkness. Instead her poetry offers renewal and birth. In "May Chant," she tells of a woman, squatting in labour, who cries for the child to:

> Come down
> to the roots of things
> and I who will
> in the darkness of germination
> stealthily gather
> his scattered members
> and bind them whole [48]

Reasserting life and germination was Pat Lowther's solution to the darkness that pursued her.

CHAPTER 9

National Recognition — Except for Ontario

*Strange, the need to be hung hooked
on some other ambiance.*

— Pat Lowther[1]

IN THE FALL OF 1972 THE LEAGUE OF CANADIAN POETS held its annual general meeting in Edmonton, Alberta. Although there is little evidence of Pat's early involvement with the League, it is likely that she had been on a least a couple of the reading tours the group organized on behalf of its membership. The fall 1972 meeting, however, could well have been the first national gathering of poets that Pat had attended.

It was at the 1972 meeting that Pat became friends with poets Fred Cogswell and Eugene McNamara. Fred Cogswell, who had a reputation for encouraging new poets, might well be called an elder statesman among English-Canadian poets. He was professor of literature at the University of New Brunswick and, for many years, editor of the literary journal *The Fiddlehead*, which had published a number of Pat's poems. He describes Pat as a "proud, independent woman," and goes on to say: "She was, in many ways, one of the

most beautiful and striking people I have ever met." Pat undoubtedly appreciated this new friendship with a poet who had lived
through changing ideas and fashions in literature. Eugene
McNamara was the poet who had sent Pat the inscribed chapbook
in 1971. He was an admirer of her work and, although they had
corresponded, this was the first time they had actually met.

After the conference, Pat and Cogswell corresponded. However, Pat's connection with Eugene McNamara was different: he
became her lover. If ever there was a long-distance romance, this
was it, since he lived in Ontario and was a professor at the University of Western Ontario. After the annual meeting, they returned
to their separate lives, thousands of miles apart. At most, they had
four rendezvous in three years. Nonetheless, their romance brought
a lightness into Pat's life, and critics say that her poetry became
stronger. Bill bissett observed that Pat's appearance was different;
she was more relaxed, as if she was letting herself and her gender
emerge. Bissett says that "flowing" is the feeling she conveyed. Pat
and McNamara's romance was to be recorded in the poems that
they wrote and the letters they exchanged. It seems that Pat made
little effort to hide the relationship from Roy.

By 1972, the League of Canadian Poets was occupying more of
Pat's time. The organization was formed in 1966 to advance poetry
in Canada and to be a voice for the interests of poets. To become a
member of the League, a poet must be published and be recommended by current members. Just being a member is a vote of
confidence. Pat's membership showed that people she valued were
appreciating her work. As Pat became more involved with the
League, she began donating her personal time to working in the
interests of Canada's community of poets. It was natural for a
woman who had worked for a political party and spoken at anti-war
rallies to work in a public way for her art. In a 1975 newspaper
interview, she pointed out that "less than ten percent of all the high
school students in Canada study Canadian literature. Canada is

probably the only country in the world that does not bother to teach
or read its own poetry, fiction or drama in most of its educational
institutions."[2]

Arlene and Gerry Lampert were the two dedicated people
behind the League of Canadian Poets. They had started out organizing the Platform for the Arts, which ran tours of writers, poets and
playwrights. As the need for a poets' organization became clear,
they responded to the challenge. With no office or operating funds,
the Lamperts did this work for the pure love of art, running the
League from the office of Gerry's advertising business. Members
paid dues to the poet elected as president to cover the cost of
newsletters and leaflets. In this way, the poets kept in touch with
one another. Then, in 1971, the Lamperts started organizing poetry
reading tours.

Inevitably, the arts work started crowding out the advertising
business. Arlene Lampert then took on more of the arts work,
which was basically sending tour lists to the poets. By the time Pat
joined the League, Lampert was working full-time on League
business, yet she still did not have a salary or an official title. Pat
and other members of the executive committee were scurrying
around to find money so that the League could pay her. They
managed to get an Ontario Arts Council grant. "It was for $2000
and we had overspent it by the time it arrived," Lampert remembers with a laugh.

As time went on, there were also grants from the Canada
Council for the League's annual meetings and to pay poets'
expenses on reading tours. For example, in 1974 the B.C.
branch of the League received $1000 from the B.C. Cultural
Fund and $2000 from the Canada Council. With this they
managed to pay the costs of eighteen reading tours. But there
were still no funds to run an organization. The cost of organizing across the thousands of miles of Canada has led many to
defeat. Telephone calls between Vancouver and Toronto alone

can eat up a small budget. Grants had to be used with ingenuity for the organization to stay alive.

Pat's volunteer work with the League helped her promote poetry in Canada; however, it did not help promote her own financial situation. She was still desperately in need of money, and her grant applications were not going well. In 1972 Pat got a short-term, junior-level grant (B Category) of $750 from the Canada Council, although she had applied for a senior-level (A Category) grant. With two publications and a promise of a third, she certainly was a professional artist, not the "promising young artist" for whom the junior-level grant is intended. A senior grant would have given her more status and $600 more in her pocket. The Canada Council grant of 1972 was not to be one of her lucky cards.

In her application to the Canada Council, Pat had proposed to:

> 1. Research and write a suite of poems dealing with celestial objects, interpreting evolution of the universe in terms of human evolution.
>
> 2. Integrate this into a script which includes visual projections and sound.
>
> 3. Performance by MacMillan Planetarium in Vancouver and possibly other planetaria later. The local planetarium curator and technician have indicated they are interested. [3]

To referee the application, the Canada Council chose D.G. Jones, poet, academic and Canada's authority on myth in poetry. Jones supported Pat's application, saying that he was struck by the "control of the line, the ring of authority of the remark, the relatively large and clean-cut general statement." He qualified his praise, however, by saying that, although Pat did a commendable job of expressing both scientific information from the outside and mythic images from the inside, "one cannot be sure that she has succeeded in digesting and integrating these two points of departure ... but in some places succeeds very well." He backed up his opinion by quoting three poems; one of them was "Coast Range." In Pat's favour, Professor Jones added that the fusion of Native myth with the landscape has been notable for West Coast artists from Emily Carr to poets such as Earle Birney, John Newlove and Susan Musgrave. He saw its connection with a general growth of environmental awareness and believed that the Canada Council should encourage Pat's work because of her ability to "give it effective articulation."[4]

The praise of D.G. Jones was not enough to earn Pat a senior-level grant. Ingluvin was experiencing financial difficulties and the press's troubles had bounded back on Pat. *Milk Stone*, which the press had had for over a year now, still had not been published and the press's failure to print the book made it look as if Pat had not written anything significant for a while. In addition, Pat had not included a statement from the MacMillan Planetarium backing up her word that they wished to sponsor the show. A letter of endorsement would have made her application stronger.

In December 1972, Pat wrote her final report for the planetarium show to the Canada Council. She said that she had completed the written script and that month she planned to work with the special-effects technician, Michael Koziniak, preparing the visual and sound effects. She added: "The short term grant from Canada Council enabled me to complete the first part of this project." Pat was political enough to let them know that the grant had not covered the full cost of doing the work, but in her usual polite way, she closed the letter "With thanks."[5] Nineteen seventy-two also brought Pat's first paid teaching job: an adult education course in creative writing for the New Westminster Board of Education.

In late September 1973, Pat got a special-delivery letter from Seymour Mayne telling her that Ingluvin had gone "splosh."[6] He suggested she send *Milk Stone* to a small publishing house in Ottawa,

Borealis Press. The publisher, Glenn Clever, was also a professor at the University of Ottawa and he invited Pat to read to his class while she was on an Eastern reading tour organized through the League. Clever was so keen on Pat's work that he also wanted to do a reprint of *This Difficult Flowring*. Pat responded that she would "much rather have two or three newer books out first."[7]

In February 1974, Pat sent a photocopy of the manuscript for *Milk Stone* to Clever along with a note thanking him for his hospitality at her reading the previous fall: "I'm sure your whole department should be congratulated on the warmth and receptiveness that your students show to visiting writers." She apologized that she did not have an original copy of her work to give him, explaining, "At this point I feel I cannot, cannot, retype this manuscript one more time." The manuscript was essentially the same as the one she had sent to Ingluvin in 1971. She had made just one change. "Burning Iris" had started out as a single poem. Pat explained: "I subsequently wrote two more, with the same title, making a set. I've inserted them into this manuscript, but they could be pulled if it would be inconvenient to include them."[8] She was self-assured about her work, but did not want to inconvenience anyone. On March 13, 1974, Clever sent Pat a contract for *Milk Stone*, which she signed and returned on March 20, with this added comment: "Those diptychs are hell for typesetting. I suggest you follow the pasteup, which I did myself, mumbling and cursing and gluing myself to anything not in motion."[9]

Once again, Pat called upon Steven Slutsky to do the artwork. The cover has a picture of a wizardly-looking woman hauling something up from a well. In the foreground a baby is tied into a basket, sleeping peacefully, as if it had just been fetched from the well. The background has an enchanted-looking building nestled against a cliff. The ground is covered with bubbles or jewels or round stones, maybe milk stones. At the top of the picture there is a new moon, surrounded by a halo, poking through a bank of clouds. Pat had hoped that the frame of the artwork would be deep blue "to carry over to the outside a sort of cold, remote feeling" and to emphasize an Ice Age setting.[10] As it turned out, the cover is shiny white with black print.

Pat called the sequence "In the Continent Behind My Eyes" the core poem of this collection.[11] It may just be the core poem of all her work. "Continent" grapples with both the external landscape of British Columbia and Pat's own internal landscape. Then, she tries to pull these two landscapes together, which, observes reviewer Diana Hayes, is the task of a shaman.[12]

"Continent" has all the Pat Lowther hallmarks. She identifies with the landscape, plays back personal memories and discusses the work of writing poetry. As the doom of the Ice Age approaches, she is the early historian, carving her people's story on the cave wall. Recording history is a human act. It is the only act that a person about to be overcome by the Ice Age can take to ensure that the story of her culture will not disappear with her bones. It is redemption in the face of apparent destruction.

By putting so much into one poem, the poet exposes her work to weaknesses. It is eleven pages long and covers a range of imaginative territory. In some places Pat has stretched too far, so that not all the parts tie clearly into the body. She starts out by talking of voices pretending to be birds. Then she moves through a landscape partly of city, partly of nature. All the while, her mind and body are intertwined, stalagmites form in her head and her feet trail weed. Her poetic eyes hang her between "backyard earth and moon." Small hints of the approaching Ice Age are everywhere: "The metronome of ice and snow still ticks." She tries to feel what it was like to perform early human rituals, such as the worship of a sacrificial bear.

In section III, Pat recounts a childhood experience and then leads us to think about the act of making a poem. There are dangers in this task, and she jerks her "foot back from the shredded edge" because she has "forgotten to account for the first metaphor." "In the Continent Behind My Eyes" does just what it says it does: it reveals the workings and intertwining of Pat's mind, trained as it was in Vancouver, where the mountains touch the sea.

It was three years after *Milk Stone* was completed before Pat finally held the book in her hand. With great relief, she sat down to send gift copies to friends. That is when she wrote something that has been much quoted and also much misinterpreted. She sent a gift copy of *Milk Stone* to poet Ralph Gustafson, signed with her name and the year, 1974. Under it she drew a tiny tombstone, with the letters RIP. Around the tombstone are jaunty tufts of grass.[13]

This is probably the origin of the story that Pat predicted the year of her death. That story has a hole in it, because the date on the book, 1974, was not the year of her death, but the year that the book was published. Nonetheless, serious people in Canadian literature repeat the story that Pat was "death haunted" and had eerie premonitions. On close examination, the drawing and in-scription do not at all give the impression of someone giving up. Instead, they make it look as if it is the writer who is doing the burying — of a work completed that had been far too long in the making.

Now that *Milk Stone* was finally published, there was the task of distributing the 500 copies that were printed. In its usual manner, Borealis sent review copies to the major newspapers in Vancouver. The result was exactly one order for one copy of *Milk Stone* from Duthie Books. Pat's friends must have asked her where they could get copies, because she wrote to Glenn Clever in January 1975, asking where it was available in Vancouver.[14] Glenn Clever says that Duthie's later ordered more copies.

The reviews of *Milk Stone* were mostly favourable. Mark Abley felt that *Milk Stone* was of mixed quality; although he said Pat's "images and rhythms are both resounding and precise," he found her sometimes banal. He summed up with: "If sometimes the reach exceeds the grasp, Lowther is rarely guilty of not daring to reach."[15] Reviewer Aviva Ravel was uneasy. She wished there were more blossoms and less frost and hoped that "the barbed seed would flower into the trumpet daffodil."[16] Ravel's understanding of *Milk Stone* is that milk and stone are in opposition to each other. Pat's effort to reconcile apparent opposites did not speak to her. Pat Lowther tried to embrace stone, bone and ice, winding her soft human form into these elements. Flower petals, water, milk and the human spirit connect to the elements of the planet.

Peter Stevens acknowledges that Pat's vision might seem bleak; he wrote that "she is aware of the basic core of existence, the skeletons, the bones and stones of life." Pointing out the singing aspect of the poetry, he says: "What shines through this volume is the clear direct sight of a singing woman, working out her responsibilities beyond the limits set by society. It is a clear-eyed and firm poetry, full of singing. Generally the vision is sustained through the book, though a few longer poems lose their focus and blur the sharp edges etched in the other poems. But *Milk Stone* holds the world in unflinching clear sight."[17]

Although Stevens makes his way adroitly through the heavy part of her work, he is tripped up by one of Pat's puns. In "The Continent Behind My Eyes," the poet hopes that evolution will "hone me / into a blade of glass / that would sing when tapped."[18] Stevens, perhaps full of Walt Whitman, misreads it as "blade of grass." With this error, he joins the impressive list of reviewers who have misread her plays on words, including the title of her first book, *This Difficult Flowring*.

Poet and critic Gary Geddes made a different point. Discussing *Milk Stone* in *The Globe and Mail*, he comments that British Columbian artists, starting with Emily Carr, find the bigness of the landscape central to their vision. Like Emily Carr, they are often ignored by what Eastern Canada calls Central Canada. Geddes quotes Emily Carr: "Canada wants something strong, big, dignified and spiritual that will make her artists better for doing it and her people better for seeing it. And we artists need the people at our back, not to throw cold water over us or to starve us with their cold, clammy silence, but to give us their sympathy and support. I don't mean money support. I mean moral support; whether the artists are doing it in the old way or in the new, it does not matter, so long as it is the big way with the spirit and the feel of Canada behind it."[19]

This same struggle continues today. Geddes mentions a number of British Columbian writers, including Pat, who were ignored by Eastern-based publishers. Not too long after he wrote his review, another of Pat's books was accepted by an Eastern publisher; nonetheless, the mind set remained. When Howard Engel, a Toronto-based writer, critic and radio personality, is asked why he never invited Pat Lowther to be on his program, he answers: "She was not outstanding. She was one of the West Coast group."

Seymour Mayne was drawn to Pat's work by her out of-the-ordinary cosmic imagination. He is taken with the way she loves to explore ideas about astronomy, astrophysics, geology and geography. By the time Pat was in her mid-thirties, she was "one of the more interesting poets writing at the time … Another five to ten years would have seen her really write, far more resonant writing … I just felt she was getting a sense of sureness of her craft." He believed that, in places, she did fulfill her potential, but that her greatest problem was the use of general images instead of specific ones. Another was a tendency to "build her comments into her work rather than let the poem do it." There were also "small, technical shortcomings, which I'm convinced she would have overcome if she had written a little bit longer, a little bit longer, a little more work … Other people think she did fulfill her promise. We need more time to study it."

Because of Seymour's regard for Pat's work, he fears that "her brutal death and the promise that was stifled somehow begin to cloud literary judgement … She was a good poet, but she was not a major poet. We shouldn't blow her out of proportion. I think she herself wouldn't have wanted to be looked at in that light." He considers "May Chant," which was published in *This Difficult Flowring,* one of her best poems. "She takes her own personal condition and universalizes it to the condition of all women through the ages. She takes the personal into the historical and writes it in a chant-like rhythm. So it grows in resonance from stanza to stanza."

CHAPTER 10

Pat's Last Year

*She had a haunting quality. She was one of those
people who walked around like she had a
very mysterious inner life.*

— Arlene Lampert[1]

SEPTEMBER 1974 BEGAN THE LAST YEAR of Pat's life. It was a year
that brought a number of important events. First, she and Fred
Candelaria became the co-chairs of the League of Canadian Poets.
That position gave Pat the responsibility of poetic leadership for
English Canada. Second, Oxford University Press agreed to publish
A Stone Diary. Publication by a prestigious Eastern house meant
that reviewers and academics would look at her work more seriously. Third, she was appointed to an advisory subcommittee for the
B.C. Arts Council. Working with a group of other artists, she was
to make recommendations on improving the accessibility of arts in
the province. This was a subject about which Pat felt passionately,
and she would have the opportunity to express her views to the
provincial government. Fourth, she was hired to teach a workshop
in creative writing at the University of British Columbia starting in

September 1975. This was a stunning prize for a woman who did not even have a high-school diploma, and it was an opportunity that might have led to Pat's financial independence.

How had Pat become head of a national organization as prestigious as the League of Canadian Poets? In 1974, Douglas Barbour and Steven Scobie had asked Fred Candelaria to stand for chair for the next two years. They needed someone from British Columbia because the 1975 annual general meeting was to be held in Victoria. Candelaria thought that the job would be too much, in addition to his work as a professor at Simon Fraser University. Barbour and Scobie responded with the idea of a joint chair, and Pat was asked to consider sharing the position. It was a particular honour because the position had never before been held by a woman.

Candelaria remembers Pat approaching him with some trepidation at the October 1974 annual general meeting of the League in Fredericton, New Brunswick. He says he encouraged her to accept the nomination. Pat also spoke to Fred Cogswell with some uneasiness about the job. She was not sure that she had the qualities to take on a leadership role in a national organization. Cogswell also encouraged her and "was glad to see her become League president … a rank commensurate with her abilities."[2] Buoyed by this moral support, Pat agreed to run and she had no trouble being elected co-chair for a two-year term. In Candelaria's words, Pat was a valued member of the League and, therefore, "she was subject to the pain of leadership." Although he maintains that the chair was not a coveted job, the poets had to choose someone who would be a credible leader. The poets of Canada made Pat their voice.

After the Fredericton meeting, Fred Candelaria and Pat divided the workload. Pat took on most of the communication with members, while Candelaria kept the books and arranged the poets' payments from the Canada Council. Pat's papers include mimeographs of letters she wrote to members. Trying to stretch the budget, she made appointments in those letters for long-distance telephone calls during discount times. Early in their term, Candelaria suggested to Pat that they do League work by meeting alternately at one another's homes. As Pat had feared, having meetings at her house did not work. Candelaria knew that Roy was jealous of Pat's position and the recognition it brought her, but he did not know about the scenes of recrimination and head-banging that followed meetings at her house. Pat did tell Candelaria that she was "just waiting for the children to grow up and she would divorce him." In Candelaria's judgement, she "was a caring parent."

Arlene Lampert, as the executive director, ran the day-to-day activities of the League from her Toronto office. The success of the organization depended on good contact between Lampert and the chair of the moment, who could be as far away as the Yukon or New Brunswick, and she says that Pat always answered letters. Her experience was not with the scatterbrained Pat that others have described. Lampert especially appreciated Pat's professionalism as Lampert was among those who understood the stress that Pat was under: "Roy was getting worse and worse and more threatening. He hadn't been working for a long time. Pat needed to find a job and that fragmented her too. I know it was a hard year for her to get through. And this League business was just another thing she had to get through. At times I wished I didn't have to write to her. I knew how harassed she was. Yet, I needed her okay."

To get Pat's approval for League business, Lampert often telephoned Pat's home. On these occasions, she often had to deal with Roy. Lampert would ring up the Lowther number, and Roy would answer. She would ask, "Is Pat there?" And Roy would sometimes say yes, sometimes no, and sometimes just hang up on her. Lampert found Roy "exceedingly rude." Occasionally she would ask him to say that she had called, but she had no faith that the messages were getting through to Pat. Nonetheless, Lampert says: "[Pat] did a fine job organizing the annual meeting in Victoria. She had booked the hotel and arranged rooms and other little bits of biz ... There were four major readings booked in another place. And some of the meetings were taking place in various spots outside the hotel, and it was all very well put together."

Poet Joe Rosenblatt was then editing a magazine in Toronto called *Jewish Dialog*. It was a quarterly that featured Canadian Jewish writers and translations from Yiddish classics. Rosenblatt had volunteered to serve on League committees. Pat wrote three letters to him, which, thanks to Rosenblatt's care, have survived.[3] The first of those letters was early in Pat's term. It is dated October 22, 1974. Pat hoped Rosenblatt and Miriam Waddington would strike a committee to work with the Writers' Union of Canada on contracts with publishers and royalties from libraries. Ever thrifty with postage, Pat enclosed some poems that she hoped he would use in *Jewish Dialog*. There was no Jewish content in Pat's poems, but Joe Rosenblatt liked them. Several of her poems did appear in his magazine in 1975 and 1976.[4]

In the second letter to Rosenblatt, written on December 3, Pat asked him to represent the League at a meeting in Toronto with some government people "regarding copyright and so on." By that time, Pat was using letterhead with the print of the Executive Committee of the League of Canadian Poets. She was careful to ask Rosenblatt to let Gerry and Arlene Lampert know whether he would be attending. Pat was not leaving any loose ends.

The last letter, dated December 31, 1974, discusses the work of Rosenblatt's committee. The letter opens: "I want to wish you a happy new year and thank you for keeping on top of things as you're doing." The second statement concerned Arlene Lampert. Pat felt they must be careful not to ask too much of her "until we can find a way to put her on a definite salary."

In March 1975, Pat wrote a letter to Arlene Lampert announcing two pieces of good news:

Dear Arlene,

I've been told unofficially I'll be appointed to an advisory sub-committee for the B.C. Arts Council or maybe the Council itself. I'll also be taking George McWhirter's place at UBC part time while he's on sabbatical. Damn good thing the League's getting a secretary.

Pat[5]

Lampert soon answered the letter, pointing out that the seat on the B.C. Arts Board was a "good foot in the door for the League." In her usual spirited way, she added: "If anyone can do it, you can. You're going to have one hell of a busy year."[6]

In June 1975, Pat gave an interview to the arts newspaper *Performance*. Chris Potter asked her if poets should work for the love of art or if they should expect remuneration. Pat's thrust in the interview is that a culture is judged by its literature: "Somebody has to do the job, just as somebody has to dispose of the garbage, so the pay should be fair." She went on to say that "no poet in Canada can live on what he gets from his poetry."[7] These were not just empty words. Pat and her colleagues had put anthology rights, contracts with publishers and national poetry reading tours on the agenda for the League's forthcoming annual general meeting in Victoria.

To address the problem of how little Canadian literature is taught in public school, she suggested a solution might be bookmobiles such as they had in Prince Edward Island. The bookmobile would "bring people concerts, book reviews, dances and fun." Pat also gave her ideas on good and bad poetry. She insisted that "good poetry is not difficult to understand." Asked what bad poetry is, she answered, "Dishonesty, not necessarily conscious dishonesty, but where the logic is not pursued, and the surface of the subject [is] bruised over." To be shallow is to bruise. In reading another writer's poem, she said, she "looks for a moment of truth, an illuminating metaphor." Pat urged Canadians to "fight [the] pseudo-culture imposed on us by radio, TV, paperbacks — it's easier to absorb than our own products." The gentle weapon she suggested for the fight was exposure to Canadian works. "A choice must be available," she concluded.

Pat was earnest in trying to find ways for poets to earn a living from their work. Suspecting that poets were getting a bad deal from publishers, she led a working group to find out if this was true. A questionnaire was drawn up and sent to poets and publishers. The response showed that many poets were signing contracts that gave them very little protection. The problems that came to light were poor distribution by publishers, no compensation for poems in anthologies and, sometimes, no royalties at all. The group recommended contracts which would allow dissatisfied poets to withdraw their manuscripts after a period of time. The goal of the working group was to ensure that contracts would protect poets in the present and future.

Pat's work with the League proved that she could organize things that were important to her. She drafted a letter to a granting agency requesting funds to send a representative to the first Cambridge International Poetry Festival in Great Britain.[8] The main purpose of the trip was to make contacts with poets' and writers' organizations throughout the Commonwealth. The representative was to arrange for a Canadian poetry book display at the festival and then travel to Scotland to meet members of the newly established department of Canadian studies at the University of Edinburgh. The letter ended with a request for a grant of $974. Most granting officers would think that proposal packed a lot of action into the dollar. Unfortunately, the final copy and the reply to the letter are not to be found.

Through reading tours sponsored by the League, Pat was starting to meet poets outside Vancouver. She met poet and editor Gary Geddes when she became ill on one of her tours and had to stay overnight at his home. Geddes does not remember the date, but since he lives in a rural area within commuting distance of Ottawa, it is likely that was where Pat was reading. Geddes explained that "Pat was so sick with some kind of flu ... I had the impression of someone who was disorganized but driven, rather frail and overextended." Under these difficult circumstances, they formed only a slight acquaintance, but Geddes was taken with her poetry. In speaking of "Coast Range" he says: "I often find the lines, 'billygoat bearded creek bumsliding down to splat into the sea' running through my head, a truly great marriage of image and sound to conjure the run-off creeks of Burrard Inlet. I'd give a dozen poems for that line."

Geddes put Pat's work into two of his poetry anthologies. The first, *Skookum Wawa*, was published by Oxford University Press before Pat's death. He gave prominence to "Coast Range" by making it the first poem in the book and accenting it with a picture of the mountain range. The second anthology was *15 Canadian Poets Plus 5*. That book, with eight of Pat's poems, was also published by Oxford University Press but would not be released until 1978, three years after her death.[9]

How had Pat moved from the small-press circuit to a major Eastern publisher? Allan Safarik tells the story this way. Back in 1972, when Margaret Atwood was in Vancouver, he had sensed that Pat and Atwood would be simpatico. He arranged for Pat to drive to the airport with Atwood after the Simon Fraser reading. His instinct was right, and Atwood offered to evaluate *A Stone Diary* for Oxford. As is often the case, there is more than one slice to the story. There are letters showing that Geddes also helped get attention at Oxford for *A Stone Diary*. The first is a letter from Geddes, found among Pat's papers, suggesting she send *A Stone Diary* to William Toye, the editorial director at Oxford. He named himself and Atwood as evaluators.[10] The second is an enquiry from Pat to Toye, saying that she was acting on a suggestion from Gary Geddes.[11] Toye replied that he liked the poems that she had in Geddes' anthology *Skookum Wawa* and hoped to publish *A Stone Diary* in the fall if the Canada Council came through with a grant.[12]

Pat's official appointment to the B.C. Arts Council on May 20, 1975, is evidence that she must have maintained good relations with the New Democratic Party after having left Phyllis Young's office two years previously. She and a group of other B.C. artists were to advise the government on arts policy. Pat wrote three drafts of a paper entitled "British Columbia Arts Council."[13] Written beneath the coffee stains are Pat's ideas on cultural policy: to bring the possibility for creative development to every person in British Columbia.

The major thrust of Pat's paper was access to the arts. The Council hoped to give everyone access to the arts by setting up regional panels composed of professional and amateur artists, as well as representatives from organized labour and low-income groups. The panels would operate in public buildings, old houses, portable huts, churches, warehouses and barns. Pat believed that if art was to "inform and enrich," it had to be encouraged at the grass-roots level. Her paper was a series of ideas on how that could be achieved. Grants to the Vancouver Symphony Orchestra could subsidize ticket prices so that everyone could afford to go to concerts. Betsy Lane chaired the board when Pat was on it, and she remembers Pat's interest in working with schools. An educational advisory committee on the arts could connect with school boards. The board talked of "large-scale purchasing of B.C. books and books by B.C. authors for distribution to schools and libraries." Board members pictured "an urgent catch-up program to bring cultural amenities to the northern regions of B.C."

Pat's childhood experience finds its way into the paper: "The artistically gifted adolescent who for one reason or another can't make it academically and drops out of school, is left in limbo, at present." She hoped all schoolchildren would have access to a range of artistic experiences in music, painting and drama, mostly to become familiar with their heritage. The other goal of the school program was to identify talented children early so that their talents could be developed, regardless of their economic status. All these ideas show that Pat was earnestly trying to find ways for artists and the public to meet and interact.

The fourth good event of this year was a temporary job as a lecturer at the University of British Columbia. How did a woman without university degrees manage that? Professor George McWhirter was due to go on sabbatical leave, and Pat had been suggested as his replacement by poet Robert Tyhurst. Tyhurst and Pat had met at poetry workshops sponsored by the Vancouver Free University. He liked her poetry and was touched by the way she helped others do their best writing. He qualified her as a fine poet and a sensitive teacher.[14] Professor McWhirter was pleased to consider Pat as his replacement. "She didn't have an aesthetic axe to grind. What she wrote herself is strong; no faking ... She was that kind of person, too; what you saw was what you got, no pretensions." Pat was appointed sessional lecturer from September 1, 1975, to May 31, 1976, at a salary of $4500 for the nine months.[15]

What was good for Pat felt very different to Roy. In his journal he complained that he had been paid much less for more work: "Add that to the Arts Board and I wondered when I would be exited [sic.]."[16] As noted earlier, Roy had been wrong about the money that Pat had received from a Canada Council grant and he was likely wrong about the financial arrangement with the Arts Board as well. Pat did not draw a salary from the B.C. Arts Board. All she received was a $100 honorarium for each meeting she attended, plus transportation costs. The meetings were often held in Victoria. Perhaps Roy saw a cheque for travel costs and thought it was a salary. In focusing on the money and his fear that a financially independent Pat might leave him, Roy seems to have underestimated his value to Pat in providing stability for the children. Pat's sister, Brenda, and her friends Hilda Woolnough, Bethoe Shirkoff,

Fred Candelaria and Fred Cogswell all confirm that Pat intended to stay with Roy until the children were grown. Roy's perception, as revealed in his journal, is that Pat's work in the artistic community put her in a position to move out and make a life for herself. He was correct that she was thinking of leaving, but he misjudged when that might happen.

Fred Cogswell spent part of 1975 in Vancouver. He was on sabbatical leave and stayed with his daughter, Carman, on Cornish Street. During that year, he became an important confidant to Pat. They would meet for lunch about twice a month at Brother John's restaurant in Gastown and talk about literature and their lives. She told him of the break-up of her first marriage and the guilt she felt about having hurt her two elder children. Although there were serious problems in her marriage to Roy, she was determined to keep it together until her two youngest children were on their own. Cogswell was drawn to Pat by her straightforwardness. "People told her the truth because she knew how to listen and to add to a conversation." He continues, "In her presence I was with someone I could respect — a kindred spirit." He adds that Pat was "free from vanity and pettiness." In a letter to Chris Lowther written in November 1995, he reminded her of an event that had occurred over twenty years earlier: "It was in the spring of the year and I went to your house. You and your sister were writing and illustrating a book about a horse. It was charming."[17]

Outside Pat's home smaller rewards clustered next to the major ones. By 1975, people from the literary community were actually knocking on Pat's door. In January, Glenn Clever of Borealis Press wrote to her, asking if she had any new manuscripts.[18] In May, she was asked to be a judge in a poetry contest run by the Burnaby Creative Writers' Society.[19]

That was also the year in which Pat and Bethoe Shirkoff became closer friends. Shirkoff describes the progression of their relationship: "In August of 1975, again needing a philosopher and turning from one friend to another to draw from them affection and encouragement, I phoned Pat." Pat agreed to come to visit one evening while Shirkoff was caring for her granddaughter, because Shirkoff wanted advice in coping with a friend's strange behaviour. They opened bottles of beer and tried to talk, but the baby was missing her mother and could not stop fretting. Shirkoff spoke about the problem until Pat held up her hand and said: "You don't need to tell me anymore. I live with someone like that." Little sobs continued from the baby. Shirkoff tells that somehow they managed to talk of how a deflected passion is to be carefully guarded, directed, "else we too could be the mad ones." Pat said that inside everyone there is great potential, especially in women, who have been held back so long. She said women have a duty to direct the force and strength of their passion and potential well. Shirkoff remarks: "What Pat exuded was calm. What her poetry revealed was enormous passion."[20]

Pat and Bethoe Shirkoff talked about all kinds of passion. A particular kind of passion had been revealed the previous year in the summer edition of *Quarry*, a literary journal that had published several of Pat's poems.[21] Although this publicity helped Pat's standing as an artist, it was disastrous for her relationship with Roy. Pat's writings were love poems and Roy knew they were not written to him. Roy had learned to live with the suspicion that Pat was having a quiet affair, but the publication of these poems told the world that the wife he could not bed was otherwise occupied. Roy's journal shows that his fragile nerves were under siege. If Pat was openly acknowledging that her marriage was as good as over, perhaps it was only a matter of time before she would leave him.

The first poem in *Quarry*, "For Selected Friends," was also included in Pat's book *Milk Stone*, which came out the same year. The person described in the poem is "a cave / splendid with crystals,"[22] but causes some fear. Beneath this poem on the same page is "Wrestling," which is more explicit about sexual involvement. The poet confesses to her lover that she is "rough with that need."[23] "Wrestling" would later appear in *A Stone Diary* as well. In "All It Takes," Pat is urging her chosen one on to a relationship. Although it is not clear whether she is urging a sexual relationship, the effect of the poem is erotic. She speaks of insertion and reinsertion and adds, "it depended how / symbolic you want to be." She concludes:

> On the other hand
> are your blunt fingers
> which quicken me
> to create only poems
> What I'm saying is
> all it ever takes is the touch [24]

Distressing as those three poems must have been for an unhappy husband, there was another one filled with anguish. "They All Laughed" describes a woman being watched by people who know she is "chirping from man to man." The poem examines different kinds of laughter. First, there is derisive laughter as people watch the woman. Then there is the woman's laughter in her "ridiculous anguish." This is followed by the forced laughter of onlookers who have "a whole jokebook / stuffed between their teeth." Finally, there is comforting laughter, as "his name fluttered / at her mouth / like secret laughter." The woman is likened to a hen in heat who has "a dissatisfied husband."[25]

Poetry was evidently the way that Pat worked out her anguish, but making it public was very hard for Roy. Her candour was consistent with her commitment to write the truth about feelings; however, given the man she was living with, it was a dangerous honesty. By coincidence, Eugene McNamara also had a poem in that same issue of *Quarry*.[26] The title, "Among the Missing," would be Roy's basis for accusing McNamara of the murder. A reading of the poem, however, shows that it is not about a death but about longing for an absent love.

Reading that issue of *Quarry* led Roy to write "September 23," a poem about the death of his marriage. The history of Pat Lowther is full of ironies. One of them is that it was probably exactly a year later, September 23, 1975, that Roy killed Pat. "September 23" appeared in the last issue of *Pegasus*, a mimeographed magazine that Roy edited.[27] It is clear Roy now knew that he was losing his wife.

Lorraine Vernon wonders if Pat wanted Roy to take the decision to separate out of her hands by pushing him to make it himself. Not only did Pat publish poems to her lover, she left letters from him around the house. Was she trying to get Roy to see that the marriage was finished? Vernon compares Pat's situation to that of a Greek tragedy. Pat's life "was racing to an inevitable disaster."

In 1972, Pat had received a Canada Council grant to write *The Infinite Mirror Trip*, a multimedia piece for the H.R. MacMillan Planetarium in Vancouver. In August 1974, the piece was finally performed. As planned, Pat wrote the poetry and Roy composed the music to accompany it. The show incorporated existing planetarium exhibits of outer space, swirling clouds and dazzling auroras.[28]

Pat's brother John helped prepare the show and recorded the sound. No musical instruments were used. A woman sang Roy's music, Pat read most of the poetry, and other voices were added for dialogue. The music was written in a sharp key with a lot of natural notes. The combination resulted in a rather strange sound, which was, of course, what Pat and Roy were trying to create. John recalls that they struggled to record in a spot where the public was going to and fro, making normal, but, to musicians, terribly distracting, noises. Mike Koziniak, the special-effects technician for the planetarium, served as program producer. The visual component had films of star clusters, nebula and gas clouds. It ended with slides of dissolving heavenly bodies. Koziniak called the piece a "noble experiment" that set the stage for future programs. Pat believed that *The Infinite Mirror Trip* was the best thing she had ever done.

One thing that was not a problem in producing *The Infinite Mirror Trip* was money, but not because some fairy godmother bearing a grant had arrived. Roy and John worked as volunteers, and Koziniak was on salary at the planetarium. For staging, the show used exhibits that were already there. Yet Pat's work was jinxed again. After the show closed, the planetarium erased the tape of the program. As in the stolen briefcase caper, Pat had not made a copy of the work for herself. Even worse, the planetarium had not advertised the program, and only one reviewer covered it. About two days before the show closed, word dripped through the grapevine: Don't miss *The Infinite Mirror Trip!* But it was too late, and many people were left regretting a missed opportunity.

After *The Infinite Mirror Trip* closed, reporter Susan Mertens wrote a lone but enthusiastic review in *The Vancouver Sun*. She pointed out that the piece "explored the ageless mystery of the relationship between inner and outer space." It played to the eye, ear and imagination at the same time. It looked at the connections between humans and the universe in a sometimes funny, sometimes mysterious way. Mertens criticized the planetarium for its poor publicity of the event and concluded: "A statistical failure, *The Infinite Mirror Trip* was an artistic success and set an imaginative precedent for further planetarium efforts."[29]

Pebble by pebble, Pat continued to increase her standing as a poet and teacher. During this period she taught creative-writing workshops in a community arts effort called Pulse. Another modest achievement was an invitation to read her poetry at the Kitsilano Public Library.

In 1974, Pat drafted a letter to the Vancouver Public Library system. She noted that, although the city offered courses in arts and crafts, there were none in creative writing. She wanted to teach a series of creative-writing workshops for teenagers. There is no information about what became of her idea, but the thinking revealed in the letter is important. Although she expected that most of the participants would be from local high schools, she urged it to be open to high-school drop-outs too. She would use "readings from Canadian literature, book displays and other visuals, and perhaps some recorded music" to set the tone.[30] Pat was continuing to experiment with combining music, sound and visual art as she had in the planetarium show. Moreover, she wanted this work to fire the imaginations of teens and offer them an opportunity for personal growth. Thinking back to Pat's own teenage years, one can easily understand that contact with a creative adult could have made a difference to her own life.

Dorothy Livesay was so heartened by the success of her first anthology of Canadian women poets that she produced another one in 1974. This second one was made up entirely of the work of twelve British Columbian women. A small press called Air, which operated from 1974 to 1977, enlisted the help of Bertrand Lachance, the Canada Council and the Jim Lawson Memorial Fund to bring out this second collection, which was called *Woman's Eye*. In her introduction, Livesay explained that this is "a way of looking *that is* distinctly from woman's eye; *and* a way of feeling *that is* centered in woman's 'I'."[31]

Livesay invited Pat to send in her work, and Pat chose "Doing It Over," "The Blind," "Octopus," "Hermit Crabs," "Craneflies in Their Season" and "Last Letter to Pablo." All but the first two poems would later appear in *A Stone Diary*. Once again Pat's poetry was in the company of works by Maxine Gadd, Elizabeth Gourlay and Dorothy Livesay. The other poets were Skyros Bruce, G.V. Downes, Marya Fiamengo, Leona Gom, Anne Marriott, Myra McFarlane, Susan Musgrave and Fran Workman.

The poets chose subjects that women have had to bring to public attention. Anne Marriott wrote about an abused child; Marya Fiamengo, about pornography; Myra McFarlane, of the despair after a miscarriage. Leona Gom added a lighter touch with "Abdication," an ironic confession about her sin of not being a feminist.

Livesay was right about readers' interest in women's poetry. The first edition of *Woman's Eye* was so popular that a reprint was issued in 1975.

The offer by Oxford University Press to publish Pat's third book, *A Stone Diary*, added to Roy's resentment of Pat's success. Virginia Tinmuth remembers that Roy said: "My work is better, but she's getting the recognition." Virginia tried to handle it lightly by replying: "Well, I guess you have to be born lucky." Roy saw no humour in the situation, nor in Virginia's irony given that Pat was anything but lucky. Ten years earlier, Pat used to invite Roy to poetry readings and gatherings, but as Roy became nastier about the work of other poets, she stopped inviting him to come along. Was Pat embarrassed by his behaviour, hoping to save other poets from pointless attacks, or was she just tired of listening to someone who believed that he alone had the truth? Maybe it was all of these factors. At home Pat listened to his rages and her body sometimes caught his punches; she had no reason to invite him on her poetry tours.

In June 1975, Pat and Roy were sitting around Virginia's kitchen table, drinking coffee, when Roy said in a complaining way: "It's okay for Pat to go out of town like this and leave me with the kids." Virginia replied: "Well, she's making money, doesn't that help out?" Roy agreed: "Oh yes, the money's okay." Virginia remembers: "I looked at Pat, and she looked so tired and thin. She looked like she needed a good time to lighten her up. So I said: 'I hope she has a little bit of fun.'" At that, Roy pounded on the table with his hand and shouted: "She's my wife! If I'm not going to have her, nobody else is going to have her." Then he stood up with such violence that he knocked his chair over. The chair barely missed knocking the cuckoo clock off the wall as it crashed to the floor. Virginia continues: "And I thought: What a reaction! I wasn't aware she had this friend back East."

Pat's family had their suspicions that she was being battered but did not know it for a fact. Pat suggested that someone was hurting her in "A Chant of Hands." She wrote, "Hands have made / face-shaped wounds in my body."[32] Then, in the spring of 1975, Pat told Allan Safarik that Roy had pushed her out a window and off a balcony. Roy's behaviour cannot be explained by a drinking problem. Neither family nor friends ever saw Roy drunk. If he drank, it was a single glass of wine, perhaps twice a year. They lay the cause of his behaviour entirely on his personality. Toward the end of his life, Roy's daughter Ruth asked him if, with all his troubles, he had ever thought of turning to drink. He replied, "I have too fine a mind to ruin it with alcohol."

Although Pat had started out trying to heal Roy, the "curst and lone,"[33] by the end of 1974 she came to understand that she could not solve his problems. In December, she wrote in a letter to a friend: "Today my husband left the house in an ambulance to be ex-rayed for possible skull fracture — self-inflicted." She went on to explain that his head-banging "had been happening off and on for many years, but increasing since the autumn."[34] Roy's self-mutilation and suicide threats were becoming more frequent. He refused to get help.

Pat was also writing to Fred Cogswell about Roy's violence toward her. Cogswell responded by advising her to leave and offered to lend her money to do so. "Pat was very proud and independent and declined the offer." Lorraine Vernon also knew what was happening. During one of Roy's shouting and head-banging attacks, Pat brought the two little girls to the home of Vernon, who says: "They stayed with us for the entire day, returning home in the evening."[35]

By 1975, people were saying that Pat was a feminist, a wise mother, a woman too devoted to poetry, a woman who knew how to put poetry on hold; that she was passionate, calm, proud, self-effacing, scatterbrained and well organized. All of these people were keen observers and all of them were right in reporting what they saw. Pat had all of these qualities. She could dive headlong into poetry at one time and tell the New Democratic Party to "write less and act more"[36] at another. She could do this because she was in charge of her mind and her feelings. Although a passionate woman, she stayed in the driver's seat and shaped her feelings into effective cargo. George McWhirter talks of Pat's efforts with a group that was trying to make recommendations to the provincial government but was stymied because of petty bickering: "She wore herself out trying to work out a consensus. But she despaired because of the bickering. She was a practical person."

In her quiet way Pat Lowther had the strength to defend the weak, including herself. As we have already seen, one bully mistook her quiet manner for weakness and tried to push her. Pat pushed back with the poem "Baby You Tell Me," a work that will be remembered long after that silly man is forgotten.[37] Pat's spirit had survived two ill-advised marriages; but she still had the ability to love. She retained her wonder over the softness of apple blossoms and the movement of planets. This was the Pat Lowther who was living out the last year of her life. The summer was to bring the most rewarding invitation of her career, an opportunity to read at a poetry festival in Charlottetown, Prince Edward Island.

CHAPTER 11

Charlottetown and After

*The country there is so beautiful and the people are
unbelievably friendly. Where I stayed they
were in the country, and they had sheep.*

— Pat Lowther[1]

THE SUN SHONE THROUGH THE BRANCHES of a 100-year-old willow
tree and under that tree, Pat Lowther was reading her poems to the
audience. This rural setting was Betty and Everett Howatt's fruit
farm at Point Tryon on the south shore of Prince Edward Island.
The mix of greenery and red earth give the Island a fairy-tale quality.
People know their neighbours, and Islanders tell visitors that they
never lock their doors.

Pat's opportunity to read in P.E.I. was due to the efforts of the
late Réshard Gool, a writer, poet and professor at the University of
Prince Edward Island, and Square Deal Publications, a small press
located in the Island's capital, Charlottetown. Square Deal had
organized a series of twelve poetry readings with funds from the
Canadian Broadcasting Corporation (CBC), the Canada Council,
and the provincial Ministry of Tourism. Nationally known poets,

such as Alden Nowlan, Al Purdy, Joe Rosenblatt, Milton Acorn and Miriam Waddington, as well as lesser-known local poets, were included in the series. In planning the readings, Gool wished to have representation from all regions of Canada and roughly the same number of men and women. "I was short of women. Unfortunately, all my life, I've been short of women," he quips. He asked Gary Geddes for help. Once again, Geddes, who had helped Pat with Oxford University Press, put her name forward.

Réshard Gool later wrote and aired a radio script about Pat's reading. His script captures the feeling that afternoon: "[There are] butterflies along hedges, birds crisp and irreverent everywhere … The woman is not really reading; she is pleading, and her words are duplicated by gestures of hands. The hands desperately massage the edges of the words as if they need more vigorous help in their birth. Stillness, candor and urgency are what Pat Lowther recalls."[2]

Early in 1975, Gool had invited Pat to be one of the readers at the festival. She accepted the invitation in a letter written on March 10 and chose July 12 as the date for her reading. Pat was enthusiastic about a book fair that would take place at the same time and asked for more details about it. She was hoping to get the British Columbia government to sponsor a similar event in her home province to promote B.C. writers.[3]

In what was to become a famous postscript, she asked if the Canada Council could buy her ticket from Vancouver to Charlottetown for her. Gool innocently asked her if she couldn't just ask for credit from a Vancouver travel agency and pay them later when the grant arrived. Pat's response so surprised Gool that he dwelt on it in his radio script: "An extraordinary irony, this. Canada is one of the richest countries in the world; yet here is Pat Lowther — a major Canadian poet, perhaps *the* very best — and she is too poor to pay for an air ticket! On the telephone she was apologetic. Could I get the Canada Council to pay her fare in advance? I asked her if she couldn't get a Vancouver travel agency to sort everything out. The idea seemed to alarm her. Could people do that sort of thing, simply charge up to 400 or so dollars, and pay later?"[4]

Until then, Gool had not understood how hard it is for people without money to get credit. He had no way of knowing that Pat's income came from public assistance. By June, Pat still did not know how she was going to pay for her ticket. She wrote to Gool saying she was looking for a "wealthy patron." She also asked him to suggest cheap accommodation as she planned to arrive the night before the reading.[5] He solved both problems by booking the ticket through a travel agency in Charlottetown and advancing the money himself. As for her accommodation, Gool and his wife, Hilda Woolnough, invited Pat to stay in their home. Even though they had never met Pat, this was just the natural thing for them to do. Woolnough is a painter and sculptor who at that time taught art at the University of Prince Edward Island. Her home is vivid testimony of her profession, and it was the perfect place for Pat to stay. The schedule and accommodation were set. The air ticket was paid for. What could go wrong?

On July 12, Pat did end up sitting under that picturesque willow tree, wearing a black, red and bronze-coloured dress. Woolnough remembers how striking the dress looked, setting off the bronze highlights in Pat's dark hair. The dress had been frantically bor-rowed from Woolnough — frantically because yet another calamity had befallen Pat. The airline had lost her luggage, including all the material that she had prepared for the reading. It was easy to provide a dress. What Woolnough could not provide were Pat's poems. Pat agonized and criticized herself for not putting her intended readings in her carry-on luggage.

Because Woolnough and Gool taught at the university, they telephoned the university librarian at home on a Sunday. They explained that it was an emergency and asked if she would open the library to see if some of Pat's books were there. In neighbourly P.E.I. form, the librarian obliged; and the frantic party did find some of

Pat's books — but not everything that Pat had planned to read was there. Some of it was as-yet unpublished.

Just a few hours before the reading, Pat sat down and wrote the missing poems out from memory. She was still writing in the truck as they drove out to the Howatt's farm. Gool kept those pages. A comparison of them with published poems of the same titles shows only small variations or discrepancies, and two of the poems were recalled with no changes at all. In spite of her ability to recall thirteen poems nearly perfectly, Pat felt that she had let people down.

Square Deal had sponsored the readings to bring poetry to the average person and to get rid of the schoolroom air that often scares people away from poetry. They used outdoor settings and modern sound systems, as well as every theatrical trick they could think of. They had people sitting in trees, playing music. Rehearsing Pat for her part, Gool had asked her to sit beside a pond and gaze into the water. Pat went along with this caper for a while. Then she broke off her rehearsal and told Gool directly, "I feel like an ass." Realizing that those effects were wrong for Pat, he told her just to behave in her own way. He noticed that she had a graceful way of moving her hands and asked if she was going to do that during the reading. Pat answered, "You make me self-conscious. Let me do it naturally. Just let me be and think about it for a bit." Then she came back and handled the reading just right, with no prompting. He adds that Pat had a natural way of reaching the audience and a distinctive voice.

Another goal of the readings was to promote less well-known poets by piggybacking them on a program with better-known writers. The July 12 reading that featured Pat also gave the public a chance to hear local poets John Smith, Larry LeClair and Réshard Gool himself.

In keeping with plans, the CBC filmed and recorded the reading. Contrary to plans, the CBC lost the film. Réshard Gool was furious. It seems that Rick Quigley, who was the editor on duty when the film arrived at the studio, left for Australia shortly after the event.

Later, the Charlottetown station manager, Dave Gunn, tried unsuccessfully to locate the film. He learned that no one had been
assigned to finish editing it, so it just slipped through the cracks and
was lost forever. Gool sputters, "CBC treats cultural tapes as dispos-
able, like the news!" On a single trip, the demon that had dug its
jaws into Pat had eaten the suitcase with her reading script as well
as the film made of the reading. These losses were added to the lost
poems in the stolen briefcase and the erased film of *The Infinite
Mirror Trip*. The demon was feasting well at Pat's expense.

The sound recording of the reading fared better than the film.
Thanks to audio technician Carl Sentner, we have the voice that
Stephen Michael Bersensky says had "warm timbre … a mellowing
quality, a soothing quality." The audio tapes are now safely in the
library at the University of Prince Edward Island. A reviewer who
wrote a few days after the event in two P.E.I. newspapers had not
heard Pat's voice with Stephen Michael Bersensky' ears. An iden-
tical series of sentences ran in both *The Patriot* and *The Guardian*.
The reports read: "Ms. Lowther was not a strong reader and her
efforts to dredge up poems from memory further weakened her
presentation. Many of her poems related to animals such as the
killer whale, hermit crab and sea anemone and reflected her love of
the West coast."[6] Although the articles are unsigned, the two
papers shared one reporter, who seemed to have little interest in
poetry. He or she is noncommittal about the three local poets, but
enthusiastic about the music by a group called The Blue Herons.

The evening after the reading, Pat sat in her hosts' living room,
talking with some of the other poets. They were discussing how the
League of Canadian Poets could best serve poetry. It was then that
Pat and Joe Rosenblatt got into a heated exchange. Rosenblatt
remembers: "I was in favour of elitist membership. I wanted a really
tough-nosed academy." But Pat had a more democratic view of
membership. So there in the Gool-Woolnough sitting room, seated
beneath Woolnough's paintings, Pat and Rosenblatt had a row

about membership in the League. Gool recounts that argument, "[Pat] was vehement, if you can say that someone as quiet as she was vehement. I mean she was passionate about the view." The heat of the exchange did not hurt Rosenblatt's admiration for Pat. He said of her: "There was this mystical landscape ... a really thriving interior."

The Gool-Woolnough house, made of wood inside and out, must have pleased Pat. To a poet's delight, the area is called Rose Valley. Woolnough has a lush garden that gives the impression of wilderness and she serves food garnished with blossoms from the garden. Everywhere there is a soft scent of home-dried herbs. The guest room is in the attic loft surrounded by sculpture in progress, flower bulbs drying for next year's garden, and some handsome pieces of antique furniture waiting to be assembled. During Pat's visit, she and Woolnough became intimate friends. Pat and Woolnough found each other so spellbinding that, after Gool had gone to bed, they would, in Woolnough's words, "stay up all night yakking." Their talks were about kids and being women. The nights sped by and it was dawn.

In Pat and Woolnough's spontaneous friendship, this P.E.I. artist may have come to understand both Pat's deep and silly sides better than anyone else. Their conversations went from the cosmic to the completely mundane. They explored together what it means to be a woman. Woolnough was convinced that women and men operate differently and that women are used to everything going on at the same time. A picture flashes in the mind of Pat composing poetry while tying children's shoes. Woolnough recounts that she can cook, organize her household and, in the back of her mind, be thinking about a drawing that she has been working on. She recalls standing in her kitchen, rolling out dough for a pie. At the same time, she was watching the light reflect on a blue glass. Then, suddenly, a spider walked by and dragged some flour on its legs. And the flour and the spider and the reflection on the blue glass gave her something she could later use in her art. By contrast, when Gool worked, he could not bear noise and distractions. But whether these were the traits of two different individuals or two different sexes is still up for debate.

When Pat visited Woolnough she was terribly preoccupied with housekeeping, but in her case, her worry was over her lack of it. Like many creative people, Pat did not have the knack of running an orderly household. According to Woolnough, "It just bugged her totally." Woolnough explains: "Because she'd go on and on about all the sort of things — these dumb things that happen in life to everybody. That somehow, she thought they were special to her … Partly because she convinced herself that she was an incompetent idiot as far as taking care of herself was concerned."

Woolnough thinks Pat felt guilty that her husband and children had to live in a mess. Laughingly, Woolnough adds, "Buttons were always coming off and zippers breaking." Maybe there were better housekeepers in Vancouver, but Pat's children have never testified that missing buttons made their lives sad. Woolnough wonders why the other adult in Pat's family could not take some responsibility for housekeeping. In the writings Pat has left us, she never asked that question.

Pat told Woolnough she dreamed of ending the housework conundrum by living on a houseboat. In that way, there would be only one room to keep tidy and things would always be in their place. After sharing this fantasy with Woolnough, Pat said, "If it were a really, really small place, even I could organize it."

In Woolnough's view, Pat was plagued with "should's." If she had to take a taxi, she would leave in distress if she did not have the right change to give the driver a tip. She just had to get her house organized. She must mend the broken zippers on her children's clothes. Perhaps these concerns sound trivial and even funny. But, together, they made for a curious lack of self-confidence in a woman of many abilities.

Woolnough was struck by Pat's lack of self-confidence. In spite of critics' praise, Pat told Woolnough that "she was just beginning to understand something about poetry." Pat was also preoccupied with self-searching. Woolnough sums up that quality by asking, "Will the real Pat Lowther stand up?" What impressed Woolnough most about Pat was her vulnerability. Woolnough says she gets a knot in her chest, "the kind you have when you don't want to cry," when she thinks about that side of Pat. Woolnough thinks Pat was vulnerable in her own life and her poetry shows that she felt the suffering of others keenly. According to Woolnough, Pat seems never to have learned to distance herself from the pain of others.

The organic universe and its artistic expression was a concern common to both Woolnough and Pat. Their work explores the structure of natural materials. Pat wrote about stone, bone and ice. In her drawings, paintings and sculptures, Woolnough explores shell, bone and plants; once she even did a series on ant hills. The work of both artists grapples with the concept of evolution. Three months before her death, Pat asked Woolnough if she would like to illustrate some of her poems.

When Pat returned home, she told her children that she thought P.E.I. was the most beautiful place she had ever seen. Pat wrote to Gool and Woolnough from Mayne Island, telling them: "We have no red earth but we do have red trees. I enclose a piece of arbutus bark to remind you of the west coast."[7] Woolnough and Gool placed that piece of bark on their mantelpiece and cherished it until it turned to dust.

The attention being lavished on Pat and the possibility that she might be becoming financially independent were unsettling Roy. His state of mind was worsened by an upcoming poetry event. The British Columbia Committee of Socialist Studies and the New Democratic Party were planning a poetry reading for September 27, 1975. The poets chosen were David Day, Patrick Lane, Peter Trower and, to Roy's distress, Pat. The topic was "Work and the

Working Life." The reading was to be held at the Ironworkers' Hall. Roy had often said that an unnamed NDP member had called him the "Poet Laureate of NDP." Brian Campbell was one of the organizers of the reading. He says that there was some discussion about including Roy. The organizers knew that Roy wanted to be on the program, but, according to Campbell, "he was not of the calibre we wanted. I was informed he was upset about that."

Roy approached several people to try to get on the program. In August he telephoned Mark Budgen, who had made arrangements for the hall and prepared a broadsheet of poems for the reading. Roy spoke to Budgen "in a forceful, demanding, excited way," saying that he was a labour poet and should be on the program. Budgen replied that choosing the poets was not in his hands and suggested that he contact poet David Day.[8] Roy decided to approach Day through MLA Rita Lalik, whom he had known for some years. Lalik's office used to run pub nights as a way to keep in touch with constituents. At one of these events, Roy asked her to help him get an invitation to the Ironworkers' reading. She recalls that "he was not very articulate" on that occasion. She asked him to write her a letter so that she would have all the facts. He delivered the letter in the second week of September[9] and then Lalik tried telephoning David Day, but was unable to reach him. "There was a time element," she remembers.

Pat's return from P.E.I. preceded what would be the last ten weeks of her life. During these final ten weeks she did things she valued and saw people who were dear to her. In mid-August she and Lorraine Vernon had their last heart-to-heart talk. Vernon says Pat told her: "When one ceases to accept responsibility for another, everything falls into place." Vernon felt that "through [Pat's] silence and her reluctance to discuss [Roy's] obvious worsening state, she had in fact, rejected him." All Pat would admit to Vernon was: "He's making it difficult for me to work."[10] This masterpiece of understatement shows that Pat finally understood that no matter how much a wife cares, she cannot be responsible for the feelings of her husband. There are no statements from Pat or any reports to show Pat criticizing Roy. Instead, she simply described his behaviour and the effect it had on her and the children. This restraint might have been from a keen sense of fair play. Or it might have been the result of self-criticism, born of the knowledge that she, herself, had chosen the wrong man.

On the evening of August 8, Pat visited Bethoe Shirkoff. Shirkoff shyly showed Pat some of her own writing. To Shirkoff's surprise, Pat told her it was good and said that she would like to use it in her creative-writing course. Shirkoff was enormously grateful for the encouragement. Pat also offered Shirkoff help finding a publisher. The most pressing thing on Pat's mind that day was her daughter's birthday. When she got home that evening, she was going to prepare for Beth's party the next day. After Pat left, Shirkoff spoke her thoughts about their visit into a tape recorder and put the tape away.

That month Pat started preparing for the creative-writing workshop she was to teach at the University of British Columbia. She met with students and read their manuscripts so that she would be able to move straight into the practical elements of the workshop. Fran Diamond, the secretary at the department of creative writing, pointed out that Pat was doing this on her own time, as her salary would not start until September.[11]

Early in September Pat sent some poems to Gary Geddes with the comment, "Return postage is too damn expensive these days. Let me know if/what you decide to keep, and I'll pick up the rest sometime when I'm in Victoria."[12] The last letter that Pat received from William Toye was dated September 9, 1975. He confirmed that Oxford planned to publish her book, but he did not like the title. He found it "flat and unappealing."[13] Pat never had time to reply.

There were at least two more important exchanges with people who valued Pat. Seymour Mayne had a long telephone conversation with her and thought she sounded sure of herself in a new way. With Oxford considering her new book and the UBC teaching job ahead, she told him she was convinced that "things were going to change." In August, Fred Cogswell and Pat had lunch together in a shopping mall. As they parted, Pat said, "In another ten years, I'll be free. And I'll only be fifty."

CHAPTER 12

The Egg of Death

... The
mind moves near it softly softly
not to jar it where it lies couched

— Pat Lowther[1]

ONE DAY IN SEPTEMBER Pat stood in front of the stove at her mother's house. "I put my arms around her, she felt so thin. I said, 'Why don't you get rid of him?' She answered, 'I'm going to, Mother.' "

By September 1975 things had come to a head for Roy: He was unhappy about Pat's having a lover and he was jealous of her position in the League of Canadian Poets. While he still could not get work, she had just started a job lecturing at the University of British Columbia. Roy's journal shows that he believed that if Pat had an income of her own she might leave him. Worse still, she might take the children with her. Roy's main status was that of father of a family. Now he felt that platform shaking. On top of all this, exclusion from the poetry reading at the Ironworkers' Hall was more than he could bear. After he had failed as a teacher and been rejected by the artistic world, he had reassured himself that at least the working class would listen to his poetry. Here also he was rebuffed. Brian Campbell believes that this rejection "was the culminating event." Roy Lowther was going over the edge.

On September 20, Don Cummins, the tenant in the basement of Pat and Roy's house, overheard Roy and Pat having a loud argument.[2] On September 22, Kathy spoke to her mother on the telephone and learned that she was suffering from a migraine.

On September 23, Pat telephoned her mother, happy about the plans for the annual general meeting of the League of Canadian Poets. She told Virginia that she was going to Victoria the next day to make the final arrangements. Pat then called Arlene Lampert in Toronto asking for last-minute information on the Victoria meeting.

Later that same afternoon, Rita Lalik made her last attempt to telephone David Day to ask if he would include Roy in the Ironworkers' Hall reading. She was unable to reach him. Lalik's next call was to Roy, to apologize for her failure. His reply was: "It's too late now anyway."[3] Between seven and eight o'clock that night, Kathy visited her mother, who was still sick with a migraine. They spent about a half an hour together, and Pat told her about plans for the League meeting. Kathy was probably the last person outside the household to see Pat alive.[4]

The night of September 23 or early in the morning of the 24th, Roy entered their bedroom, where Pat lay in bed. Using the most ordinary of household tools, a hammer, he bludgeoned Pat to death.

For Pat Lowther

He raised his arm
Lifting the flaming sword above his head
Flowers and bright-plumaged birds
Leopard and maiden

Flared into life and burst behind his eyes
And it was Michael
Who brought the hammer down [5]

Roy had already written in his journal that Pat "was a cancer for us to be rid of."[6] Perhaps at the moment, the act of murder felt cleansing. Then, like a speeding car, it had a power beyond the driver. Roy continued to batter Pat's head after the blood stopped spurting against the flowered wallpaper. He pounded and pounded: a blow for every published poem, a blow for her job, a blow for every friend, a blow for every real or imagined lover, a blow for her Canada Council grant, a blow for the Fishermen's Hall reading, a hard blow for the upcoming Ironworkers' Hall reading, a blow for being chair of the League, a cascade of blows to blot out the Roy Lowther that he refused to see.

When Beth and Chris awoke on the morning of September 24, they found their mother "gone." Pat had told them that she was planning to go to Victoria that day, but they also knew that their mother would never leave without kissing them goodbye. They wanted to go into the bedroom to see for themselves that she was gone. They did not understand when Roy refused them entry. The children left for school, and Roy set to his task of hiding the evidence.

The outside world would not leave Roy alone that morning. At about 8:15, Arlene Lampert telephoned from Toronto, trying to give Pat the information she had requested: "I wanted to catch her before she went off to work. I figured out when I thought she'd be awake but not left yet. So I phoned Roy. As I always did, I said, 'Is Pat there?' And he said 'No' in his usual terrible manner. And in my usual chummy manner, I said, 'Oh, I hoped to catch her before she went off to work. Has she gone to work?' And he grumbled, 'No, she's not at work; she's not home either.' I said, 'Would you tell her it's Arlene, that it's urgent and to call me back?' And then he slammed [the phone] down on me. I waited all day and she didn't call, and I waited all the next day and she didn't call again."

Lampert knew that Pat had planned to go to the Empress Hotel in Victoria to complete arrangements for the League meeting that day. To do that, Pat would have needed some of the information that Lampert had prepared for her. Pat had also planned to see Bill Bartlett, director of the Open Space Gallery-Theatre, and Charles Lillard, poet and professor at the University of Victoria. Neither man saw her that day. The convention manager of the hotel did not see her either.

Pat Sighting Number 1: Someone said he saw Pat on September 24 at the Empress Hotel in Victoria. This piece of false information was at first accepted by police, and it slowed down their investigation. It became the first of several mistaken reports that surfaced after Pat's disappearance but before her body was found. It took no time for myths to grow around Pat Lowther.

Roy started to cover his tracks by putting Pat's body in the cupboard of the adjoining bedroom, Kathy's former bedroom closet. Then, on September 25, after the children were asleep, Roy carried Pat's body down the back stairs of the house and put it into the trunk of his car.

Later, in court, Roy said that he came home and found Pat dead. He denied killing her, but he did admit to disposing of the body. His journal details how he did it.[7] The entries are an account told without emotion and laced with comments about the landscape and Pat's poetry. Not being an experienced cleaner, he did not do a good job washing the blood spots off the walls, ceiling and floor. In Brenda's words, "Roy spot washed the walls," leaving generous evidence for the police. Then he put the blood-soaked pillow and the bloodstained cloths into a laundry box but found that the box was too heavy to put into his car, so he transferred them to another box, later explaining to the court that he "was rather fond of" the laundry box.[8] At this point, he made enough noise to disturb the children. "I talked to them a little bit and they went back to sleep."[9]

Next, he tried washing the blood off the mattress but with little success. So he taped a piece of a pink blanket and bit of white cloth over the huge bloodstain and took the mattress off the bed. The Lowthers did not have a bed frame; they had put an old yellow mattress on the floor and topped it with a newer blue one. At first, it was the stain on the blue mattress that gave Roy trouble. Then he found that there was also a stain on the yellow one and he taped a piece of cloth over that stain as well. He decided to get rid of only the blue mattress and, with difficulty, he moved it into the backyard. He left it leaning against the car with the telltale taped end on the ground. As Roy looked over his work, he saw that two large drops of blood had landed on the back steps. He tried to clean them off but only succeeded in creating a large brown smear — it is almost as if those bloodstains willed themselves to be Pat's witnesses.[10]

Roy finished his tasks at about four or five in the morning and then went back into the house to get some rest. About three hours later, on September 26, he sent his children off to school. While they were out, Roy finished what he thought would be the last of his cover-up work. *The Vancouver Sun* of April 20, 1977, told how he covered the bloodstained mattress with a blanket and put it onto the roof of his car. As he was tying it on, the woman who lived next door walked to the gate of her garden and they said hello to each other.[11] Then Roy headed for Furry Creek.

Roy drove his car full of evidence through West Vancouver and stopped once to rearrange the concealing blanket. He felt a driver behind him was showing an uncomfortable interest in the mattress. After he got onto the Squamish Highway, he found a parking lot in Porteau Cove, where he dumped the incriminating blue mattress. Once again, he felt that a motorist was looking at him. The box with the bloodied pillow and stained cloths was left at a roadside dump on his return trip to Vancouver. None of these items was ever found.

Roy arrived at Furry Creek some time between 10:30 and 11:00 A.M., intending to leave Pat's body at the dam site. Finding her body too heavy to carry uphill, he dragged it about fifty feet through the woods to the side of the creek. Then he dropped it over. The body landed on a rock about three feet above the stream. He thought that the body would stay there, out of sight until the spring. Then he threw Pat's purse down after her and tossed her briefcase into some bushes.[12] The account in Roy's journal ends with a business-like inventory of the contents of Pat's briefcase.

Roy had not considered the possibility of heavy autumn rain. It did rain heavily that year, and the swollen waters of Phyllis and Marian Lakes blended with Furry Creek to make the creek rise. Pat's body was swept off the rock and floated down the creek, where it was later seen by a fisherman. Pat would have known that rivers rise and fall. Roy Lowther was not so in tune with his world.

The violence done to Pat's body and the disposal of her blood and bones like last week's garbage thrust one of Pat's poems to mind. "The Dig" tells of archaeologists who are studying the bones of ancient women, but are ignorant of suffering:

> Their bones should thrash
> in the diggers' baskets,
> should scream against the light. [13]

September 25, 1975, was scheduled as the third session of Pat's creative writing class at UBC. Pat Lowther's space at the front of the classroom was empty. Professor Robert Harlow, then acting head of the creative writing department, admitted to feeling "a little pissed off" that she had not been in class and had not telephoned to cancel. He said: "I phoned her up. Roy answered and he called me Bob. In the words of my mother, Roy didn't know me from Adam, yet he called me Bob. I asked if Pat was there and if I could speak to her. Roy answered in a peculiar voice that she wasn't there. I asked him where she was and he answered, 'She's in Victoria. Maybe she went East. You know how marriages go sour.' Then he added something to the effect that she sleeps around."

Harlow felt later that Roy was building his story during the telephone conversation. Harlow talked to a former student, Ron Riter, who was a reporter for *The Vancouver Sun*. As he talked about the disappearance, he found himself saying, "I don't think she's missing. I think she's dead." They contacted the police to tell them that it was probably a murder case. Without any evidence, the police had trouble believing it was anything but the case of an unhappy wife having left her marriage. That same day, September 25, Roy telephoned Pat's aunt, Elsie Wilks, saying that there were problems at home. Elsie agreed to let Roy and the children stay at the cabin on Mayne Island for a while.

Arlene Lampert still needed to talk to Pat and tried unsuccessfully to reach her early in the evening of September 25. She felt it was strange that Pat was not home to get her two young children to bed. The telephone was finally answered about 9:15 P.M., Vancouver time, or just after midnight, Toronto time. This is how Lampert describes that second telephone call: "Roy answered in another peculiar way. He sounded panic stricken that I was even calling. He said, 'I don't know where she is. I think she's in Ottawa with Joy Kogawa. I think she's run off. You know she's got a lover, don't you?' I remember him saying that to me. And I just gulped. I didn't know what to say. Am I supposed to say 'yes,' am I supposed to say 'no'? I don't remember what I said, but it really took me back to hear that accusing tone. Then he said, 'I think she's run off with her lover. I think she's in Windsor. I think she's in Toronto ... She's disappeared, and I'm very worried.'"

Lampert, like Harlow, knew something did not sound right. The League annual general meeting was to take place in less than two weeks and Lampert was sure that Pat would have notified her if she could not fulfill her duties. In addition, Lampert was "back East," and she had not heard from Pat.

The university authorities took other actions. Students read a strange notice on the bulletin board saying that an instructor, Pat Lowther, had disappeared and a reward was offered to anyone who would come forward with information that might help to find her. No one claimed the reward. Then, that Friday, Harlow became worried enough to telephone Pat's family. He spoke to Brenda and told her he was concerned. Brenda told him that she too was concerned, and that she and another relative were going to dig up the Lowther's backyard.

On September 27, what Brian Campbell calls "the culminating event" took place at the Ironworkers' Hall. No poets named Lowther were at 2415 Columbia Street that night. So Jeni Couzyn read Pat's poems: "Kitchen Murder" and "Two Babies in Two Years." Both poems are about problems in the everyday lives of women.

Pat Sighting Number 2: On September 27, someone claimed to have seen Pat at an NDP fundraising dinner. When the police followed it up, they found that someone who did not know Pat had made the claim. The myths were growing.

September 27 just would not lie down and be quiet. Kathy's birthday was three days away, and she had every reason to expect some special event with her mother. *Criminal Reports* records that Kathy Domphousse visited the Lowther home on September 27.[14] She met Roy as he was getting out of his car and asked him if her mother was at home. He answered that she had gone "back East" and had left the morning of September 24. It was not like Kathy's mother to go out of town without telling her family, or to miss her daughter's birthday. "I went to see Mum on September 27 and Roy didn't even let me into the house. He met me at the bottom of the stairs and told me that my mother had gone East. She didn't own a stick of luggage. Whenever she needed any, she'd borrow it from me or my grandmother." Pat had not borrowed a suitcase from either of them. Kathy's worry now turned to fear.

Kathy also remembered a second exchange with Roy in the days following her mother's disappearance. She drove to the house on

46th Avenue and parked behind Roy's car. Roy was standing there quietly with his hands in his pockets. Despite the hostility between the two of them, Kathy had enough feeling for Roy to know that something was wrong. She was silent for a moment. Then she asked, "What's happening?"

"Nothing."

She asked again, "What's happening?"

"Nothing. We're just trying to keep things together here."

She remembers looking at him for a minute. Perhaps that gaze was as much as he could bear. He ended the meeting by saying, "Well, I guess we'll see you." Kathy, realizing she would learn no more in that interview, said, "Okay," got into her car and drove off.[15] Roy's version of the meeting is essentially the same. But he added one point: "I had no intention whatever of telling Kathy anything at that time, not even what I was telling others. I simply wanted her out of there."[16]

Accidentally lost work had been a problem throughout Pat's short life — the stolen briefcase, the misdirected suitcase, the destroyed recording of *The Infinite Mirror Trip*, the CBC film gone missing in Charlottetown — but after her death, much of her work was deliberately destroyed.

Roy's journal details what he did with Pat's papers. Pat had kept her files and letters for the League of Canadian Poets on the kitchen table. Roy wrote that between September 25 and 27 he put those, together with copies of book manuscripts and letters from McNamara, into two garbage bags. "I intended to take them to the dump at the foot of Quebec Street or Manitoba Street for recycling," he wrote. He also wrote that he intended to "get rid of most of it" and turn over her files to the League, "but I had never finished it." Instead, he put some of the papers into a bag and took them to the cabin on Mayne Island, from where they were eventually removed by police as evidence. Police also removed papers from the garbage bags left in the garage. Roy added that there was some material that had "not surfaced at the preliminary [hearing]."[17] With all these hands moving the papers around for their different reasons, it is hard to say how much was kept intact and how much was lost. Arlene Lampert confirms that, despite Roy's claims that he wanted to be a good citizen and return files to their rightful owners, all the League files in Pat's care disappeared with her.[18]

Once Roy was in jail, Kathy took matters into her own hands. "I took bunches of papers out of the house ... I didn't have any storage space, but Alan did." She and Alan put these papers into a trunk in his attic, where they stayed from 1975 to 1995, when they became the basis for *Time Capsule*. It is a good thing Kathy and Alan had the foresight to do this because, later, when Roy was out on bail, he emptied the house of everything, including a beautiful old piano that Pat had bought, which he gave to a friend of his. According to Kathy, the piano was the only thing of value in the house. As for Pat's papers, we will simply never know how many of Pat's single copies of finished and unfinished poetry were destroyed.

On September 27, Roy arrived at the cabin on Mayne Island with the two children and two cats. Beth remembers that the cats, in their excitement, befouled everything in sight. Pat's aunt, Elsie Wilks, helped them out while they were on the Island. She let them use her refrigerator and telephone, lent them a lamp and generally looked out for them. People who knew Elsie Wilks say that she was an open-hearted person, the sort that others confide in, so Elsie had no trouble getting Roy to talk about his marriage problems. She said that Roy seemed upset that Pat had left him, but his tales of woe were confusing. He did not like Pat's poetry; nonetheless, he felt hurt because Pat would not let him go to her readings. When Elsie asked him if he would like Pat to return, he said, "No, certainly not." When she asked if he was jealous of Pat, "he just put his head down and did not answer."[19]

Chris was then seven years old and has a fuzzy memory of that time. She said that after they settled into the cabin, her father paced the room for several hours. Then he told her and Beth that their mother was dead and they would never see her again. She now thinks that she and Beth did not fully understand the meaning of his words. They were accustomed to Pat's occasional absences when she went on reading tours. They were also accustomed to their father's erratic behaviour. Perhaps they thought this was just another period to get through.

Early in the disappearance, the police did not have the authority to enter the Lowther house. Everyone worried that, as time passed, evidence would disappear. Therefore, the police asked the family to look for evidence. On September 27 or 28, Kathy broke into her mother's home to have a look around. The police had instructed her what to look for: photos, anything to show suspicion of foul play. She was surprised to see that her mother did not appear to have taken anything with her. If Pat was moving East, Kathy wondered, why were all her clothes, including her winter coat, still in the closet?[20] Later that evening, Kathy brought her questions to her grandmother. "I was making new slip covers, putting the finishing touches on them," Virginia says. Kathy and Virginia puzzled over Roy's story that Pat had gone East. It did not make sense. Virginia decided to join Kathy in searching the Lowther house.

On September 29, Roy telephoned Brenda. He said he wanted to speak to her as the "level-headed one" in the family. Brenda had had very few dealings with Roy, and she found the call frightening. In their conversation, he often paused as he was speaking. "It made my heart thump in the back of my throat," she says. Brenda asked where her sister was, and Roy asked her why she was worried. Brenda found herself replying, "I don't know. Is anybody dead?" Roy told her there was nothing to worry about. He, however, was an unhappy man because his wife had a sweetheart in the East who was writing her love poems and letters. Brenda responded that she "didn't think that poems, letters and a once-a-year meeting was a very torrid affair."[21] Like everyone close to Pat, Brenda knew that her sister's main concern was keeping the children's lives stable.

Brenda asked more about Pat's whereabouts and Roy said that, on September 24, Pat had received an emergency telephone call and had to go to Victoria. He went on to say that, the next day, he received a telephone call from his imaginary Pat in an imaginary Victoria telling him that she was going East and did not know when she would be back. Brenda knew her sister well enough to tell him that Pat would not leave the children for very long. To that Roy replied, "I don't think she's coming back."[22]

A couple of days later, Virginia and Kathy made another search of the Lowther house. Going through Pat's clothes, the only thing that Virginia noticed missing was a crocheted shawl. Kathy had given Pat slacks and a top for her birthday in July. "Pat loved them. She had them on every day … and we saw them lying folded on the dresser." When Brenda telephoned Roy on September 30 and told him what Kathy had found, Roy replied that Pat had bought some new blouses and it was still warm back East. Brenda was not convinced.

On October 1, Kathy formally notified the Vancouver police that Pat was missing. Earlier that day, she and Brenda had gone to the police station and spoken to Detective Menzies. After that, joined by Virginia and Pat's brother John, they had made another search of the house and found two important clues. One was a note from Roy to Pat, taped to the dining-room table. The note had not been there on earlier visits. The second was a yellow mattress with a patch taped over it. When they peeled back the tape, they found a bloodstain. The fooling around was over. They told the police about the mattress and Kathy gave the note to the investigating detectives. Finally, the police had the authority to enter and investigate.[23]

Meanwhile Roy telephoned Brenda and suggested calling hospitals. How did this square with his story that Pat had gone East?[24]

The next day Roy talked with a financial worker from the Vancouver Resources Board about his welfare payments. Now that Pat was gone, he had to make new arrangements. He told the worker that Pat had deserted him and the children. He added that his wife had a lover and that he and she "more or less condoned" the practice.[25]

After Kathy told Roy that she had found her mother's clothes in the house, Roy realized he needed to protect himself. While Roy was still on Mayne Island, he got Don Cummins, the basement tenant, to help him. Kathy relates: "I went [to the house] with my boyfriend of the time. Don had moved upstairs, per Roy's instructions. Don was sleeping in a sleeping bag in the living room. The whole place was lit with candles. We knocked on the door. He phoned Roy on Mayne Island. Roy told him, 'Guard the house. Keep that little so-and-so out.' I wanted in. I wanted to look for things. He wasn't having any of it. I didn't get in that day. I just made a big noise, jumped up and down on the porch."

On another occasion Kathy and Brenda tried to break in. Anxiety was running high: "I never laughed so hard because of all the tension. We tried to break a flimsy-looking back window and couldn't. We couldn't even break it with a brick! We were nearly hysterical by then. We found blood in a basement bathroom. It was either Roy's or Mum's."

Pat Sighting Number 3: Another false report circulated that Pat had been seen in the creative writing department at UBC.

With the suspicion of murder on the table, the family decided to try to find the body and made good on their plan to dig up the backyard. Kathy relates: "We were digging up the backyard, searching for anything. There was a freshly turned bit of earth." They later learned that the owner was putting in a garden, but, at the time, it looked suspicious. Kathy continues, "It was pouring. I was there with Arden and Gramma. Some of us had towels on our heads — it was raining so hard." By this time, more than the family was in action. "Then we looked up and there were reporters in the back alley. It made us feel like a bunch of fools."

Then, Uncle Bill Wilks used his divining skills. Roy had taken Pat's hairbrush with him when he went to the cabin on Mayne. Alan Domphousse says, "Bill put the hairbrush on the ground and [the wires he used as an instrument] kept pointing in a certain direction. The best he could come up with was West Vancouver." Bill went to the police station and gave them a demonstration. Alan says, "They more or less ignored him. Pat's body was eventually found in Howe Sound in West Vancouver."

Wilks' book, *Science of a Witch's Brew*, has a section called "Finding the Missing."[26] In it, he relates taking hair from Pat's hairbrush, putting his index finger on the hairs and getting a bearing northward to Point Grey, which is near the University of British Columbia. He was unable to determine the exact line because of obstructions. (He was on Mayne Island at the time.) Several days later he went to Vancouver and stood on the shoreline at Point Grey. He "was dismayed to discover that the bearing line had now altered and was pointing to downtown Vancouver." At first he did not know what to think. Then he says he had a "flash of under-standing. Her body had been found and the police had taken it to the morgue." A telephone call to the police showed that his intuition was correct.

In her search for her mother, Kathy made an appointment with a clairvoyant. The woman, who was from England, was in town staying with her sister. When Kathy appeared at the appointed time, the clairvoyant refused to see her. Two days later she telephoned Kathy to apologize and said the only help she could give was that she saw a small bridge and a creek or a brook. In Kathy's words, "It didn't mean anything to me at the time, but it certainly did when they found her."

On October 7, Roy returned to Vancouver to move more things to Mayne Island and to do the family laundry. One of the things he took away with him to the Island was the blood-stained yellow mattress with the taped patch.[27]

The League of Canadian Poets held its annual general meeting, as scheduled, at the Empress Hotel in Victoria on the Canadian Thanksgiving weekend, October 11 through 13. Joe Rosenblatt says, "Pat's absence was like a cobalt cloud hanging over the group." But life had to go on, and so Charles Lillard took over her duties as chair. While Lorraine Vernon was taking the ferry from the mainland to the island to attend the meeting, she kept thinking about Pat in water. Allan Safarik remembers: "The undercurrent of her not being there was very strong. Everybody just sort of came together ... Everyone was concerned. I suspected she had been murdered." Lampert knew about the troubles in Pat's marriage. That knowledge, punctuated by her recent telephone talks with Roy, drove her to one conclusion. Rosenblatt says that a distraught Lampert kept saying, "I know he's killed her."

Pat Sighting Number 4: During a lunch meeting, there was an announcement. Elizabeth Gourlay recalled that a woman with amnesia had been found wondering around Victoria. The group convinced itself that this was Pat.

On October 13, 1975, a family on a fishing trip found Pat's nude and decomposed body in Furry Creek. The news reached the anguished group of poets, still assembled in Victoria. Fred Cogswell laments, "Her death was more a shock than a surprise." When he returned to Fredericton, he sent police copies of letters that Pat had sent to him, establishing Roy's violence and threats against her.[28] Joe Rosenblatt believed then, and still believes, that Roy killed her because "he knew there was greatness there. It was the genocide of the muse."

CHAPTER 13

Dealing with a Murder

*If the poet is to live, it's to live by words that go
beyond this kind of biographical circumstance.*

— Seymour Mayne[1]

WHEN PAT WAS FOUND IN FURRY CREEK, her nude body was
wedged under a large cedar log.[2] The RCMP officer who responded to the call likely did not intend to be poetic when he
reported: "Her left hand was in the water; her right hand was
down in among the rocks." Pat's body was returning to the
elements; touching cedar, water and stone in her beloved Furry
Creek.

Vancouver Police Inspector Kenneth Hale was then a young
sergeant working on detective investigations. The note that had
suddenly appeared taped to the dining-room table became part of
the investigation. It read: "Pat. I hope you return soon and are well.
Some sort of solution will have to be worked out for this problem
with Legal Aid. We are living on Mayne Island. The children are
happy and are attending school there. I have moved only the things
we needed and some pictures and records. You can reach us at

[phone number]. Everyone has been extremely worried about your disappearance. Please contact us."[3]

Hale did not claim to be an expert in language, but on October 15, writing in his duty notebook, he wondered, "Shouldn't it have said something like, 'I'm glad you're back,' or something in the present?" If Roy expected Pat to read the note at their home, why did he say, "I hope you return soon"?

When Hale and his partner, R.E. Chapman, went to the house on 46th Avenue, they found 117 blood spots on the bedroom wall. Now there were several things that did not add up. The woman who was said to have voluntarily "gone East" had a bedroom full of bloodstains. There was the strange note. There was also the question of the mattresses. If Roy believed his wife might walk back into their home, why was there no mattress in the bedroom? On October 15, Detectives Hale and Chapman visited Roy on Mayne Island and questioned him.

Hale's duty notebook records Roy's responses to information given to him by police and his answers to their questions. They told him that a body had been found in Furry Creek, which they believed was Pat's. When they asked him if he thought she might have committed suicide, Roy responded, "No, she definitely didn't commit suicide." The detectives asked Roy more questions and noted that he appeared to be getting angry. When they asked him when he had last visited Furry Creek, Roy said he had not been there for the past two years.

Hale repeated something that Arlene Lampert had reported Roy as having said. He had threatened that if Pat's lover came to Vancouver, "it would be the worst for him. His wife and family would find out." Roy's response was, "Yes, I might have said something like that, but I wouldn't do it." Hale asked Roy about the strange note he had left for Pat. He did not have an answer about the confusion of the present and future tense. Roy later admitted in his journal that, on reflection, leaving that note on the table was "mildly odd ball."[4]

When the police asked Roy why he had taken the mattress from the house if he expected Pat to return, he had an answer. It seems there was a better one in the basement, or Pat could have slept on the chesterfield. But there was also the yellow mattress outside the cabin for the police to see, the same one Roy had taken from Vancouver on his October 7 trip. It was wet on both sides and had reddish-brown stains. Hale asked Roy about the stains and whether he had washed it. Roy denied knowing anything about the stains and said he had not washed the mattress. He suggested that Pat might have washed it "because it was old."[5] He also suggested that it might be damp from dew, as he had moved the mattress on top of his car. Chapman reminded Roy that the mattress had been moved three weeks earlier.

Chapman then asked, "Did you kill your wife?" The duty notebook entry reads: "Lowther jumped up walked to window looked out. Returned to chair." Predictably, Roy said he had not. Roy asked, "Am I a suspect?" The detective replied, in television cop show fashion, "I suspect everybody. It's my job." Roy willingly drew a map of the Furry Creek area to help the police in their investigation. Chapman asked Roy if he had brought a hammer from the house in Vancouver. He said that he had, because he wanted to build the children a bookcase. The police told Roy that they were going to seize the hammer. Chapman handed it to Hale, who put in into a plastic bag and placed it in his briefcase.[6] The prime clues were now the bloodstained wallpaper, the hammer and the travelling mattress.

Because the body was so badly decomposed, the only way to positively identify it was by dental records. Hale remembers the difficulty there because "Mr. Lowther first gave us the name of the wrong dentist," and the investigation had to be delayed until the right dentist was found. On October 17, 1975, *The Vancouver Sun* ran a short story saying, "Homicide detectives have positively identified the body found last week near Squamish as missing poet Pat Lowther."[7]

On October 21, Hale, Chapman and two social workers went to Mayne Island in an RCMP launch and arrested Roy.[8] "I felt sad taking him away from his children. He was devoted to his kids. You could tell he was a good father, but he also used the kids as a shield," Hale recalls. Social Services arranged to take the children into care. Chris remembered being cold as she and Beth were taken away in the RCMP launch. She has no memory of anyone talking to them or trying to comfort them as she and Beth huddled together crying. This time they knew their mother was dead.

On November 15, Chris Potter, who had interviewed Pat only a few months earlier, wrote a eulogy in *Performance*, the Vancouver monthly arts newspaper: "To use the instinctive words of sorrow is to place inadequacies on paper, and these resound hollowly around the mind." Potter spoke to Michael Yates, one of Pat's colleagues from UBC and owner of Sono Nis Press. The quality Yates remembered most about Pat was calmness. It showed in her writing, in her care for her children and in her work with the New Democratic Party. Yates credited Pat with building the League of Canadian Poets into "a major force in Canadian literature." Potter also pointed out the high regard poets had for Pat and the publication of her work in literary magazines in other countries. Yet, he said, Pat Lowther's work could not be found in Vancouver book stores: "Pat had to buy her own copies from Toronto."[9] Potter's assertion fits with the already noted experience of Borealis Press, which initially got only one order from Vancouver when *Milk Stone* was released.

The worst fears of friends, family and colleagues had come true. The shock and anger that set in were expressed in a letter by Dorothy Livesay. She had been in Winnipeg when she learned the news by reading it in the Canadian Press item of October 13. She wrote a letter to *The Globe and Mail* which said, in part: "Her death under such very strange circumstances is a body blow to the cause of poetry in Canada. Although only beginning to be known in the east, she has for ten years been producing the most stirring, lyrical, and meaningful and committed poetry of any written by man or woman in Canada or the world."[10]

The letter goes to on to say that Pat was devoted to justice, civil rights and the kind of socialist society that South American poets had championed. Livesay also complained that the International Poetry Festival, which was to be held in Toronto that month, had neglected to invite Pat. In fact, the festival had not invited "any Canadian woman poet to participate."

Social Services made Beth and Chris wards of the province and put them into a foster home in Victoria. After they had been there for three days, their grandmother learned about it and swept into action. Virginia believed that, in their mother's absence, she should care for the girls, and she headed for Victoria with the intention of getting custody of the children. "I had baby-sat them every weekend since they were babies." When she arrived, she got a warm welcome from the foster family, who even put her up for two nights. In spite of their kindness, the worry over her grandchildren coupled with the grief over Pat's death put Virginia in a state of great stress. She remembered that she could not relax on the ferry ride back to Vancouver, for she did not know what the future had in store for the children. Once they were on the dock in Vancouver, Virginia began to relax. It was a long time before she would get official custody of Beth and Chris. After getting custody, she did keep their status as wards of the province, as she was advised that the children would derive some advantages from this arrangement.

Shortly after the children had settled into their grandmother's house, the family was sitting on the chesterfield in the living room, when Beth asked, "Where's our daddy?" To Virginia fell the job of saying, "Well, you know what happened to your mother. The police think your daddy did it, and he's been arrested." Then from seven-year-old Chris, "Oh no, he wouldn't do that!" Then nine-year-old Beth asked, "Gramma, what do you think?" Virginia had to respond, "I think he did it." Then Beth thought for a while and said, "I think he did it too. Who else hated Mother? Nobody else hated her." Chris cried, and then Beth cried, and their grandmother did her best to comfort them.

A grandmother doing her best with two badly hurt little girls is what the next ten years would bring for all of them. The girls lived for some of the time with their grnadmother in the house on 10th Street in North Vancouver, and the children attended Pat's old elementary school, Ridgeway. They also spent some time together at a foster home and when Chris was thirteen, she spent eleven months in a group home. Beth lived in several foster homes and never returned to her grandmother's house. She and Chris were unable to live together. Sadly, it's not uncommon for children of trauma to take their distress out on each other.

Chris writes of a recurring dream that she had in which she would open a closet and find her mother in it. "She stood, again slightly swaying, with even more of a faraway look in her eyes ... In the dream it was decided (by one or another family member) that my mother was 'on her way to heaven.' For some reason, this closet was one of her stops along the way. I obediently shut the door, or woke up."[11]

On Friday, October 24, Pat's sorrowing family, friends and local poets gathered at a memorial service conducted by Dr. Phillip Hewitt at the Unitarian Church on West 49th Avenue. Lorraine Vernon, Rona Murray and Hilda Thomas were among the mourners. Allan Safarik read the poem "Death of a Poet."[12] Marya Fiamengo had intended to read some of Pat's work, but as she prepared for it, she found herself writing a tribute to Pat, which opens with a line from Pat's poem "Woman":

Requiem for Pat Lowther — October 24, 1975

Earth and salt water,
bless and absolve
the bruising of this flesh

which walked the hard road
of genesis. [13]

After Bethoe Shirkoff came back from the service, she picked up
the tape that she had started the night before Beth's birthday and
reminisced about her talks with Pat. She ended the tape with, "Oh
God, I'm sorry that woman is dead! … What a loss for our country!
What a loss for humanity!" *The Vancouver Sun* reported the service
and repeated the rumour that Pat Lowther had last been seen in
Victoria on September 24.[14] Gossip was being elevated to the
written word.

At the time of the service, the family did not know when Pat's
funeral could be held. They had arranged for a funeral to be held on
Thursday, October 23, at the Boat Memorial Chapel in North
Vancouver, but had to cancel it because the body had not been
released by the authorities. To the further distress of her family,
parts of Pat's body, such as her dented skull, were needed as
evidence in the trial. It was not until after Roy's murder trial, nearly
two years later, that Pat's exhausted bones would finally be cre-
mated.

At last Eastern literary critics started to take notice of Pat
Lowther. Using the poem "It Happens Every Day" as a focus, Robert
Fulford devoted his syndicated column of October 25, 1975, to her.
The article is about Pat's untimely death and the sad loss for poetry.
To describe her poetry, he uses words like "harsh," "tough," "memorable."[15] Perhaps because of the manner of her death, her humour
and delicacy seem not to have spoken to him. Quotations from that
column were used by Oxford on the back cover of *A Stone Diary*.
Even *Maclean's* sauntered in with tardy praise. On November 3, the
magazine ran an article with a photograph of Pat. Although the
focus of the piece, "When the poet dies …," is Pat's work, it did take
the discovery of her battered body to squeeze a few hundred words
out of this national magazine.[16]

People who had supported Pat's work were angry at the delayed praise. Brian Brett, co-publisher of *The Age of the Bird*, wrote, "It is typical that it took her violent death for the gods of Toronto to notice her."[17] Seymour Mayne laments, "She had an uphill battle getting recognized. The terrible irony of her life was that ... with her brutal death, all of a sudden people began to turn attention to her work." He said with distaste, "As soon as she dies ... all the hyenas of literature ... are baying at the moon and saying how wonderful she was. Well, where were they when she needed them, when those of us who were trying to help her needed them too? They weren't there."

Réshard Gool in Charlottetown was hurt and so angry at the conduct of the media that he refused an interview with CBC, which during Pat's life had turned down Gool's efforts to have her works put on the air. After her murder, someone from the corporation asked Gool to make a statement. He responded angrily, "I don't particularly want to talk about her. She was a friend and I think the interest you people have in her is prurient." His anger was largely because of earlier rebuffs and partly because the request was from a news program representative, not from the CBC arts staff. "And you're concerned more with the murder than with the woman's poetry. Otherwise you wouldn't ask me to summarize her life in two minutes. I'm not prepared to do that."

In early November, Allan Safarik put together a documentary called "Pat Lowther: Woman, Mother, Artist" for Peter Gzowski's national program on CBC FM radio, as a Canada-wide memorial to Pat. Patrick Lane, Seymour Mayne, Hilda Thomas, George Woodcock and Pat's mother were all present in a studio in Vancouver. Milton Acorn spoke from Toronto, and Dorothy Livesay from Winnipeg. Their comments were interlaced with clips of the audio tape of Pat reading her poems in Prince Edward Island.[18]

Hilda Thomas told of how she felt on hearing that Pat's body had been found: "I went about preparing dinner and I felt about ninety years old." Dorothy Livesay repeated lines from her much-quoted tribute to Pat in *The Globe and Mail*: "Her death is a body blow to the cause of poetry in Canada." Safarik repeated that he had once asked Pat, "For God's sake, why don't you get your teeth fixed?" Pat had answered, "I can't afford to." Marya Fiamengo rejoined, "Her teeth were a metaphor for her life."

The poets kept returning to Pat's lack of help and recognition. George Woodcock remarked that she was not recognized because her poetry is austere and "intellectually precise." Milton Acorn accused the "Eastern Literary Mafia" of murdering Pat artistically with neglect while she was alive. Of Pat Lowther the poet, Marya Fiamengo intoned: "She loved language, she read widely, and her reading fed her imagination. It wasn't the sterile directed reading of a PhD program; she read where her imagination took her. This in turn nurtured her. She did what the best women poets do. They make matter sacramental. They celebrate themselves as women."

The next day on Peter Gzowski's show, poet Andy Wainright added his ideas. Wainright had never known Pat, but he criticized the documentary: "On CBC last night they made you human, stripping away your poetic mask, making you wear their own: Pat the welfare girl whose teeth were bad."[19] A hurt and angry Allan Safarik came on the program the third day accusing Wainright of being an unfeeling stranger at a funeral. He said, "I would suggest, if you don't try to make someone human, there's no point in talking about them in any other way."[20]

Pat's death left Oxford University Press in a difficult situation. William Toye had told Pat, in a letter sent to her on September 9, that they would publish her book.[21] They were still working out the details when she was killed. One major detail was the contract, which Pat had not signed. Who would get the royalties from the sale of *A Stone Diary*? In an ordinary situation, a deceased writer's royalties would go to the next of kin. However, if one suspects cause of death at the hands of that same kin, it is another matter entirely.

It took nearly two years for the murder to come to trial. During that period, Roy Lowther might claim the royalties, modest though they would be. To make matters worse, Pat did not have a will. The poets who had been Pat's friends wanted her children, not Roy, to get whatever benefits might come from her work. Oxford turned the matter over to its lawyers. They in turn negotiated with the Public Trustee of British Columbia, whose job it was to protect the interests of the estate.

Oxford also wanted to make sure that the copy that Pat had sent to them was her final version. William Toye asked Allan Safarik for help. Safarik agreed to check Oxford's proposed manuscript against whatever versions he could find among Pat's papers to see if she had made any late changes. Safarik wrote to Toye in July 1976, "I feel sure that she was a meticulous worker and that if there are changes she would have sent them to you quickly after the first submission of the manuscript."[22] Over a year after Pat's death, in November 1976, the Public Trustee of British Columbia signed the contract, and Oxford was able to produce the book.[23] The royalties from *A Stone Diary* were sent to Virginia for the children.

After Pat's cremation, Kathy kept her mother's ashes for many years. In 1995 she and her partner, Russ, scattered the ashes at Prospect Point in Stanley Park, where Pat is now mingled with the ocean, the air and the earth.

CHAPTER 14

On Trial

She was poised for a marvelous leap. I suppose that's why such men do it — they can't stand the idea of their women taking to flight, becoming airborne.

— Margaret Atwood[1]

ON OCTOBER 18, 1975, ROY LOWTHER WAS CHARGED with the murder of his wife. The counsel for the Crown was John Hall; Roy's lawyer was A.G. Henderson. Roy pleaded not guilty, and at first bail was denied. Later the Supreme Court granted him a release on bail until his preliminary hearing, in April 1976.[2]

Roy was out on bail. Although the owner of the house on 46th Avenue had allowed him in to get his belongings, he could no longer live there. He was broke and his in-laws were not likely to take him in. Living in his car in a parking lot — that might work. Roy found himself in the Kitsilano beach parking lot with a car that would not start. When he tried to open the hood, it would not budge. He flagged down two police constables, who kindly helped him open the hood. As the officers left, they looked back to see Roy holding on to the front bumper of the car as it started to crawl backwards.

When he could hold on no longer, the car started to move in a circle. Then it gained speed and gamboled in a larger circle. Moving at about twenty-five miles an hour, it kept making bigger and bigger circles. Then it waltzed over the curb and tangoed into a garbage can. With each circle, it did a Highland fling into the police car. It took no time for a crowd of delighted onlookers to gather and cheer the romping car each time it smashed the cruiser. Within a few minutes the police moved their cruiser into its path and stopped the performance. "I guess I left it in gear when I tried to start it," Roy explained. The helpful constables were left to write a report explaining $2500 worth of damage to the police car.[3] A good mechanic could probably explain the waltzing car; some would prefer to believe that Pat's spirit had let loose cosmic imps.

In April, Roy had his preliminary hearing for the murder charge. Attorney A.G. Henderson, who later became the Honourable Mr. Justice Henderson of the British Columbia Supreme Court, was then a partner in the law firm assigned by the Legal Aid Society of British Columbia to defend Roy. His first impression — "a difficult client" — proved painfully true. "Mr. Lowther wanted his lawyers to go into a tremendous amount of detail with him in discussing strategy and tactics." This was coupled with what Henderson calls "paranoia about the justice system and about lawyers." Roy made it clear that he did not trust lawyers in general or Henderson and his associate, Ann Roundthwaite, in particular, to act in his best interests.

Preparing the defense resulted in "many, many hours talking to him about things that were of marginal or no relevance, including repeated explanations, on his part, of what was wrong with society and the justice system." Mr. Henderson concedes that Roy was sincere in his beliefs. He could not trust the justice system because he did not trust the state.

Not only did Roy try to educate his lawyers, he continually surprised them. While preparing for the trial he would talk "for thirty or forty minutes at a stretch without letting you get a word in edgewise and then he would conclude his dissertation by saying, 'However, you're a great lawyer; you're doing a great job for me,' or words to that effect." Then, just when the lawyers felt they were relating well to Roy, "he'd be off again, telling you about how you were a tool of the state."

Although the preliminary hearing started on the first day of April 1976, it would be nearly two years between the murder and the actual trial, which took place in April 1977. Kathy remembers how Roy sat in the courtroom, "making millions and millions of notes." When she went up to testify, Roy was sitting right below her. When she spoke into the microphone, she surprised herself because her voice sounded exactly like her mother's. "It startled *me*. He put his pen down and he looked up at me. And I know that's exactly what he thought too."

Another witness at the preliminary hearing was Pat's colleague Professor Robert Harlow. He said that, as Pat's supervisor, he would have known if she had intended to cancel her workshop or planned to go East.

Arlene Lampert came to Vancouver to testify and told of the two telephone exchanges she had with Roy at the time of the murder. On both occasions Roy had sounded extremely anxious.[4] Lampert repeated the contradictory statements Roy had made during the second call. First, he said that Pat was in Victoria. Next, he said she was in Ottawa. Then, he said he did not know where Pat was.

When Pat's disappearance was first reported, Roy's stories had won him some sympathy from police. Thinking that Pat might have deserted the family to be with her lover, the police minimized the fears of foul play. Roy described real and imagined love affairs throughout his journal as if Pat hid a lover under each one of her typewriter keys.

Roy Lowther's murder trial lasted from March 28 to April 22, 1977. The trial began in a predictable way. Roy said he knew nothing of Pat's death until the police informed him that they had found a body. Crown Attorney John Hall began to build his case against Roy, giving professional jealousy as the motive.

The first few days of the trial saw a parade of police experts testify on the finer points of identifying the body and the manner of death. Among them were forensic dentist Dr. Laurence Cheevers; pathologist Dr. Thomas Harmon; coroner's technician Ralph Barton Bastien; and fingerprint specialists John Marshall of the coroner's office and Michael O'Donnell of the RCMP. John Elsoff spoke about his laboratory work on the blood spots taken from the Lowther house. There had also been a small amount of blood stuck between the handle and the head of the hammer that had been taken from Roy. Elsoff testified that it was human blood.[5] *Pat's blood.*

> for the rush and pressure
> of blood like a great river
> gathering volume
> falling among caverns
> in the listening skull [6]

If Pat's life had been full of ironies, unwinding the circumstances of her death revealed especially cruel ones. In life, Pat had not been able to afford the dental care she needed. Yet when police were working to identify the body, it was her battered teeth and fractured dental plate that answered the question as to who she was. Dr. Harrison, the dentist whom Pat had seldom seen, gave the court her records. Based on that evidence, the forensic dentist Dr. Laurence Cheevers could testify, "Having examined the evidence presented to me, I have concluded that the cadaver number 929-75 and Mrs. Pat Lowther are one and the same person." He also noted, "She has not obviously seen a dentist in the last few years."[7] Laboratory work took the fingerprints from the hands that Shirkoff had called delicate. The fingerprints backed up the dental findings. There was no doubt that the body was the husk of Pat Lowther.

Still, it was necessary to prove exactly how a living person became a recovered body. Dr. Harmon gave the jury a demonstration. He stepped down from the witness box and showed the jurors a part of Pat's skull, labelled Exhibit Number 6. With Pat's occipital bone in one hand and the hammer, Exhibit Number 7, in the other, he showed them that the hammer head fit into a dent in the skull.[8]

In Pat's life, she wrote of blood and bone. In her death, Pat's spattered blood and shattered bones told her story. Officials numbered and sorted her bones, typed her blood and placed their expert conclusions among the twenty-seven exhibits that made up the physical evidence.

The people still hurting from Pat's death had to tell what they knew of her life. On April 15, Don Cummins, the tenant in the Lowther's basement, was called to the stand. The prosecutor asked him if Pat had ever made sexual advances toward him. He answered, "No, she wasn't that kind of a lady."[9] Virginia was grateful to the end of her life to Cummins for being the only one at the trial who countered Roy's charges that Pat had "a roving eye."

"Lies, he never had to recant those lies!" Virginia agonized about Roy's testimony. She remembers approaching Crown Attorney Hall privately and saying that Roy was compounding lie upon lie about Pat. He responded with, "Leave him alone." Attorney Hall did not explain to Virginia that his strategy was to let Roy have free rein to show his character to the court. The strategy worked. Virginia received some comfort during one of the recesses when the wife of a reporter approached her and said, "We don't believe him. Nobody believes him." As the trial moved along, one by one, the lies Roy had told to Pat's family, the police and Robert Harlow were exposed.

Rita Lalik of the New Democratic Party and Mark Budgen, one of the planners of the Ironworkers' reading, gave testimony that added to the Crown's case of poetic rivalry. Lalik turned over a letter Roy had written to her. In the letter Roy said that he deserved twenty minutes at the reading, "as a writer of poems about the working man."[10]

Only three months before Pat's death, one of Virginia's chairs had fallen victim to Roy's anger. The *Province*, on April 16, ran the headline "Witness Recounts 'Melodramatic' Vow." Virginia told the court that her remark about hoping that Pat was having some fun when she went to readings caused Roy to pound on the table and shout, "She's my wife! If I'm not going to have her, nobody else is going to have her."[11] Roy's character was being laid out for the jury. Years later Allan Safarik wrote to Chris Lowther about his view of Virginia throughout the ordeal. "The shock of what happened revealed your grandmother to be a woman with a backbone of steel. I admire her as much as any person I ever met."[12]

Eugene McNamara was called to give evidence and had to tell the court details of his relationship with Pat. Here, too, Pat's poetry preceded her life. McNamara said that he had started reading Pat's poetry in the 1960s. They had begun a correspondence in the 1970s, but did not meet until 1972. It wasn't until November 1973 that the relationship became romantic.[13] By then, Roy's behaviour had destroyed his second marriage as it had his first. McNamara testified that, in the two years of their romance, he and Pat had met about once a year. He also said that he had received a telephone call on September 12, shortly before Pat was killed. It was from a man giving a name that sounded like Tom Errinson or Harrison. The purpose of the call was to stop McNamara from going to the League meeting in Victoria and the caller threatened to tell McNamara's wife of his affair if he did go. Eugene McNamara decided to stay away.[14]

The courtroom probably echoed with more poetic references during this trial than it had in a decade of criminal cases. McNamara was asked to explain the title of his book of poetry *Diving for the Body*, as well as the poem "Among the Missing."[15] Both titles are startling, considering Pat's disappearance and the way her body had been hidden. However, a poet's stock-in-trade is language that moves people. The defense lawyer tried to connect McNamara's book with Pat's murder, but Justice Gould said that the titles of McNamara's work were irrelevant and inadmissible. Roy had written a poem titled "September 23" in which he speaks of death, but Roy's poem did not become part of the evidence either.[16] A small mercy was Justice Gould's decision that the love letters between Pat and Eugene McNamara were not necessary as court evidence.

Arlene Lampert was summoned to Vancouver again in 1977 to tell her story at the murder trial. Her description of the two telephone calls and Roy's panicky, contradictory statements were important evidence. Roy had told police that he had been in all evening, but Lampert testified that she had been calling all evening and the telephone was not answered until after nine o'clock at night, Vancouver time. Lampert later admitted to being worried about seeing Roy Lowther, whom she had never met: "If I make eye contact with that man, I won't know what to say. I'll feel like, I can't do that to another human being; in spite of what he did. But no, he was ... so unconnected with her death ... or seemed to be. He was so proud. The court was filled. He was sitting ... looking behind him, he couldn't contain the smile on his face. He was trying to look serious, but he just couldn't contain himself. He was so proud to be the centre. It was his day. And he was getting all the attention and it was just such a strange response from him. It helped me. It helped me to say everything that I needed to say because I looked at him and I thought ... I don't care if they hang him from a tree! Just ice cold about her death, absolutely no connection."

Kathy saw Roy's behaviour the same way. She remembered two lawyers firing questions at him. Roy broke into a big smile and said, "Gentlemen, gentlemen, please, one at a time." When the Crown asked him questions, he often replied with word games.

Perhaps it was predictable that this much-reported story involving murder and romance would include strange telephone calls aimed at the jury. There were two. On April 15, the clerk of the court informed Justice Gould of the first call. The call was from a Mrs. Rhinehart saying that she knew Roy Lowther and that she also worked with a juror. Implying that the juror may have known Lowther through her, she suggested that there might be a conflict of interest. The juror was called into the judge's chambers in the presence of both lawyers. Questioning her, they learned that Rhinehart had taken over part of the woman's job. The two did not actually work together; in fact, they hardly knew each other. Judge Gould decided that it was of no consequence and instructed the juror accordingly, "If she phones you, tell her to mind her own business."[17] The second call came to the office of another jury member. His secretary received a message from someone whose name may have been Jack Denny. He instructed the juror not to go to court that day, as the session had been postponed. This juror then presented his information to the judge, counsels for the defense and the Crown, but the lawyers agreed to let the matter drop. After dealing with the second mischief-making report, Justice Gould gave his candid opinion. "I think there are some nuts involved."[18]

There is no evidence to identify the sources of the telephone calls, but there is one more piece of information. The trial transcript that Roy used is now in possession of the Lowther family. It was among Roy's papers and his handwritten notes are in the margins. Beside Judge Gould's comment about "nuts," Roy wrote "bigotry thing." Beside the lawyers' agreement to let the matter drop, he wrote, "No one told me of this incident my lawyer [sic]. I was not asked if I knew Jack Denny."

Detectives Chapman and Hale gave testimony about their investigation before and after Pat's body was found. Reading from his duty notebook, Hale repeated the questions they had asked Roy and the answers he had given. They told of discussing the strange note with him. The note became Exhibit Number 10. Hale was always on good terms with Roy and, like other observers, he could see that Roy's lawyers did not want Roy to talk at his trial. At the end of the hearings, on April 18, Roy approached Hale and said, "You stood up in the witness box. Could I?" Hale admits to playing with Roy's vanities and responding, "Sure you can. Why don't you go stand in it now and see how it feels?" There, in the empty courtroom, Roy stepped into the witness box. The next day, Roy took the stand. It was clear that he wanted a platform to talk about his ideas. Pat's death was not on the top of Roy's list.

Roy's surprises for his lawyers before the trial were nothing compared with what he did when he took the stand. When he had been charged, Roy had claimed to know nothing about Pat's death. However, on April 19, Roy astonished everyone by volunteering the information that he had made up the story given to police. Before his arrest, Roy had told investigating officers that he had not been to Furry Creek for about two years. Now he admitted publicly to having disposed of the body. Even the Toronto papers ran headlines such as, "Poet Feared Arrest, Dumped Wife's Body in Creek, Court Told."[19] Until this point he had been telling Pat's family, her employer and the police that she had told him she was leaving him. Now he admitted that Pat's "going East" telephone call from Victoria was a lie.[20] Roy's new story went like this: Pat had suffered from a migraine the night before, so he did not disturb her in the morning. He got up with the children and sent them off to school. Then he went out for a walk in Queen Elizabeth Park. When he returned from the park, he found Pat murdered. "Someone had come in and hit her over the head."[21]

Kathy said that Roy accused one of her boyfriends of the murder. At one point Roy was asked how blood spots got in the basement bathroom. Kathy remembers that he stood up dramatically in court and said, "That's Steve So-and-So's blood or no one's." Kathy continues, "He was trying to get people to go with his theory that she had been raped or attacked — there was some sort of sexual attack before she was killed." He also tried to accuse Eugene McNamara.

Roy explained that he had not called for help or notified authorities because, in his words, he had "walked into the trap of all time." He knew that husbands are suspect in such cases. At that point, he told the court that he had hidden Pat's body in the closet and later disposed of it in Furry Creek. Now it was on the record that Roy Lowther was capable of lying to police.

Roy described loading Pat's body into the trunk of his car and added, "There was a full moon. That I remember."[22] Maybe the detail felt literary to him. To the average person, horrified by murder, it sounded grotesque. He explained that the mattress found by the police detectives was underneath the one Pat had been lying on. The mattress on top was the one he had dumped along the Squamish Highway. The crown attorney asked him if he worried about having a murderer on the loose. Roy replied that he had not thought about that danger.[23] Roy tried to gain sympathy by saying that he had been living under terrible stress and by claiming that Pat had been getting into the "free love" world and had developed schizophrenia. He did not seem to realize that the jealous and damaging statements he made about Pat were an admission that he had a motive for the murder. Bethoe Shirkoff attended much of the trial and kept a journal. On April 22, 1977, she made this entry: "The salacious and incredible statements which Roy inadvisedly made, were printed on the front pages of two local papers. Obviously, in his self-incriminating, contradictory way, he was able to say in court what his lawyers had told him not to say."[24] As Alan Domphousse says, "They didn't want him to take the stand. He demanded to take the stand. That's where he hung himself."

Once Roy's willingness to make up stories was evident, Crown Attorney John Hall was able to build a convincing argument that Roy had a motive for the murder. Hall argued that the motive was mainly jealousy of Pat's professional success. She was becoming recognized as a poet. Furthermore, her employment at the university had put her in a position to be able to leave the marriage. In addition to the jealousy was the embarrassment of knowing that Pat had a lover. The publication of the poems in *Quarry* a year before had made an open secret of her romance. The Ironworkers' reading was the final straw. Trade unionists had shown that they were more moved by Pat's poetry than by Roy's.

Defense Attorney Henderson did his best to defend Roy by pointing out that there was no evidence that Lowther had *planned* to kill his wife. He tried to diminish the motive of poetic rivalry. "But I ask you, do you really think that one poet would kill another because of rivalry over poems? It's just not credible."[25]

In an interview given several years after the trial, A.G. Henderson was asked if he thought Roy was sane. He replied, "Oh definitely." He pointed out, however, that there are at least two meanings to the term "insane." The first sense is a restrictive legal definition that has hardly changed since 1867. The second sense is a modern psychological one. Henderson said that, within the legal meaning of insanity, "[Roy] wasn't even on the borderline. He was perfectly sane. In fact, I would say he was more sane than half of the murder cases I've defended." Of the modern psychological meaning he says, "That's a little bit tougher of a question because I think he had paranoia. I'm not a psychiatrist, but I think he had some degree of paranoia about the justice system and possibly you could say he was insane in that limited respect. My suspicion is that even a psychiatrist would say, even in the non-legal sense, that he was sane."

Many years before the murder, Roy had been diagnosed with an illness called anxiety hysteria. Psychiatrist Dr. David Norman was asked if anxiety hysteria could cloud a person's judgement so that he would not know he was committing murder. He replied that the term is an old one, not much used now. By itself, anxiety hysteria would not lead a person to commit murder.

During breaks in the trial, Roy sat in the lobby outside the courtroom, where he was free to talk to the public. Knowing him from NDP meetings, Bethoe Shirkoff struck up a conversation with Roy one day. She wrote in her journal that he had "sudden flashes of resentment against Pat. So if he continued like that with someone he knew to be a friend of Pat's and not his, when he was on trial for her murder, he is either mad or dumb. And he is not stupid."[26]

Looking over the court transcripts reveals one person as standing out amidst the horror. Pat's daughter Kathy, about to turn eighteen at the time of the murder, was a spicy twenty-year-old at the time of the trial. Her court testimony crackles with integrity. She spoke plainly and retold events sharply. Innocent of the niceties of courtroom language, Kathy answered the judge with "okay," while others were murmuring, "Yes, m'lord." Since Kathy had lived in the Lowther home for about nine years, she had more power than anyone else to smash Roy's version of reality.

Kathy's strength comes out during the cross-examination. One of Roy's lawyers was trying to get her confused by asking how many telephone conversations she had had with her mother in September. She answered, "I don't recall." Then he came at the question from a different angle and asked, "You're certain of that?" Even people more experienced in life are often rattled by this kind of cat-and-mouse questioning. Kathy was not rattled. Instead she answered, "I'm certain I don't recall." There was nothing the lawyer could do but go on to the next question.[27] That exchange was just a warm-up for another time when she was asked by the defense counsel to read a note written in Roy's handwriting, which must have been illegible. She said she could not make it out and then innocently asked him, "Can you?" While the defense objected to her question in the usual manner, he was probably somewhat unhinged by the girl's straightforwardness. At any rate, he likely spoke in a tone different from his usual voice because the next statement records the judge as saying, "I'm sorry, Mr. Doust, I didn't hear you."[28]

On April 15, 1977, newspaper reports carried Crown Attorney Hall's summation. He pointed to Roy in the prisoner's box and told the jury, "He is a man with a very queer view of life and he was on a set of rails heading to this tragic event." He cited Roy's jealousy at his wife's success in poetry as the motive. He reminded the jury that Roy had been convicted of a violent offence against his first wife that resulted in denial of access to his children. Hall called Roy's story "fantastic and improbable." Roy's strutting in the court came back to haunt him. Hall added, "I suggest he enjoyed fencing with counsel and I note the occasional quip he would slip out."[29] The lawyers gave their closing remarks, and Justice Gould made his charge to the jury. Referring to testimony Roy had given that he was a lifelong communist, Justice Gould asked the jurors to put aside their political prejudices. That was the best that the defense could expect.

On April 22, 1977, Roy Lowther was convicted of committing murder, which is "against the peace of our Lady the Queen her Crown and Dignity." The sentence was life imprisonment. Once again, he insisted that he was innocent and said, "God help you if the real killer ever has the guts to confess." This last remark was too much for Justice Gould, who cautioned Roy, "You say you did not kill your wife but the jury did not believe you, and you are saying that the jury has just now committed a massive miscarriage of justice. I must say I don't believe you either."[30]

After Roy was convicted, Defense Counsel Henderson believed that he had grounds to appeal. The law has often been soft-hearted when a murder is committed and a lover is in the picture. If provocation could be established, the murder charge might be reduced to manslaughter. The appeal claimed that the judge had misdirected the jury by not telling them that they could convict Roy of the lesser charge. Although Henderson filed a notice of appeal for Roy, he added, "I never had any intention of acting for him on the appeal itself. I had pretty well come to the end of my patience by the time the trial was over." Another lawyer, James Hogan, took over the case.

While Roy was in prison, he wrote volumes of instructions to his lawyers. His stated reason was to give them background information for the appeal. He did not seem to understand that an appeal has to be made on a point of law. Instead, he pictured a whole new trial in which the court and the world would hear every detail of his political and personal philosophy. He also told his lawyers how to break down the credibility of the witnesses who had given damaging testimony against him.

Roy's appeal was dismissed on August 22, 1978; however, the issues raised were unusual enough that the case was written up in *Criminal Reports*, a legal journal that reports significant decisions.[31] The appeal was based on two issues. First, that the judge had erred by not telling the jury that they could find Roy guilty of the lesser crime of manslaughter, and in so doing, the judge had usurped the role of the jury. Second, that the judge had not directed the jury to take provocation for the murder into consideration. The Court of Appeal found no evidence for manslaughter or provocation and went on to say that, in the absence of evidence, it was the duty of the judge to refrain from putting provocation to the jury. Roy was sentenced to life at Williams Head Penitentiary near Victoria on Vancouver Island. "Life" meant he would be eligible for parole in fifteen to twenty-five years. Speaking of Roy's time in prison, Hale muses, "I guess he was a good prisoner. He was choirmaster in prison."

To the end of his life, Roy refused to take responsibility for his actions. He dug up information on his admitted infractions of moving a dead body and tampering with evidence.[32] In 1980, Ruth, Roy's daughter by his first marriage, re-established contact and visited him in prison. She tells that he kept a huge casebook, trying to show his innocence. Roy did, however, approach the Reverend Gordon Walker and asked him to write to the Tinmouth family on his behalf. Reverend Walker's October 1977 letter said that Roy wanted the family's forgiveness and asked the children to write to him.[33] When Pat's mother received the letter, she was struggling to raise two sad little girls. The letter only caused her hurt and anger. She says, "I didn't even bother to answer it."

The goal of modern penal practice is rehabilitation, not punishment. The first step in rehabilitation is admission of wrongdoing. Ruth explains that, in an attempt to be paroled, Roy did tell prison authorities that he had killed Pat. But it was only a tactic. It was also only a tactic to have Reverend Walker be an ambassador to the Tinmouth family. Roy Lowther died of a pulmonary embolism in prison in May 1985.[34] Ruth was with her father a few hours before his death. One of the last things he said to her was, "Find Pat's killer."

CHAPTER 15

The Continent
Pat Left Behind

Poets don't live in time. They live in eternity.

— Stephen Michael Bersensky[1]

PAT LOWTHER DIED WHEN HER LIFE WAS MOVING at top speed. Her life and work had grown to a considerable continent. Here is an account of what happened to the features of her continent: her work, studies about her work, her family and friends, Mayne Island, posthumous books, awards and tributes, legends and myths.

There are so many Pat Lowther legends that the story of her life could approach saga proportions. Brian Brett remembers that, for a short time, the drama of Pat's murder "was a sort of cult thing" among some people in Vancouver. As with any set of legends, only some have any basis in fact. One task of this book has been to track them down and separate fact from fiction. The most widely known legend is Pat's supposed prediction of the year of her death.

Many people wondered if Pat willed or foresaw her death, or even if she had a resigned acceptance of her fate. All across Canada in 1975, there were rumours about an uncanny inscription in a copy of Milk Stone. It supposedly read, "Pat Lowther R.I.P. 1935—1975." Paul Grescoe repeated the story in his article "Eulogy for a Poet" in *Canadian Magazine*.[2] Someone said that the inscribed book was given to poet Lorraine Vernon. Vernon was indeed given a copy of *Milk Stone* by Pat, but it had no such inscription and she has since passed that book along to Pat's daughter Chris. Chris made it clear that the fabled inscription is not in the book. This legend is really an embroidered retelling of the real inscription on a copy of *Milk Stone* given to Ralph Gustafson in 1974. With the tombstone sketch, Pat was laying to rest a tough period in her life in a light-hearted way. Moreover, the real inscription did not have the year of her death, 1975; rather, it had the year of publication of the book, 1974.

Losses of Pat Lowther poetry, sometimes permanent, sometimes temporary, are also legendary. The most repeated story is the loss of Pat's reading material on the trip to Charlottetown. That story is true and fits in with her many lost poems, stolen briefcase and erased films. Pat's husband also destroyed much of her work between the time of her death and his arrest for her murder.

There is the story of the moving truck that was to take Pat and the children away from her violent man. That truck never actually rolled up to her door. Allan Safarik and Seymour Mayne told me that, like in most pieces of urban folklore, a friend of a friend owned a truck. They did offer it to Pat, but she did not pick up the offer.

There were at least four sightings of Pat after her death. However, once her body was found, people stopped "seeing" her.

Did Pat did have a tap root into a special level of awareness? Though the legend claiming that Pat predicted the year of her death can be dismissed as simply myth-making, it is not so easy to cast off other premonitions. She did have continuous dark premonitions, as well as foreknowledge that was not at all dark but simply resulted from the workings of a logical and intelligent mind, and she may have had an enlightened premonition about the manuscript that she called *Time Capsule*, her project at the time of her death.[3]

Pat's voice, reading from *Time Capsule* in Charlottetown, is preserved on tape. In a cheerful voice Pat says that it is "envisioned as a complex kind of witness ... buried and dug up in the future." That is literally what would happen to the manuscript. It survived Roy's attempts to destroy her work; it survived the police investigation; it survived Kathy's hurried packing of the things on 46th Avenue; and it came to rest finally in a trunk in Alan's attic. Twenty-two years later, her daughter dug it up, and *Time Capsule* became a witness for Pat's voice. Pat may have had an awareness beyond that of most people, but it never led her to unhook her thinking mind or to throw herself at the mercy of unseen forces. Her awareness simply led her to try to connect herself, other people, the earth and the universe to one another in a life-giving way.

Early in 1977, with a Canada Council grant in hand and the legal details in place, Oxford University Press published *A Stone Diary*. Brian Brett, always a supporter of Pat's work, wrote a review in the Vancouver *Province*. He noted that Pat had published three books in her lifetime, "all of them excellent and all of them absolutely unnoticed by the literary gods that be, for she was an outsider and took no part in the political idiocies necessary for success."[4] Brett later said that the release of *A Stone Diary* reopened many wounds. Milton Acorn was among Pat's still-grieving friends and, according to Brett, "Milton went nuts."

In 1977 things were different. Acclaim such as Pat had not seen during her lifetime followed the Oxford publication. There were good reviews in the popular press, including *The Canadian Forum*, *The Toronto Star* and *The Ottawa Citizen*. Robert Fulford once again nodded at Pat's accomplishment and called the book a memorial "to a poet of exceptional talent."[5] Literary journals such as *Quill and Quire*, *Queen's Quarterly* and *Canadian Literature* were full of praise. Even the British literary journal *Ambit* reviewed it with the comment, "Her writing was lucid, and about something definite. There is much to admire in *A Stone Diary*."[6]

In 1977 the editors of Oxford entered Pat's name for the Commonwealth Poetry Prize, an annual contest for writers living in the British Commonwealth. Although she did not win it, librarian Michael Foster wrote that Pat was on the short list and "several of the judges thought highly of Ms. Lowther's book."[7] As a result of the contest, Pat's books are now in three British libraries: the Commonwealth Institute, the Arts Council of Great Britain's Poetry Library and the Poetry Society of Great Britain.

Pat's mother, Virginia Tinmuth, and
Pat's oldest daughter, Kathy Lyons. (1978)

In 1980, poet Dona Sturmanis was interviewing Pat's old friend Ward Carson about his inventions for an article she had been commissioned to write for *The Province*.[8] As they chatted, Sturmanis mentioned to Carson that she had been a poetry student in the UBC creative writing department at the time of Pat's death. He entrusted her with a packet of Pat's unpublished poems. Some were carbon copies from Pat's typewriter; some were in Pat's own handwriting. That packet became the main part of Pat's fourth book, *Final Instructions: Early and Uncollected Poems*, which Sturmanis co-edited and published with the collaboration of Professor Fred Candelaria, co-chair of the League with Pat and editor of the literary journal *West Coast Review*.[9] The title comes from a poem by the English poet C. Day Lewis. He had written a poem called "Final Instructions" in the 1930s. Pat had copied Lewis's poem and left it with her papers.

In the introduction to the book, the editors say, "We consider this book a posthumous tribute to a very fine poet and humane woman whose talents and warm personality touched the hearts of many." They also acknowledge that the book does not contain her best work; rather it presents her early work. The poems are important for readers and students of literature who want to follow Pat Lowther's development as a poet. The book was released at a memorial ceremony marking the fifth anniversary of Pat's death in September 1980 at the Literary Storefront. Dona Sturmanis organized and hosted the event and arranged for Pat's faithful friends Lorraine Vernon, Dorothy Livesay and Allan Safarik to read.[10]

Christopher Dafoe reviewed *Final Instructions* and included Pat in the category of writers with the ability to see beyond the physical. "They are aware of what lies beyond the object observed, the emotion felt." Agreeing that *Final Instructions* does not contain Pat's most mature work, he found this ability "even in these early attempts at vision." Dafoe commented that, at the time of Pat's death, "many observers wondered whether she would, in the future,

Author Joy Kogawa, speaking at the launch of *Time Capsule*. (1997)

be best known for her poetry or for the dramatic nature of her leave-taking ... Happily, no morbid cult seems to have grown up around the name of Patricia Lowther. She continues to be admired as an outstanding poet."[11]

Some people did try to preserve Pat's poems. In 1987 A.G. Henderson, the lawyer who had defended Roy found four of Pat's poems in Roy's file: "Elegy for the South Valley," "Watershed," "Losing My Head" and "Mysteries." He sent them to Professor Hilda Thomas, asking if she could determine whether they had been published or to arrange for their publication. Thomas could confirm that "Watershed" had been published.[12] Then in 1994 Arlene Lampert gave several apparently unpublished poems to Della Golland: "His eyes exaggerate," "Context," "Their Hands" and "1913." The first two had been published in *Jewish Dialog*.[13] "Their Hands" and "1913" would become part of *Time Capsule*.

In May 1997, Polestar Book Publishers unveiled *Time Capsule: New and Selected Poems*[14] at a standing-room-only event at the Havana Gallery in Vancouver. Guest readers were Brian Brett, Toby Brooks, Cathy Ford, Maxine Gadd, Joy Kogawa, Chad Norman and Kate Braid, who also hosted the event.

As Pat had hoped, *Time Capsule* does serve as a witness for her to speak to the future. It also has selections from her earlier books. Much of Pat's earlier work meditated upon early history and evolution. In *Time Capsule*, Pat takes on the task of projecting herself into the future. Lorraine Vernon worked as a consultant on the project, which, she says, helped bring closure to her own grief. The book was widely reviewed in the media and prompted a CBC interview with Beth and Chris. Writing in *Quill and Quire*, Amy Barratt hailed the "the maturity, the wisdom of this voice."[15]

The League of Canadian Poets has established an annual award in Pat's name. The Pat Lowther Memorial Award goes to the best

Pat's daughters, Beth Lowther (left) and Chris Lowther,
at the launch of *Time Capsule*. (1997)

book of poems written by a Canadian woman each year. When the award was first established in 1981, the prize was simply a gift copy of all the other poems in the contest. The following year, the League of Canadian Poets was able to raise $300 to add to the prize. They did this by holding a "series of gala poetry readings." Poets of the standing of Earle Birney, Eli Mandel, Jay Macpherson, Erin Mouré and Mary di Michel gave benefit readings.[16] Over time the amount of the prize has increased to around $1000, but just as important as the money is the honour, recognition and stimulus given the deserving women poets.

The award ceremony of August 25, 1985, was unlike any other. First, Lorraine Vernon donated a copy of the poem "A Water Clock" typed on Pat's typewriter. Vernon says that Pat gave her the poem simply because Vernon had said she liked it. The League had a limited edition of the poem made up as a broadside and sold it at the award ceremony. The proceeds added to the award for the following year.

In 1985, fundraising for the Pat Lowther Award was being done by the Feminist Caucus of the League. The caucus was trying to get the organization to pay more attention to women poets and women's issues. Pat's mother, sister and daughters were there to hear the twelve women poets from British Columbia who were chosen to read selections from Pat's work. Elizabeth Gourlay made her contribution by memorizing and reciting "Poem: For All the Mad Poets." That year, Paulette Giles won the award for her book *Celestial Navigation*, which was also recognized with a Governor General's Award for Poetry as well as the Gerald Lampert Memorial Award.[17] Allan Safarik hosted the evening and shared his memories of Pat. Safarik and Peter Trower were the only men invited to speak. Trower said of the experience, "Apart from us, it is wall-to-wall ladies, appropriate enough under the circumstances, but a tad intimidating."[18]

The 1987 award ceremony was held at the Harbourfront in Toronto. Gary Geddes was one of the readers, and he talked about his feelings about Pat Lowther, the poet. He was among the poets who felt guilt at Pat's death. He wondered if his attention to her work had contributed to Roy's jealousy. Geddes told the audience that, like Pat, he considered Pablo Neruda an icon. He had made a trip to Chile that year. There, in the sands of La Isla Negra, in front of Neruda's home, he wrote the words of Pat's poem "Last Letter to Pablo."[19]

Another feature of the 1987 award was the donation by Margaret Atwood of her poem "Another Night Visit (for Pat)."[20] Proceeds from the sale of the poem were added to the prize. One hundred copies were handprinted at the Monroe Press as a broadside. The poem is a mixture of recollections of Pat, overlaid with details of her death. It has illustrations by Rosalind Goss. In 1989, Margaret Atwood read at a benefit for a Kingston, Ontario, shelter for battered women and later wrote of the experience: "Carolyn Smart read the 'Night Visit' as an intro — it was chilled — I felt Pat was right there in the room."

After Pat's death, her work began to appear in many anthologies. The most important are listed in the appendix. One, however, deserves special mention. In 1986 eight of Pat's poems were included in an anthology *Un pajaro es un poema* (a bird is a poem).[21] This book was put together by the Canadian embassy in Chile as a way of introducing Chileans to Canadian culture. Here Pat's name was among others such as Earle Birney, Irving Layton, Dorothy Livesay and Gwendolyn MacEwen. Editor Lake Sagaris translated the poems into Spanish, and the English and Spanish version are printed side by side. Sagaris included all Pat's poems to Pablo Neruda, but excluded "Chacabuco, the Pit," which is strongly critical of the Chilean government.

Through it all, Pat's children managed to grow up about as well as anybody. Going from the eldest to the youngest, Alan and his wife, Linda, have three teenage children: Paul, Lindsey and Sarah. Lindsey has written a poem to the grandmother she

Pat's son, Alan Domphousse. (2000)

never knew. Alan still plays guitar and thinks carefully before he speaks.

Kathy now works in sales for a packaging company. She lives with her partner, Russ James, whom she "intends to stay with for the rest of my [her] life." Sometimes she thinks of returning to water-colour painting.

Beth Lowther declares, "I am a feminist first. It has more to do with my mother's death than her life. It's about the life not lived." Beth says of her mother, "She stepped out of her perceived role. I believe she was assassinated. It was political." Since forty-five percent of murdered woman are killed by their men in anger over, or fear of, separation, it is hard to disagree with Beth. Had Pat been a man, her success would likely been welcomed, and even celebrated, by her mate. Pat would probably be alive today. Beth holds, as well, the environmental concerns that she learned from both of her parents. Determined that her mother's voice will not be silenced, Beth helped her sisters dig up her mother's last manuscript from an attic trunk and guided it to the publication that would later become *Time Capsule*. Beth has a little boy, Rowan. In the acknowledgement to *Time Capsule*, Beth thanks Chris Jang for teaching her "that 'father' is not a bad word."

"We live in a wild, sacred place," says Chris Lowther. She and her partner, Warren Rudd, live in a bay of Clayoquot Sound, British Columbia. Chris carries on the Wilks family tradition as an activist, and is concerned about feminism and the earth. Her determination

Pat's oldest daughter, Kathy Lyons. (2000)

to save the rainforest of Clayoquot Sound by civil disobedience earned her two years' probation. She has served on the board of Friends of Clayoquot and has helped out with their newsletter. Chris says she is compelled to do these things because she believes, "I / we are possessed by the rainforest."

Chris is convinced that she must explore the full measure of her sorrow before she can pass through it. From this conviction, she has written a book of poems that explores the trauma resulting from her mother's death and the pain of growing up without her mother. *New Power* was published in 1999 by Broken Jaw Press. One of the

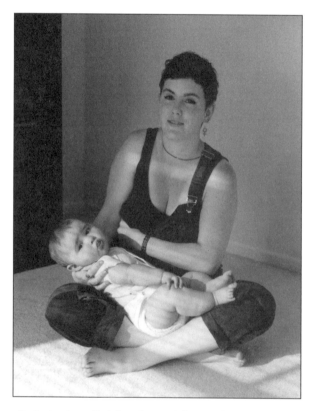

Pat's daughter, Beth Lowther, with her son Rowan. (1995)

Pat's youngest daughter, Chris Lowther. (1999)

poems, entitled simply "Mother," received an award from the League of Canadian Poets in 1996.[22] The Lowther name gave her no special advantage because all work for the contest was judged blind. Chris has also become involved with a supportive organization called Motherless Daughters.[23]

Ruth Lowther Lalonde, Roy's daughter by his first marriage, is now a teacher of English as a Second Language. As a child, she suffered greatly from her father's outbursts, or what she calls his fear-anger sickness. "That's what drove him so batty: hatred ... Every time I hear any hating, angry words from those people who are obviously hurting, well, they sound just like him!" As an adult, she is determined not to be ruled by hatred and revenge.

There is relief in the voice of Virginia Tinmuth, Pat's mother, as she says, "There's no reason why this story shouldn't be told. The girls know about it. They've accepted the fact that it happened." Pat never told her mother that she was being beaten. Virginia says that, from childhood, Pat had been a very private person. It would have been just like Pat to spare her mother, who had a heart condition, from the stress of knowing. Virginia sees clearly one of the reasons Pat stayed in the marriage. "I think she stayed with him for the children. He had a hold on those children."

In her 90th year, on May 21, 1998, Virginia Tinmuth passed away peacefully in her sleep. Some people will remember her as a miner's daughter who became a dancer and political activist. Her children and grandchildren will remember that she stood behind them through the good times and bad, and never wavered from what she knew was fair and decent behaviour. She raised four children, including a disabled son who outlived medical predictions. She endured her husband's early death, her daughter's horrifying murder and the accidental death of a grandchild. Virginia Tinmuth remained what Allan Safarik called "a woman with a backbone of steel."

Bill's daughter Tracey and her husband raise sheep on Mayne Island and Bill's son Barry and his wife still live on Mayne Island. Because of Mayne's unique and fragile natural features, some of Bill Wilks' land was bought from the family in 1996 by the Pacific Marine Heritage Legacy and some was donated. The Pacific Marine Heritage Legacy is an organization that pulls together the British Columbia Ministry of Environment, Lands and Parks with Parks Canada. Its purpose is to protect marine and coastal areas.

While the woman, Pat Lowther, can no longer touch the people and places that were dear to her, the voice of Pat Lowther, the poet, goes on:

In the silence between the
notes of music
something is moving [24]

Pat Lowther's Publications

Anthologies and Journals

1959. *Alberta Poetry Year Book*. Includes "Requiem for a Phoenix."

1961. *Alberta Poetry Year Book*. Includes "Pastorale," "Spring Sunday" and "Alpha Beta."

1964. *Alberta Poetry Year Book*. Includes "The Sewing Machine and the Umbrella."

1966. *Best Poems of 1965: Borestone Mountain Poetry Awards* (Palo Alto, CA: Pacific Books). Includes "A Water Clock."

1968. David Robinson & Jim Brown (eds.), *Poets Market* (Vancouver: Talon Books / University of British Columbia Press). Includes "Amphibia."

1968. J. Brown & D. Phillips (eds.), *West Coast 68* (Vancouver: Talon Books); reprinted as *West Coast Seen*. Includes "Notes from a Far Suburb," "Visit to Olympus" and "Child, Child."

1969. Alan Purdy (ed.), *Fifteen Winds: A Selection of Modern Canadian Poems* (Toronto: Ryerson). Includes "On Reading a Poem Written in Adolescence."

1970. Michael Yates (ed.), *Contemporary Poetry of British Columbia* (Vancouver: Sono Nis / Department of Creative Writing, University of British Columbia). Includes "Prometheus."

1971. *Best Poems of 1970: Borestone Mountain Poetry Awards* (Palo Alto, CA: Pacific Books). Includes "The Chinese Greengrocers" and "Penelopes."

1971. Dorothy Livesay & Seymour Mayne (eds.), *40 Women Poets of Canada* (Montreal: Ingluvin). Includes "tv," "Mr. Happyman Is Coming," "Killing the Bear" and "Woman."

1973. Elaine Gill (ed.), *Mountain Moving Day* (Trumansberg, NY: The Crossing Press). Includes "Morality Play," "The Piercing," "Remembering How," "The Earth Sings Mi-Fa-Mi" and "Regard to Neruda."

1974. Dorothy Livesay (ed.), *Woman's Eye* (Vancouver: Air). Includes "Doing It Over," "The Blind," "Octopus," "Hermit Crabs," "Craneflies in Their Season" and "Last Letter to Pablo."

1975. Gary Geddes (ed.), *Skookum Wawa: Writings of the Canadian Northwest* (Toronto: Oxford University Press). Includes "Coast Range."

1975. Walter Lowenfels (ed.), *For Neruda, for Chile: An International Anthology* (Boston: Beacon Press). Includes "Anniversary Letter to Pablo."

1978. Gary Geddes & Phyllis Bruce (eds.), *15 Canadian Poets Plus 5* (Toronto: Oxford University Press). Includes eight of Pat's poems, including "Chacabuco, the Pit."

1978. John Robert Columbo (ed.), *The Poets of Canada* (Edmonton: Hurtig). Includes "Greetings from the Incredible Shrinking Woman" with the observation that the poem was "the first use of the technical resources of the plane as a total art form."

1979. Ingrid Klassen (ed.), *D'sonoqua: Anthology of Women Poets of British Columbia* (Vancouver: Intermedia). Includes three of Pat's poems from *This Difficult Flowring*. Klassen comments in the introduction: "What these poets have in common is that they believe in the power of language and that their medium is poetry."

1986. Allan Safarik (ed.), *Vancouver Poetry* (Vancouver: Polestar). A volume in celebration of Vancouver's 100th anniversary. Includes "Intersection," "Slugs," "Coast Range" and "Kitchen Murder."

1986. Lake Sagaris (ed.), *Un pájaro es un poema* (Santiago: Manuel Montt). Includes eight of Pat's poems in English and Spanish as part of a project of the Canadian Embassy in Chile introducing Chileans to Canadian culture.

1989. Rosemary Sullivan (ed.), *Poems by Canadian Women 1989* (Toronto: Oxford University Press). Includes five of Pat's poems: Pat's best-known poem, "Coast Range," as well as "A Stone Diary," "Anniversary Letter to Pablo," "Leaning from a City Window" and "Octopus." Sullivan notes that the collection represents "the cumulative work of one and a half centuries" showing women's concerns.

1995. Sabine Campbell, Roger Ploude & Demetres Tryphonopou (eds.), *Fiddlehead Gold: 50 Years of The Fiddlehead Magazine* (Fredericton, NB: *The Fiddlehead* / Goose Lane). Includes "The Chinese Greengrocers."

Prose by Pat Lowther

1974. "The Face," *Prism International* 13 (Spring 1974), pp. 39-41.

[N.D.] "Red," unpublished short story [loose document #300].

[N.D.] "The Wonderful Thing," unpublished short story [Pat Lowther's old notebook, entry #34].

Books of Poetry by Pat Lowther

1968. *This Difficult Flowring* (Vancouver: Very Stone House).

1972. *The Age of the Bird* (Burnaby, BC: Blackfish), published as a limited edition broadside.

1974. *Milk Stone* (Ottawa: Borealis).

1977. *A Stone Diary* (Toronto: Oxford University Press).

1980. Dona Sturmanis & Fred Candelaria (eds.), *Final Instructions: Early and Uncollected Poems* (Vancouver: *West Coast Review* / Orca Sound).

1997. *Time Capsule: New and Selected Poems* (Victoria: Polestar).

About Pat Lowther and Her Writing

Papers on Pat Lowther's Work

1986. Jean Mallinson, "Woman On / Against Snow: A Poem and Its Sources," *Essays in Canadian Writing* 32 (Summer), pp. 7-26.

1989. Della Golland, "Gathering the Light: A Search for Literary Knowing," unpublished paper, Ontario Institute for Studies in Education, Toronto.

1994. Della Golland, "Metaphor as a Second Language: Vision and Revision in the Poetry of Pat Lowther," unpublished M.A. thesis, Graduate Department of History and Philosophy of Education, University of Toronto.

1997. Keith Harrison, "Notes on, 'Notes from Furry Creek,'" *Canadian Literature* 155 (Winter), pp. 39-48.

Tributes to Pat Lowther

1975. *Event* 4, 3 (International Women's Year Issue, Summer), pp. 69-73.

1975. Peter Gzowski, "Pat Lowther: Woman, Mother, Artist," *Gzowski on FM*, producer Allan Safarik, CBC FM, Vancouver, November 2.

1976. "Pat Lowther: A Tribute," poems and reflections by Elizabeth Brewster, Stephen Michael Bersensky, Marya Fiamengo, Robert Gibbs, Anne Marriott, P.K. Page & Lorraine Vernon, *CV II* 2, 1 (January), pp. 15-17.

1981. The Pat Lowther Award was established in 1981 by the League of Canadian Poets. It is given annually to the best book of poetry by a Canadian woman.

1995. "The Triumph of Pat Lowther: A Commemorative Reading Honouring the Poet Who Died 20 Years Ago," coordinated by Toby Brooks and Della Golland in collaboration with the League of Canadian Poets, June 4.

1995. Carole H. Leckner, "A Tribute to Pat Lowther," *Museletter* (The League of Canadian Poets), December.

1995. Sabine Campbell, Roger Ploude & Demetres Tryphonopou (eds.), *Fiddlehead Gold: 50 Years of The Fiddlehead Magazine* (Fredericton, NB: *The Fiddlehead* / Goose Lane Editions). Two of Pat Lowther's poems, "Penelopes" and "The Chinese Greengrocers," were included in this fifty-year-anniversary book.

Poems Dedicated to Pat Lowther

1974. Patrick Lane, "After — (for Pat Lowther)," *Beware the Months of Fire* (Toronto: House of Anansi).

1978. Margaret Atwood, "Another Night Visit," in Barry Dempster (ed.), *Tributaries an Anthology: Writer to Writer* (Oakville, ON: Mosaic Press / Valley Editions, 1978), p. 60.

1978. Marya Fiamengo, "Requiem for Pat Lowther," read at the Memorial Service, October 24, 1975; also in *West Coast Review* 12, 3 (January), p. 15.

1978. Patrick Lane, "For Pat Lowther," in *Tributaries an Anthology*, p. 62.

1978. Dorothy Livesay, "Book Review for Pat Lowther," in *Tributaries an Anthology*, p. 63.

1978. Seymour Mayne, "For Pat Lowther (1935-1975)," *Tributaries an Anthology*, p. 64; also published in *The Impossible Promised Land* (Oakville: Mosaic Press / Valley Editions, 1981).

1978. Gail McKay, *The Pat Lowther Poem* (Toronto: Coach House).

1988. Daniel David Moses, "Our Lady of the Glacier" (retitled "Grandmother of the Glacier"), *First Person Plural* (Windsor, ON: Black Moss).

1991. Leona Gom, "Patricia's Garden — for Pat Lowther," *Leona Gom: The Collected Poems* (Victoria: Sono Nis).

1995. Carole Leckner, "For Pat Lowther Reading at Emanuel College," *Museletter* (The League of Canadian Poets, December).

1996. Christine Lowther, "Mother," originally published in *Vintage 96* (League of Canadian Poets), p. 57; also published in *Undertow* (Fall 1996), p. 18; *The Fiddlehead* 194 (Winter 1997), p. 5; and her own book, *New Power* (Fredericton, NB: Broken Jaw Press, 1999), pp. 17–19.

1998. Chad Norman, "The Dim Church Benefits," *Prairie Journal of Canadian Literature* 30.

1999. Christine Lowther, "What's Left for Me," *New Power*, pp. 62-63.

[N.D.] Hilda Thomas, "For Pat Lowther," unpublished.

Timeline

1935   • Patricia Louise Tinmouth born July 29; family lives at intake station above North Vancouver

1939   • Sister Brenda born

1941   • Family moves into North Vancouver; Pat starts first grade at Ridgeway Elementary School

1946   • Brother Arden born

1947   • Family moves to Mayne Island for four months before returning to North Vancouver

1949   • Brother John born

1951   • Pat leaves high school at age 16 to work as a keypunch operator

1953 (approx)   • Pat marries William Domphousse; stops working

1954   • Alan Domphousse born April 1

1956   • Katherine (Kathy) Domphousse born September 30

1957   • Pat takes a course in creative writing at a community college; meets Ward Carson

1959   • "Requiem for a Phoenix" wins *Alberta Poetry Year Book* First Prize in "short poetry" class

1959 (approx)   • Pat divorced from William Domphousse; moves into her parents' basement with Kathy; returns to work as a keypunch operator

1961   • Ends relationship with Ward Carson; meets Roy Lowther
      • Awards: *Alberta Poetry Year Book*: "Alpha Beta" wins "short poem" class; "Pastorale" gets Third Honourable Mention in "short poem" class; "Spring Sunday" gets Honourable Mention in "short poem" class

1962 • "After Rain" and "Diamonds" published in *Full Tide*

1963 • Marries Roy Armstrong Lowther July 20; lives at
5823 St. George St with daughter, Kathy; Alan lives with his
father; Roy teaches music for the Maple Ridge School Board
• "Recollections of Three Dumb Angels" & "On the
Bridges" published in April issue of *Full Tide*
• "Stone" & "With Ferns in a Bucket" published in
December issue of *Full Tide*

1964 • "The Sewing Machine and the Umbrella" wins *Alberta
Poetry Year Book* First Prize in "humorous verse" class

1965 • "A Water Clock" published in summer issue of *Northwest
Review*

1966 • Heidi Elizabeth (Beth) Lowther born August 9
• "A Water Clock" published in Borestone Mountain
Poetry Awards' *Best Poems of 1965*
• "Poem for Schizophrenics" published in the winter edition
of *The Fiddlehead*
• "A Water Clock" & "with ferns in a bucket" published in
the summer edition of *The Fiddlehead*

1967 • Family moves to 46th Ave East in July; Christine Louise
(Chris) Lowther born November 19
• "History Lessons" published in the summer edition of *The
Fiddlehead*

1968 • Roy loses his job with the Maple Ridge School Board
• *This Difficult Flowring* published in June
• "Amphibia" published in *Poets Market*
• "Notes from a Far Suburb," "Visit to Olympus" & "Child,
Child" published in *West Coast 68* (reprinted as *West
Coast Seen*)

1969 • Roy loses his job at Porter School in June and family goes
on social assistance
• Pat receives her first Canada Council grant to prepare "a
second book of poems" (*Milk Stone*)
• "On Reading a Poem Written in Adolescence" published
in *Fifteen Winds*
• "Growing Seasons" published in *Quarry*

1970   • Pat's father, Arthur Tinmouth, dies of heart attack
          April 25; Pat elected second vice-president of NDP Area
          Council in September
       • "The Chinese Greengrocers" & "Penelopes" published in
          January/February issue of *The Fiddlehead*
       • "Prometheus" published in *Contemporary Poetry of British
          Columbia*

1971   • "The Chinese Greengrocers" & "Penelopes" published in
          Borestone Mountain Poetry Awards' *Best Poems of 1970*
       • "tv," "Mr. Happyman Is Coming," "Killing the Bear" &
          "Woman" published in *40 Women Poets of Canada*
       • Fall edition of *Blackfish* contains 12 of Pat's poems

1972   • Daughter Kathy leaves home
       • Pat gets her first job teaching creative writing, for the New
          Westminster Board of Education
       • Pat becomes active in the League of Canadian Poets
       • Poetry reading with Margaret Atwood at SFU
       • Pat receives her second Canada Council grant for "*The
          Infinite Mirror Trip*"
       • "The Age of the Bird" published by Blackfish, in the form
          of an artistic broadsheet

1973   • Pat administers the constituency office of NDP MLA
          Phyllis Young
       • "Morality Play," "The Piercing," "Remembering How,"
          "The Earth Sings Mi-Fa-Mi" & "Regard to Neruda"
          published in *Mountain Moving Day*

1974   • Pat elected co-chair of League of Canadian Poets in
          October
       • "Doing It Over," "The Blind," "Octopus," "Hermit Crabs,"
          "Craneflies in Their Season" & "Last Letter to Pablo"
          published in *Woman's Eye*
       • *Milk Stone* published in the spring
       • "For Selected Friends," "Wrestling," "All it Takes" & "They
          all Laughed" published in the summer edition of *Quarry*
       • Performance of *The Infinite Mirror Trip* at the
          H.R. MacMillan Planetarium in August in Vancouver
       • *A Stone Diary* accepted by Oxford University Press

1975   • Appointed to a subcommittee of the B.C. Arts Council
       • Hired to teach a creative writing course at University of
         British Columbia in September, teaches two classes
       • Reads at festival in Charlottetown, P.E.I., July 12, 1975
       • Scheduled to read at Ironworkers' Hall, September 27
       • Murdered September 23 or 24

1977   • Roy Lowther convicted of murder April 22
       • A Stone Diary published

1980   • Final Instructions published

1985   • Roy Lowther dies in prison on July 14

1997   • William Domphousse dies of a stroke in May
       • Collected works published as Time Capsule in May

1998   • Virginia Tinmuth dies May 21

Notes

Chapter 1: First Things

1. Pat Lowther, "Coast Range," in Garry Geddes (ed.), *Skookum Wawa: Writings of the Canadian Northwest* (Toronto: Oxford University Press, 1975), p. 2. [All quotations of poetry in this book reproduce the style, format and punctuation of the original.]

2. Letter to Christine Lowther from Bethoe Shirkoff, January 18, 1996.

3. Gail McKay, in an interview with Robert Harlow, September 1975.

4. George Woodcock, "Purdy's Prelude and Other Poems," *Canadian Literature* 64 (Spring 1975), p. 94.

5. All quoted material in this book that has not been individually referenced comes from interviews and correspondence with the author, listed on pp. 279-282.

6. *The Fiddlehead* 72 (Summer 1967), p. 4.

7. Family documents have both spellings; in this book, the name is spelled Tinmouth for consistency except for recent references to Virginia, who reverted to Tinmuth in the last twenty years of her life.

8. "Song," *A Stone Diary* (Toronto: Oxford University Press, 1977), p. 40.

9. Paul Grescoe, "Eulogy for a Poet," *Canadian Magazine* (June 5, 1976), p. 16.

10. "Watershed," *Event* 4, 3 (International Women's Year Issue, Summer 1975), p. 69.

11. *This Difficult Flowring* (Vancouver: Very Stone House, 1968), p. 8.

12. *Milk Stone* (Ottawa: Borealis, 1974), p. 24.

13. Ibid., p. 41.

14. Unpublished poem found among the papers that Roy Lowther kept, with the notation "Workbook, Fall '74."

15. *Milk Stone*, p. 24.

16. *A Stone Diary*, pp. 41-44.

17. "Slugs," *A Stone Diary*, pp. 44-45.

18. *A Stone Diary*, p. 40.

19. Ibid., p. 10.

20. *Milk Stone*, p. 44.

21. *This Difficult Flowring*, p. 12.

22. Pat Lowther's old notebook, entry #9.

23. *Final Instructions: Early and Uncollected Poems*, edited by Dona Sturmanis & Fred Candelaria (Vancouver: *West Coast Review* / Orca Sound, 1980), p. 57.

Chapter 2: A Husband and Two Babies

1. Interview with Stephen Michael Bersensky, June 6, 1995.

2. Fred Cogswell, *The Fiddlehead* 108 (Winter 1976), p. 2.

3. "Stone" first appeared in *Full Tide* 28, 1 (December 7, 1963, p. 13), a periodical publication of the Vancouver Poetry Society; it was later published in *Final Instructions*, p. 18.

4. *Alberta Poetry Year Book* (1959), pp. 39-40.

5. Dona Sturmanis wrote an article about Carson's ideas, "Investigation of an Inventor," in *The Province*, March 30, 1980.

Chapter 3: Poetry in Vancouver

1. Paul Grescoe, "Eulogy for a Poet," *Canadian Magazine* (June 5, 1976), p. 17.

2. This letter was among the papers found in Alan's attic after his mother's death; it has no inside address or date, and the ink was faded.

3. *Alberta Poetry Year Book* (1961) included "Alpha Beta," "Spring Sunday" & "Pastorale" on pages 28, 58 & 31 respectively.

4. Ibid.

5. Ibid., p. 31.

6. *A Stone Diary*, pp. 91-92.

7. *Milk Stone*, p. 46.

8. *This Difficult Flowring*, p. 40.

9. Ibid., p. 25.

10. *Alberta Poetry Year Book* (1961), p. 31.

11. Beth Lowther, "Introduction," *Time Capsule: New and Selected Poems* (Victoria: Polestar, 1997), p. 18.

12. *Full Tide* 27, 1 (December 1, 1962), p. 4.

13. Paul Grescoe, "Eulogy for a Poet," *Canadian Magazine* (June 5, 1976).

14. *Final Instructions*, p. 51.

15. *Full Tide* 27, 2 (April 6, 1963), pp. 4-5; "On the Bridges" also in *Final Instructions*, p. 35.

16. Unpublished poem #202.

17. Unpublished poem #203.

18. *Final Instructions*, p. 57.

19. Ibid., p. 30.

20. Ibid., p. 27.

Chapter 4: Enter, Roy Lowther

1. "To Capture Proteus," *Milk Stone*, p. 78.

2. *Milk Stone*, p. 44.

3. Roy Lowther's journal, vol. II, biographical section.

4. Bruce Ramsey, *Britannia: The Story of a Mine* (Brittania Beach: Britannia Beach Community Club, n.d.).

5. Pablo Neruda, Section V, "The Sand Betrayed," *Canto General*, trans. Jack Schmitt (Berkeley: University of California Press, 1991).

6. Pat Lowther's old notebook, entry #19.

7. Unpublished poem #34.

8. Christine Lowther, "Mother," *New Power* (Fredericton, NB: Broken Jaw Press, 1999), pp. 17-19.

9. *A Stone Diary*, p. 29.

10. Roy Lowther, "Trial Separation," *Alberta Poetry Year Book* (1966), p. 11.

11. Unpublished poem #199.

12. Unpublished poem #154.

13. *Full Tide* 28, 1 (December 7, 1963), pages 13 & 12 respectively.

14. *Alberta Poetry Year Book* (1964), p. 52.

15. *Northwest Review* (Summer 1965).

16. *Best Poems of 1965: Borestone Mountain Poetry Awards* (Palo Alto, CA: Pacific Books, 1966), p. 56.

17. Unpublished poem #198.

18. The form was part of a research project in which the organization The Voice of Women helped Dr. Murry Hunt of the University of Toronto collect baby teeth for research on the amounts of strontium 90 ingested by Canadians: *The Vancouver Sun*, February 20, 1965; in the United States the organization Women Strike for Peace held large demonstrations with placards saying, "Pure Milk, Not Poison": *Voice of Women/Voix Des Femmes Ontario Newsletter*, Fall 1997.

19. "Doing it Over," *Final Instructions*, p. 71.

20. Letter to Dorothy Livesay from Pat Lowther, November 26, 1966.

21. Draft; final version published in *Milk Stone*, p. 40.

22. Réshard Gool, "Pat Lowther," radio script, p. 8.

23. Garry Geddes & Phyllis Bruce (eds.), *15 Canadian Poets Plus 5* (Toronto: Oxford University Press, 1978), p. 363.

24. *The Fiddlehead* 70 (Winter 1966), p. 47.

25. *The Fiddlehead* 69 (Summer 1966), p. 2. "With ferns in a bucket" was first published in *Full Tide* in 1963 and later appeared in her first book, *This Difficult Flowring*. In both earlier versions the poem is in lowercase letters. In the *Fiddlehead* version, even the title has no uppercase letters. In the book, the usual words in the title are capitalized.

26. Testimony of Kathy Lyons, *Regina v. Roy Lowther*, vol. IV, April 2, 1976, p. 257.

27. *Time Capsule: New and Selected Poems* (Victoria: Polestar, 1997), p. 235.

Chapter 5: Another Baby and Some Poets

1. "Doing It Over," *Final Instructions*, p. 71.

2. Published posthumously in: Paul Grescoe, "Eulogy for a Poet," *Canadian Magazine* (June 5, 1976), p. 18.

3. Very Stone House files, National Archives of Canada, MG 31, D 253, FA 2099, 1966-69.

4. Ibid.

5. *This Difficult Flowring*, p. 18.

6. Roy Lowther's journal, vol. II, biographical section.

7. *The Fiddlehead* 72 (Summer 1967), p. 4.

8. Bethoe Shirkoff, *Pat Lowther, 1935–1974* [sic], unpublished manuscript, p. 10.

9. P.K. Page, *Contemporary Verse II* 2/1 (1976), p. 16.

10. *Milk Stone*, p. 71.

11. First published in *The Fiddlehead* 83 (January/February 1970), p. 53; chosen for *Best Poems of 1970: Borestone Mountain Poetry Awards* (Palo Alto, CA: Pacific Press, 1971), p. 67; reprinted in Sabine Campbell, Roger Ploude & Demetres Tryphonopou (eds.), *Fiddlehead Gold: 50 Years of The Fiddlehead Magazine* (Fredericton, NB: The Fiddlehead / Goose Lane, 1995).

12. Testimony of Roy Lowther, *Regina v. Lowther, Preliminary Inquiry Record of Proceedings*, April 6, 1976, vol. V, p. 381.

13. Unpublished poems #72, #55 & #157 respectively.

14. Virginia Tinmuth, "Pat Lowther: Woman, Mother, Artist," *Gzowski on FM*, producer Allan Safarik, CBC FM, Vancouver, November 2, 1975.

15. Unpublished poem #52.

16. "Our Lowther Story," unpublished essay by Ruth Lowther Lalonde, March 26, 1994.

17. Unpublished poem #29.

18. Lorraine Vernon, *Contemporary Verse II* 2,1 (January 1976), p. 17.

19. Lorraine Vernon, review of *This Difficult Flowring*, *The Vancouver Sun*, August 15, 1969.

20. *This Difficult Flowring*, p. 25.

21. Della Golland, "Metaphor as a Second Language: Vision and Revision in the Poetry of Pat Lowther," unpublished M.A. thesis, Graduate Department of History and Philosophy of Education, University of Toronto, 1994, p. 26.

22. Appreciation to Enid Valerie for this interpretation.

23. Ibid.

24. Garry Geddes & Phyllis Bruce (eds.), *15 Canadian Poets Plus 5* (Toronto: Oxford University Press, 1978); Paul Grescoe, "Eulogy for a Poet," *Canadian Magazine* (June 5, 1976); Len Gasparini, review of *The Difficult Flowering* [sic], *The Canadian Forum* 55 (January 1969).

25. David Robinson & Jim Brown (eds.), *Poets Market* (Vancouver: Talon Books / University of British Columbia Press, 1968).

26. Alan Purdy (ed.), *Fifteen Winds* (Toronto: Ryerson, 1969), p. 59.

27. J. Brown & D. Philips (eds.), *West Coast 68* (Vancouver: Talon Books, 1968); reprinted as *West Coast Seen* (Vancouver: Talon Books, 1969).

28. *Milk Stone*, p. 14.

29. Jean Mallinson, "Woman On / Against Snow: A Poem and Its Sources," *Essays in Canadian Writing* 32 (Summer 1986), pp. 7-26.

30. Della Golland, "Gathering the Light: A Search for Literary Knowing," unpublished paper, Ontario Institute for Studies on Education, 1989.

31. Edward Carpenter, "Image Making in Arctic Art," in Gyorgy Kepes (ed.), *Sign, Image, Symbol* (New York: George Braziller, 1966), p. 220.

32. *Milk Stone*, p. 14.

33. Carpenter, in Kepes (ed.), p. 16.

34. *Milk Stone*, p. 16.

35. Paul Riesman, "The Eskimo Discovery of Man's Place in the Universe," in Kepes (ed.), p. 229.

36. *Milk Stone*, p. 14.

37. Della Golland, "Metaphor as a Second Language," p. 97.

Chapter 6: Victories in the Mire

1. Interview with Beth Lowther, March 26, 1996.

2. Letter to Dorothy Livesay from Pat Lowther, December 15, 1968. In 1968, Pat applied for a Canada Council Award. On the Gzowski radio program "Pat Lowther," Livesay said she had twice supported Pat's application with the Canada Council. This may be the reason Pat felt it important to thank her.

3. Alberta Social Services, *Breaking the Pattern: How Alberta Communities Can Help Assaulted Women and Their Families* (Edmonton: Alberta Social Services, November 1985), p. 17.

4. Roy Lowther's journal, vol. II, p. 55.

5. Lorraine Vernon, Statement to Police, October 15, 1975, p. 2.

6. Domestic Violence Project, Family Service Association of Toronto, 1981.

7. Domestic Abuse Intervention Project, 206 West 4th St, Duluth, Minnesota, 218-722-4134.

8. Unpublished poem #47.

9. Maria Crawford & Rosemary Gartner, *Women Killing: Intimate Femicide in Ontario* (Toronto: Women We Honour Action Committee, Ontario Women's Directorate, April 1992). Crawford and Gartner found that some 45 percent of the men who murdered women in Ontario between 1974 and 1990 gave as the motive for killing "anger at estrangement."

10. Unpublished poems #173 & #193 respectively.

11. Letter to Christine Lowther from Allan Safarik, August 30, 1995.

12. Letter to Dorothy Livesay from Pat Lowther, July 30, 1969.

13. Roy Lowther's journal, vol. II, biographical section.

14. Letter to the Canada Council from Pat Lowther, September 10, 1968.

15. Roy Lowther's journal, vol. I, p. 56.

16. Letter to Dorothy Livesay from Pat Lowther, April 23, 1969.

17. *Quarry* 19, 1 (Fall 1969); later published in *Milk Stone*, p. 62.

18. Unpublished poem #120.

19. Letter to Dorothy Livesay from Pat Lowther, July 30, 1969.

20. Lorraine Vernon, Statement to Police, October 15, 1975, p. 2.

21. Ibid., p. 3.

22. Letter to Patrick Lane from Pat Lowther, 1973; referenced in Paul Grescoe, "Eulogy for a Poet," *Canadian Magazine* (June 5, 1976), p. 19.

23. William Wilks (ed.), *Science of a Witch's Brew* (Mayne Island, BC: Mayne Island Evergreen Estates, 1979).

24. *A Stone Diary*, p. 16.

25. Ibid., p. 22.

26. Pat Lowther's old notebook, entry #8.

27. *The Fiddlehead* 83 (January/February 1970), pp. 50-53; also in *Best Poems of 1970: Borestone Mountain Poetry Awards* (Palo Alto, CA: Pacific Books, 1971), pp. 67 & 69.

28. Michael Yates (ed.), *Contemporary Poetry of British Columbia* (Vancouver: Sono Nis / Department of Creative Writing, University of British Columbia, 1970), p. 85.

Chapter 7: Moving Mountains

1. Andreas Schroeder used this phrase in a column in *The Province* in 1970, but the specific date is uncertain. In a letter dated March 20, 1997, Schroeder verified the phrase and gave me permission to quote him "on the understanding that the statement refers to her during her lifetime."

2. Elaine Gill (ed.), *Mountain Moving Day* (Trumansburg, NY: The Crossing Press, 1973).

3. Ibid., p. 81.

4. Ibid.

5. Daphne Marlatt, "Musings with Mothertongue," *Touch to My Tongue* (Edmonton: Longspoon Press, 1984), pp. 45-49.

6. Bethoe Shirkoff, unpublished manuscript, p. 2.

7. Ibid., p. 3-4.

8. Seymour Mayne, "For Pat Lowther (1935-1975)," *Tributaries an Anthology: Writer to Writer* (Oakville, ON: Mosaic Press / Valley Editions, 1978), p. 64; also in Seymour Mayne, *The Impossible Promised Land* (Oakville, ON: Mosaic Press / Valley Editions, 1981), p. 118.

9. "In Praise of Youth," *This Difficult Flowring*, p. 33.

10. The poem was eventually published by Polestar in 1997 as part of *Time Capsule*, titled "Posthumous Christmas Eve," p. 200.

11. *A Stone Diary*, pp. 67-73.

12. Dorothy Livesay (ed.), *40 Women Poets of Canada* (Montreal: Ingluvin, 1971), pp. 77-83.

13. The practice of killing a sacred bear is widespread. It extends from the Ainu of Japan across North America and Siberia to Lapland. See: A. Irving Hallowell, "Boreal Hunting People of America and Asia: Bear Ceremonialism in the Northern Hemisphere," *American Anthropologist*, January-March 1926.

14. Roy Lowther's journal, vol. II, p. 38.

15. Pat Lowther's Final Report to the Canada Council, June 21, 1971.

16. *The Age of the Bird* (Burnaby, BC: Blackfish, 1972); also in *Time Capsule*, pp. 43-49.

17. Letter to Milton Acorn from Allan Safarik, August 18, 1971; Milton Acorn Papers, National Archives of Canada, MG31 D175 V.2.

18. Patrick Lane, "Lives of Poets," *Geist* 4, 17 (Spring 1995), p. 30.

19. Milton Acorn Papers, National Archives of Canada, MG31 D175 V.2.

20. Milton Acorn, "Pat Lowther: Woman, Mother, Artist," *Gzowski on FM*, producer Allan Safarik, CBC FM, Vancouver, November 2, 1975.

21. Réshard Gool, "Pat Lowther," radio script, 1977.

22. The Chilko Kid, *The Peak* (November 1, 1972), p. 8.

23. Margaret Atwood, "Another Night Visit," in Barry Dempster (ed.), *Tributaries an Anthology* (Oakville, ON: Mosaic Press / Valley Editions, 1978), pp. 60-61; written as a tribute for Pat Lowther; The League of Canadian Poets later used it as a fundraiser for the Pat Lowther Award.

24. Letter to Seymour Mayne from Pat Lowther, January 5, 1973.

25. Letter to Eugene McNamara from Pat Lowther, June 1973.

26. Letter to Christine Lowther from Bethoe Shirkoff, January 18, 1996.

Chapter 8: Pat's Vision and *Realpolitik*

1. Interview with bill bissett, June 5, 1988.

2. Robert Fulford, review of *A Stone Diary*, *Saturday Night* 92, 4 (May 19, 1977), p. 71.

3. Bethoe Shirkoff, unpublished manuscript, p. 3.

4. See: James Petras & Morley Morris, *The United States and Chile* (New York: Monthly Review Press, 1975).

5. Pablo Neruda, Section V, "The Sand Betrayed," *Canto General*, trans. Jack Schmitt (Berkeley: University of California Press, 1991). For a closer look at Anaconda Copper Company, see: Edwin Dobb, "Pennies from Hell," *Harper's*, October 1996, pp. 39-54.

6. "In the Continent Behind My Eyes," *Milk Stone*, p. 22.

7. Manuel Duran & Margery Safir, *Earth Tones: The Poetry of Pablo Neruda* (Bloomington: Indiana University Press, 1981), p. 56.

8. Ben Belitt (ed. & trans.), "Ode to a Lemon," *Selected Works of Pablo Neruda* (New York: Grove, 1961), p. 235.

9. Ibid., p. 117.

10. Ibid., pp. 148-149.

11. Robert Bly, *Neruda and Vallejo: Selected Poems* (Boston: Beacon Press, 1971), pp. 8-10. Robert Bly, a poet of the Black Mountain School, was also influenced by Neruda's work. Bly translated some of Neruda's poetry into English.

12. Brian Brett, review of *A Stone Diary*, *The Province*, August 15, 1977.

13. "Last Letter to Pablo," *A Stone Diary*, p. 58.

14. Letter to Eugene McNamara from Pat Lowther, September 22, 1973.

15. Walter Lowenfels (ed.), *For Neruda, For Chile: An International Anthology* (Boston: Beacon Press, 1975), p. 230.

16. Letter to Eugene McNamara from Pat Lowther, December 31, 1973.

17. Originally published in *The Canadian Forum*, October 1974; later reprinted in *A Stone Diary*, pp. 16-26. All subsequent quotes of poetry in this chapter come from "Chacabuco, the Pit" unless otherwise noted.

18. Allende may have committed suicide just before the military forces reached him. He had sent his family out of the country but courageously stayed behind. Suicide has been something of a Chilean tradition as a way to defy unjust authority, and it is quite possible that, in acceptance of the inevitable and in support of his principles, Salvador Allende embarrassed the military by taking his own life.

19. Interview with Chilean-Canadian writer & publisher Leandro Urbina, May 1985.

20. George Pendle, *A History of Latin America* (Harmondsworth: Penguin, 1976).

21. Sylvannus G. Morley & George W. Brainerd, *The Ancient Maya*, 4th ed. (Stanford: Stanford University Press, 1983), pp. 469-470.

22. Joan Jara, *Victor: An Unfinished Song* (London: Jonathan Cape, 1983), pp. 249-251.

23. Philip Birnbaum, *A Book of Jewish Concepts* (New York: Hebrew Publishing Co., 1964), p. 186.

24. Bethoe Shirkoff, unpublished manuscript, p. 4.

25. Len Gasparini, *The Canadian Forum*, January 1969.

26. "To a Woman Who Died of 34 Stab Wounds," *A Stone Diary*, p. 65.

27. Ibid.

28. Claire Martin, *In an Iron Glove* (Toronto: Ryerson, 1968), p. 60. This is the story of Martin's life with an abusive father.

29. *Final Instructions*, p. 51.

30. Ibid.

31. "The Insider," *This Difficult Flowring*, p. 41.

32. *Milk Stone*, p. 46.

33. "Socrates for Mayor" was never published; it was found among Pat Lowther's papers.

34. *A Stone Diary*, p. 74.

35. Brian Brett, review of *Milk Stone*, *The Province*, April 15, 1977.

36. Peter Gzowski, "Pat Lowther: Woman, Mother, Artist," *Gzowski on FM*, producer Allan Safarik, CBC FM, Vancouver, November 2, 1975.

37. Beth Lowther, "Introduction," *Time Capsule*, p. 18.

38. *This Difficult Flowring*, p. 31.

39. *Final Instructions*, p. 48.

40. Untitled poem #197.

41. Paul Grescoe, "Eulogy for a Poet," *Canadian Magazine* (June 5, 1976), pp. 13-19.

42. Margaret Atwood's letter to *Ms.*, April 4, 1977; Pat Lowther file, Oxford University Press, Toronto.

43. Scott Lawrence, *The Vancouver Sun*, April 22, 1977.

44. "Coast Range," *A Stone Diary*, pp. 35-37.

45. *This Difficult Flowring*, p. 19.

46. Unpublished poem #111; probably written in the 1960s [capital letters and absence of apostrophe as in original].

47. Untitled, unpublished poem #196.

48. *This Difficult Flowring*, p. 8.

Chapter 9: National Recognition — Except for Ontario

1. "Ion," *Time Capsule*, p. 194.

2. Chris Potter, *Performance*, June 16, 1975.

3. Canada Council Files, National Archives of Canada, RG 63, vol. 1242, A-72-1276 1972-73.

4. Letter to Joanne Roffey of the Canada Council from D.G. Jones, July 29, 1972.

5. Canada Council Files, Pat Lowther Financial Representative, December 7, 1972–3, RG 63, vol. 1242, file 721276.

6. Letter to Pat Lowther from Seymour Mayne, September 21, 1973.

7. Letter to Pat Lowther from Glenn Clever, February 8, 1974.

8. Letter to Glenn Clever from Pat Lowther, February 13, 1974. There is some confusion about whether this tour was in the fall of 1973 or 1974. Arlene Lampert testified at Roy's trial that she had arranged a tour of southern Ontario for Pat in the fall of 1974: *Regina* v. *Lowther, Appeal Book Record of Proceedings*, April 14, 1977, vol. I, pp. 188-196. However, Pat wrote a letter to Glenn Clever on February 13, 1974. In my talk with Clever, he was not sure when Pat was in Ottawa, but thought it was probably the autumn of 1973.

9. Letter to Glenn Clever from Pat Lowther, March 20, 1974.

10. Ibid.

11. *Milk Stone*, pp. 18-28. All subsequent quotes of poetry in this chapter come from "In the Continent Behind My Eyes" unless otherwise noted.

12. Diana Hayes, review of *Milk Stone*, *Event* 8, 1 (1979), pp. 162-173.

13. That copy of *Milk Stone* is among the Ralph Gustafson books & papers in the Rare Books Collection of the McLennan Library, McGill University. My appreciation to Betty Gustafson for directing me there.

14. Letter to Glenn Clever from Pat Lowther, January 25, 1975.

15. Mark Abley, *Contemporary Verse II* 1, 2 (Fall 1975), pp. 35-36.

16. Aviva Ravel, review of *Milk Stone*, *The Fiddlehead* 105 (Spring 1975), p. 118.

17. Peter Stevens, review of *Milk Stone*, *The Globe and Mail*, March 1, 1975.

18. *Milk Stone*, p. 24.

19. Gary Geddes, *The Globe and Mail*, May 7, 1975.

Chapter 10: Pat's Last Year

1. Interview with Arlene Lampert, September 26, 1987.

2. Letter to Christine Lowther from Fred Cogswell, November 19, 1995; all quotations from Cogswell in this chapter are from this letter unless otherwise stated.

3. Joe Rosenblatt's papers, National Archives of Canada, MG 31 D51, vol. 24, 1963–78.

4. *Jewish Dialog*; the Hanukah [December] 1975 issue includes "His eyes exaggerate" [no capitals in original] & "Context," p. 73; the Passover [Spring] 1976 issue includes "1969," "1952" & "Newsreel," p. 85.

5. Letter to Arlene Lampert from Pat Lowther, March 18, 1975.

6. Letter to Pat Lowther from Arlene Lampert, March 25, 1975; the name was soon to change from the B.C. Arts Board to the B.C. Arts Council.

7. Chris Potter, *Performance* (June 16, 1975).

8. Undated, handwritten letter with no salutation.

9. Gary Geddes (ed.), *Skookum Wawa: Writings of the Canadian Northwest* (Toronto: Oxford University Press, 1975); Gary Geddes & Phyllis Bruce (eds.), *15 Canadian Poets Plus 5* (Toronto: Oxford University Press, 1978).

10. Letter to Pat Lowther from Gary Geddes, April 2, 1975.

11. Letter to William Toye from Pat Lowther, May 22, 1975; Pat Lowther file, Oxford University Press.

12. Letter to Pat Lowther from William Toye, July 18, 1975; Pat Lowther file, Oxford University Press.

13. Drafts of "British Columbia Arts Council" are in the keeping of Beth Lowther.

14. Dona Sturmanis, unpublished manuscript, p. 86.

15. Pat Lowther Faculty Reference file, Department of Creative Writing, University of British Columbia, 1975.

16. Roy Lowther's journal, vol. I, p. 88.

17. Letter to Christine Lowther from Fred Cogswell, November 19, 1995.

18. Letter to Pat Lowther from Glenn Clever, February 8, 1975.

19. Letter to Pat Lowther from John Hebgin, Chairman, Burnaby Creative Writers' Society Contest Committee, May 28, 1975.

20. Bethoe Shirkoff, unpublished manuscript, pp. 7-8.

21. *Quarry* 23, 3 (Summer 1974), pp. 46-48.

22. Ibid., p. 48; also in *Milk Stone*, p. 58.

23. Ibid.

24. Ibid., p. 47.

25. Ibid., p. 46.

26. Eugene McNamara, "Among the Missing," *Quarry* 23, 3 (Summer 1974), p. 58.

27. Roy Lowther (ed.), *Pegasus*.

28. Pat Lowther, *The Infinite Mirror Trip*, music by Roy Lowther, performed August 1974 at H.R. MacMillan Planetarium, Vancouver.

29. Susan Mertens, review in *The Vancouver Sun*, August 27, 1974.

30. Handwritten, undated letter among Pat Lowther's papers with no salutation.

31. Dorothy Livesay (ed.), "Introduction," *Woman's Eye* (Vancouver: Air, 1974) [italics as in original].

32. *This Difficult Flowring*, p. 34.

33. Unpublished poem #34.

34. Letter to Eugene McNamara from Pat Lowther, December 11, 1974.

35. Lorraine Vernon, Statement to Police, October 15, 1975.

36. Bethoe Shirkoff, unpublished manuscript, p. 2.

37. *This Difficult Flowring*, p. 19.

Chapter 11: Charlottetown and After

1. Pat Lowther's words, repeated by Kathy Lyons February 27, 1989.

2. Réshard Gool, "Pat Lowther," radio script.

3. Letter to Réshard Gool from Pat Lowther, March 10, 1975.

4. Réshard Gool, "Pat Lowther," radio script.

5. Letter to Réshard Gool from Pat Lowther, June 10, 1975.

6. *The Patriot*, July 16, 1975; *The Guardian*, July 17, 1975.

7. Letter to Hilda Woolnough & Réshard Gool from Pat Lowther, July 27, 1975.

8. Testimony of Mark Budgen, *Regina* v. *Lowther, Appeal Book Record of Proceedings*, April 14, 1977, vol. I, pp. 197-206.

9. Letter to Rita Lalik from Roy Lowther, September 15, 1975.

10. Lorraine Vernon, Statement to Police, October 15, 1975.

11. Fran Diamond, Statement to Police, November 7, 1975.

12. Letter to Gary Geddes from Pat Lowther, September 12, 1975; Pat Lowther file, Oxford University Press.

13. Letter to Pat Lowther from William Toye, September 9, 1975.

Chapter 12: The Egg of Death

1. "The Egg of Death," *This Difficult Flowring*, p. 31.

2. Testimony of Don Cummins, *Regina* v. *Lowther, Appeal Book Record of Proceedings*, April 13, 1977, vol. I, p. 89.

3. Testimony of Rita Lalik, *Regina* v. *Lowther, Appeal Book Record of Proceedings*, April 15, 1977, vol. I, pp. 224-229.

4. Dona Sturmanis, unpublished manuscript, p. 99.

5. Hilda Thomas, "For Pat Lowther," unpublished poem.

6. Roy Lowther's journal, vol. I, p. 90.

7. Ibid., pp. 9-11.

8. *The Vancouver Sun*, April 20, 1977.

9. *The Vancouver Sun*, April 21, 1977.

10. Roy Lowther's journal, vol. I, p. 14.

11. Roy Lowther's journal, vol. I, p. 15.

12. *The Vancouver Sun*, April 20, 1977.

13. *A Stone Diary*, p. 91.

14. *Criminal Reports, Regina* v. *Lowther* (1978), 7 C.R. (3rd) 238 (B.C.C.A.).

15. Testimony of Kathy Lyons (Domphousse), *Regina* v. *Lowther, Preliminary Inquiry Record of Proceedings*, April 2, 1976, vol. IV, pp. 264-266.

16. Roy Lowther's journal, vol. I, p. 25.

17. Roy Lowther's journal, vol. II, pp. 38-39.

18. Letter to Detective Hale from Arlene Lampert, October 15, 1975.

19. Testimony of Elsie Wilks, *Regina* v. *Lowther, Appeal Book Record of Proceedings*, April 15, 1977, vol. I, pp. 239-251; also in *The Province*, April 16, 1977.

20. *The Vancouver Sun*, April 14, 1977.

21. Testimony of Brenda Tinmouth, *Regina* v. *Lowther, Appeal Book Record of Proceedings*, April 13, 1977, vol. I, pp. 106-129; also in *The Vancouver Sun*, April 14, 1977.

22. *The Vancouver Sun*, April 14, 1977.

23. *Criminal Reports, Regina* v. *Lowther* (1978), 7 C.R. (3rd) 238 (B.C.C.A.), p. 241; also in *Regina* v. *Lowther, Preliminary Inquiry Record of Proceedings*, April 2, 1976, vol. IV, pp. 271-308.

24. *The Vancouver Sun*, April 14, 1977.

25. Testimony of Eileen Langley, *Regina* v. *Lowther, Appeal Book Record of Proceedings*, April 14, 1977, vol. I, pp. 182-186.

26. William Wilks (ed.), *Science of a Witch's Brew* (Mayne Island, BC: Mayne Island Evergreen Estates, 1979), pp. 119-207.

27. Roy Lowther's journal, vol. II, p. 30.

28. Letter to Christine Lowther from Fred Cogswell, November 19, 1995.

Chapter 13: Dealing With a Murder

1. Interview with Seymour Mayne, May 11, 1987.

2. Statement of Robert Andre Courvoisier given to the RCMP in Squamish, October 13, 1975, in P.C. 29C2.

3. *Criminal Reports, Regina v. Lowther* (1978), 7 C.R. (3rd) 238 (B.C.C.A.), p. 241; also in *Regina v. Lowther, Preliminary Inquiry Record of Proceedings,* April 2, 1976, vol. IV, pp. 271-308.

4. Roy Lowther's journal, vol. II, p. 35.

5. *The Vancouver Sun,* April 19, 1977.

6. Testimony of Kenneth Hale, *Regina v. Lowther, Appeal Book Record of Proceedings,* April 14, 1977. vol. I, pp. 269-275; testimony of R.E. Chapman, vol. I, pp. 252-266.

7. Testimony of Dr. Laurence Cheevers, *Regina v. Lowther, Preliminary Inquiry Record of Proceedings,* April 1, 1976, vol. I, pp. 14-83.

8. *Criminal Reports, Regina v. Lowther* (1978), 7 C.R. (3rd) 238 (B.C.C.A.), vol. 7, p. 241.

9. Chris Potter, eulogy in *Performance,* November 15, 1975.

10. Dorothy Livesay, letter in *The Globe and Mail,* October 21, 1975.

11. Christine Lowther, "Introduction," *Time Capsule,* p. 20.

12. I was unable to confirm whether Allan Safarik wrote "Death of a Poet" or if it was ever published.

13. Marya Fiamengo, "Requiem for Pat Lowther — October 2, 1975," *West Coast Review* 12, 3 (January 1978), p. 15.

14. *The Vancouver Sun,* October 25, 1975.

15. Robert Fulford, *The Toronto Star,* October 25, 1975.

16. Jacques Hamilton, *Macleans,* November 3, 1975.

17. Brian Brett, review of *A Stone Diary, The Province,* August 15, 1977.

18. "Pat Lowther: Woman, Mother, Artist," *Gzowski on FM,* producer Allan Safarik, CBC FM, Vancouver, November 2, 1975.

19. *Gzowski on FM,* November 3, 1975.

20. Ibid., November 4, 1975.

21. Letter to Pat Lowther from William Toye, September 9, 1975.

22. Letter to William Toye from Allan Safarik, July 20, 1976; Pat Lowther file, Oxford University Press.

23. Registered letter to William Toye, Oxford University Press, from McCarthy & McCarthy, Barristers and Solicitors, November 8, 1976.

Chapter 14: On Trial

1. Letter from Margaret Atwood, May 2, 1989 [italics in original].

2. *The Vancouver Sun*, December 20, 1975.

3. *The Vancouver Sun*, January 2, 1976; also in *The Province*, January 2, 1976.

4. Testimony of Arlene Lampert, *Regina* v. *Lowther*, *Preliminary Inquiry Record of Proceedings*, April 1976, vol. V, p. 386.

5. Testimony of John Elsoff, *Regina* v. *Lowther*, *Preliminary Inquiry Record of Proceedings*, April 1, 1976, vol. III, pp. 140-162.

6. "Cataracts," *A Stone Diary*, p. 93.

7. Testimony of Dr. Laurence Cheevers, *Regina* v. *Lowther*, *Preliminary Inquiry Record of Proceedings*, April 1, 1976, vol. I, pp. 14-83.

8. Testimony of Dr. Thomas Redo Harmon, *Regina* v. *Lowther*, *Preliminary Inquiry Record of Proceedings*, April 2, 1976, vol. III, pp. 161-201; also in *The Vancouver Sun*, April 13, 1977.

9. Testimony of Don Cummins, *Regina* v. *Lowther*, *Appeal Book Record of Proceedings*, April 13, 1977, vol. I, pp. 89-97.

10. Letter to Rita Lalik from Roy Lowther, September 15, 1975.

11. Testimony of Virginia Tinmuth, *Regina* v. *Lowther*, *Appeal Book Record of Proceedings*, April 15, 1977, vol. I, pp. 231-238; also in *The Vancouver Sun*, April 16, 1977.

12. Letter to Christine Lowther from Allan Safarik, August 30, 1995.

13. Testimony of Eugene McNamara, *Regina* v. *Lowther*, *Appeal Book Record of Proceedings*, April 14, 1977, vol. I, pp. 163-165.

14. *Regina* v. *Lowther, Statements of Witnesses*; interview between Eugene McNamara & R. E. Chapman, October 6, 1975.

15. Eugene McNamara, *Diving for the Body* (Ottawa: Borealis, 1974).

16. Roy Lowther (ed.), *Pegasus*.

17. *Regina* v. *Lowther, Appeal Book Record of Proceedings*, April 15, 1977, vol. I, pp. 336-338.

18. Ibid., p. 338.

19. *The Globe and Mail*, April 20, 1977.

20. *The Province*, April 22, 1977.

21. *The Globe and Mail*, April 20, 1977.

22. *The Vancouver Sun*, April 21, 1977.

23. *The Vancouver Sun*, April 21, 1977.

24. Beth Shirkoff, unpublished journal, entry dated April 22, 1977.

25. *The Province*, April 22, 1977.

26. Beth Shirkoff, unpublished journal, entry dated April 23, 1977.

27. Testimony of Kathy Lyons (Domphousse), *Regina v. Lowther, Preliminary Inquiry Record of Proceedings*, April 6, 1976, vol. V, p. 356.

28. *Regina* v. *Lowther, Preliminary Inquiry Record of Proceedings*, April 3, 1976, vol. IV, p. 301.

29. *The Vancouver Sun*, April 23, 1977; *The Province*, April 22, 1977.

30. *The Vancouver Sun*, April 23, 1977.

31. *Criminal Reports, Regina v. Lowther* (1978), 7 C.R. (3rd) 238 (B.C.C.A.).

32. Roy Lowther's journal, vol. I, p. 48.

33. Letter to the Tinmouth family from Reverend Gordon Walker on behalf of Roy Lowther, October 28, 1977; found among Roy Lowther's papers.

34. *The Vancouver Sun*, July 18, 1985.

Chapter 15: The Continent Pat Left Behind

1. Interview with Stephen Michael Bersensky, June 6, 1995.

2. Paul Grescoe, "Eulogy for a Poet," *Canadian Magazine* (June 5, 1976).

3. *Time Capsule* was published posthumously by Polestar in 1997.

4. Brian Brett, review of *A Stone Diary*, *The Province*, August 15, 1977.

5. Robert Fulford, review of *A Stone Diary*, *Saturday Night* 92, 4 (May 1977), p. 71.

6. Jim Burns, review of *A Stone Diary*, *Ambit* 73 (1978), p. 79.

7. Letter to Richard Teleky, Oxford University Press, from Michael Foster, *The Librarian*, The Commonwealth Institute, September 1, 1977.

8. Dona Sturmanis, "Investigation of an Inventor," *The Province: The Magazine*, March 30, 1980.

9. *Final Instructions: Early and Uncollected Poems* was published simultaneously by Sturmanis' publishing house, Orca Sound Publications, and the 1980 issue of the literary journal *West Coast Review* 15, 2 (Fall 1980). They were helped with grants from the Leo and Thea Koerner Foundation, the Government of British Columbia & Simon Fraser University.

10. Dona Sturmanis, unpublished manuscript, p. 172.

11. Christopher Dafoe, review in *The Vancouver Sun*, March 12, 1981.

12. "Watershed," *Event* 4, 3 (International Women's Year Issue, Summer 1975), p. 69.

13. *Jewish Dialog*; the Hanukah [December] 1975 issue includes "His eyes exaggerate" [no capitals in original] & "Context," p. 73; the Passover [Spring] 1976 issue includes "1969," "1952" & "Newsreel," p. 85.

14. *Time Capsule* (Victoria: Polestar, 1997).

15. Amy Barratt, *Quill & Quire* (July 1997).

16. Marian Engel, *The Globe and Mail*, February 18, 1986.

17. Paulette Giles, *Celestial Navigation* (Toronto: McClelland & Stewart, 1984).

18. Peter Trower, *Poetry Canada Review* 7 (Winter 1985–86), p. 12.

19. *A Stone Diary*, pp. 56-58.

20. Margaret Atwood, "Another Night Visit," in Barry Dempster (ed.), *Tributaries an Anthology* (Oakville, ON: Mosaic Press / Valley Editions, 1978).

21. Lake Sagaris (ed.), *Un pájaro es un poema* (Santiago: Manuel Montt, 1986).

22. Christine Lowther, "Mother," originally published in *Vintage 96* (League of Canadian Poets, 1996), p. 57; also in *Undertow* (Fall 1996), p. 18; *The Fiddlehead* 194 (Winter 1997), p. 5; and her own book, *New Power* (Fredericton, NB: Broken Jaw Press, 1999), pp. 17-19.

23. Motherless Daughters, Cherokee Station, Box 20710, N.Y., USA 10021-0074.

24. "In the Silence Between," *A Stone Diary*, p. 94.

Interviews

The following people were interviewed as part of the author's research:

Margaret Atwood
> May 2, 1989 letter

bill bissett
> June 5, 1988

Stephen Michael Bersensky
> June 6, 1995

Brian Brett
> March 24, 1996

Brian Campbell
> February 23, 1989; April 1, 1996

Fred Candelaria
> April 1, 1996

Ward Carson
> May 28, 1997; May 31, 1997

Glenn Clever
> July 3, 1996

Fred Cogswell
> June 1988; November 19, 1995 letter; May 25, 1996

Judith Copithorne
> May 31, 1997

Alan Domphousse
> February 27, 1989; March 25, 1996

Howard Engel
  December 27, 1988

Maxine Gadd
  March 29, 1996; April 16, 1996 letter

Gary Geddes
  May 19, 1988 letter

Réshard Gool
  June 19-20, 1988

Elizabeth Gourlay
  June 24, 1987; June 29, 1987

Paul Grescoe
  April 1, 1996

Chris Gudgeon
  March 10, 1997 letter

Kenneth Hale
  July 19, 1987

John Hall
  June 29, 1987

Robert Harlow
  February 22, 1989

A.G. Henderson
  June 28, 1987

Bill Henwood
  February 27, 1997

Michael Koziniak
  March 1989

Rita Lalik
  March 31, 1996

Arlene Lampert
  September 26, 1987

Elizabeth (Betsy) Lane
April 5, 1998

Ed Livingston
June 5, 1997

Beth Lowther
January 7, 1994; March 18, 1996; March 26, 1996; April 1, 1996;
April 25, 1996 letter; May 14, 1996 letter; July 15, 1996 letter;
August 26, 1996 letter; January 31, 1997 letter; May 29, 1997;
March 31, 1999

Christine Lowther
January 21, 1995 letter; October 22, 1995 letter; March 21, 1996;
January 21-23, 2000; voluminous correspondence 1995-present

Ruth Lowther Lalonde
February 19, 1995; July 12, 1995 letter; October 24, 1995 letter;
February 14, 1996 letter; March 31, 1996; May 31, 1996;
November 3, 1996 letter; August 1, 1997 letter

Kathy Lyons (*nee* Domphousse)
February 27-28, 1989; March 29, 1996; November 10, 1996;
December 29, 1996; June 22, 1997; August 11, 1997 letter;
September 17, 1998 letter

Seymour Mayne
May 11, 1987; March 20, 1997

George McWhirter
February 22, 1989

Dr. David Wylie Norman
October 1, 1996

Joe Rosenblatt
March 24, 1996

Allan Safarik
September 29, 1987; February 24, 1989; September 29, 1989

Bethoe Shirkoff
February 3, 1997; February 3, 1997 letter; May 29, 1997

Hilda Thomas
February 23, 1989

Brenda Tinmouth
February 22-23, 1989; April 1, 1996; December 29, 1996

John Tinmouth
March 18, 1996

Virginia Tinmuth
February 22-23, 1989; March 25, 1996

Leandro Urbina
May 1985

Lorraine Vernon
March 18, 1996; March 26, 1996; June 1, 1997

Bronwen Wallace
May 18, 1988

Maureen Wight
February 27, 1998

Barry Wilks
November 3, 1996

Hilda Woolnough
June 19–20, 1988

Permissions

Margaret Atwood, "Another Night Visit," in Barry Dempster (ed.), *Tributaries an Anthology: Writer to Writer* (Oakville, ON: Mosaic Press / Valley Editions, 1978), p. 60; permission from the author.

Marya Fiamengo, "Requiem for Pat Lowther," *West Coast Review* 12, 3 (January 1978), p. 15; permission from the author.

Pat Lowther, "Angel," "Baby You Tell Me," "A Chant of Hands," "The Egg of Death," "In Praise of Youth," "The Insider (A Poem for Voices)," "May Chant," "On Reading a Poem Written in Adolescence" & "Two Babies in Two Years," from *This Difficult Flowring* (Vancouver: Very Stone House, 1968); permission from Pat Lowther's children.

Pat Lowther, "In the Continent Behind My Eyes," "The Last Room," "Touch Home," "Toward a Pragmatic Psychology," "Wanting," "Woman" & "Woman On / Against Snow," from *Milk Stone* (Ottawa: Borealis, 1974); permission from the publisher.

Pat Lowther, "Cataracts," "Chacabuco, the Pit," "City Slide / 7," "Dark," "The Dig," "In the Silence Between," "Intersections," "It Happens Every Day," "Last Letter to Pablo," "Levitation," "Notes from Furry Creek," "Rumours of War," "Slugs," "Song" & "To a Woman Who Died of 34 Stab Wounds," from *A Stone Diary* (Toronto: Oxford University Press Canada, 1977); permission from the publisher.

Pat Lowther, "The Comet," "Doing It Over," "Luck," "Poetry," "A Simple Song of Love" & "Stone", from Dona Sturmanis & Fred Candelaria (eds.), *Final Instructions* (Vancouver: *West Coast Review* / Orca Sound, 1980); permission from the publishers.

Pat Lowther, "For Selected Friends" & "Posthumous Christmas Eve;" Christine Lowther, "Introduction;" & Lorraine Vernon, "Afterword;" from *Time Capsule* (Victoria: Polestar, 1997); permission from the publisher.

Pablo Neruda, "A Lemon" & "Some Beasts," from Ben Belitt (ed. & trans.), *Selected Works of Pablo Neruda* (New York: Grove Press, 1961); permission from the publisher.

Pablo Neruda, "Anaconda Copper Company," from Section V, "The Sand Betrayed" of his *Canto General*, trans. Jack Schmitt (Berkeley: University of California Press, 1991), p. 177; permission from the publisher.

Bethoe Shirkoff, "Pat Lowther, 1935-1974," unpublished manuscript; permission from the author.

Hilda Thomas, "For Pat Lowther," unpublished poem; permission from the author.

Lorraine Vernon, "On the Business of Being: A Practical Friend," *Contemporary Verse II* 2, 1 (January 1976), p. 17; permission from the author.